YOUNG HOUSE LOVE

YOUNG
HOUSE
LOVE

243 WAYS TO PAINT, CRAFT, UPDATE
& SHOW YOUR HOME SOME LOVE

SHERRY & JOHN PETERSIK

ARTISAN

NEW YORK

To Clara and Burger.

No house is complete without you.

Copyright © 2012 by Sherry and John Petersik
Photographs copyright © 2012 by Kip Dawkins, except as specified on page 336,
which constitutes an extension of this page
Illustrations copyright © 2012 by Emma Kelly

Published by Artisan
A division of Workman Publishing Company, Inc.
225 Varick Street
New York, NY 10014-4381
artisanbooks.com

Published simultaneously in Canada by Thomas Allen & Son, Limited

———————————————————————

Library of Congress Cataloging-in-Publication Data

Petersik, Sherry.
  Young house love : 243 ways to paint, craft, update, and show your home some love / Sherry and
John Petersik.
    p. cm.
  Includes index.
  ISBN 978-1-57965-478-8
  1. Dwellings—Remodeling—Miscellanea. 2. Interior decoration—Miscellanea.
3. Housekeeping—Miscellanea. 4. Dwellings—Maintenance and repair—Miscellanea.
5. Petersik, Sherry—Homes and haunts—Miscellanea. 6. Petersik, John—Homes and haunts—
Miscellanea. I. Petersik, John. II. Title.
TH4816.P476 2012
  747—dc23
2012009849

———————————————————————

Design by Alissa Faden and Michelle Ishay-Cohen
Wood letters on front cover by Ron Ateah

Printed in China

10 9 8 7

CONTENTS

PREFACE

Hi. We're Sherry and John Petersik (picture us tipping our hats to you with a not-smarmy grin). Fancy meeting you here. First off, thanks for picking up our book. And second of all, we kind of think you're awesome. And you're having a great hair day. But enough flattery. You might be wondering who the heck we are and what sort of impressive degrees or decades of formal training we have when it comes to renovating and decorating. The answer is none. Nada. Zilch. Picture a big ol' goose egg in the design degree/formal training column.

See, when we began renovating and decorating our first home back in 2006, we were naive twenty-five-year-olds with a dream of turning our cute little 1,300-square-foot brick ranch in Richmond, Virginia, into a home that we loved. Initially the goal was just to make it not resemble a dark, wood-paneled hunting lodge with dated curtains and oppressive brick, but eventually we decided we could do even better than that, so our goal morphed into the desire to create a whole-house transformation that we could be proud of.

We searched in vain for a book that would fill our idea-hungry minds with suggestions for personalizing and falling in love with our home. Nothing too fancy and over-the-top for cheapos like us (yes, we're happy to refer to ourselves as cheap) or full of info about box pleats and professional upholsterers (what are box pleats, anyway?). We just wanted a book to spark our imaginations and spur us on with ideas that we could actually implement in simple, not-intimidating-at-all language. Oh yeah, and we didn't have a bank account like The Donald's.

The den in our first house, before and after.

The kitchen, before and after.

Our living room, before and after.

So accessible and doable ideas on a budget = the sweet spot. But tons of the home-makeover books we picked up led us to believe that this would be the biggest and most expensive project of our lives. Cue the sweaty palms. We wanted affordable ideas, but we couldn't settle for things that looked shoddy and amateur. Understandable, right? Basically, we wanted cheap that didn't look cheap. Luxe for less, if you will.

Sadly, we left the bookstore empty-handed. So we just decided to jump in and get started. To learn as we went and course-correct along the way. To tackle one small project at a time to avoid becoming cash poor and woefully overwhelmed. And to break down big projects into a series of bite-sized chunks. Over time we gained confidence and expertise. (Here's where you can start imagining the *Rocky* music playing in the background.) We're proud to say that over the past five years, not only did we completely transform that first house of ours *and* live to tell the tale, but we also hosted our very own completely DIY wedding in the backyard of our beloved casa.

And in 2010 we took our three-"person" family (yes, we count Hamburger, our nine-pound Chihuahua, as a person) to four when we welcomed a sweet baby girl named Clara.

A few months after completing our best DIY project to date (that would be our daughter), we sold our completely overhauled first house to move into another needs-lots-of-work home. It was sad to leave our first love behind, but it was also insanely exciting.

Why? Because we're bad at sitting on our hands and were downright giddy to start the entire crazy/fun journey of taking an old seen-better-days house and turning it into a holy-buckets-we-love-it home all over again. And this time we got to do it with our pooch *and* our baby by our side.

If you recognize our cheesy mugs, you might be familiar with our blog, *Young House Love* (younghouselove.com). Back in 2007 we started our online DIY diary of sorts just to chronicle our home-related adventures for friends and family. We didn't know a thing about blog coding or site maintenance, which was about as much as we knew about renovating and decorating. Somehow it blossomed into a bustling little site that has now become a full-time job for both of us. As in, we blog about all of the house-related projects we take on (the trials, tribulations, failures, and victories) to the world at large like it's our job. Because it *is* our job. And nobody's more surprised than we are that we have

regular followers. And not just our moms and dads, but people we don't even know. To the tune of about 5 million hits a month. Crazytown. So here's where we stop to send out a big, wet kiss to everyone who stops in to see what we're up to. Love you. Mean it.

When the opportunity to write a book presented itself, we immediately knew what we wanted to do. Well, not *immediately.* First we pinched ourselves and squealed like tweens for about forty-eight hours. Then we got unbelievably intimidated and considered saying no to avoid probable humiliation. But after a week of letting it sink in, we got it together and began acting like normalish human beings again. (Okay, anyone who knows us is probably guffawing at the idea that we just called ourselves normalish.) Anyway, the point is that we eventually started toying with the idea that we could write the book that we always wanted to buy. And we're not gonna lie, it got us all sorts of excited.

We loved the idea of tossing out a ton of suggestions for others who were feeling stuck or uninspired or just plain overwhelmed with the state of their home. You know, things that worked for us, stuff we learned along the way, and both classic ideas and more specific DIY projects in the hope that others would fall just

as hopelessly in love with their four walls as we had with ours. And with that, we set out to write a book full of doable, affordable, not intensely intimidating ideas to take any house to the next level. Basically, it's the exact book that we looked for back when we were just starting out on this whole making-our-house-a-home journey six years ago.

So after 2,190 days of living, learning, and tackling a major home makeover almost entirely on our own (and then excitedly embarking on another one), here it is. That book. I guess we're such suckers for DIY that we decided to tackle it ourselves. And we hope it'll come in handy for anyone out there who is looking to make their house a bit more homey (and less homely). Because we can totally relate to the feeling of being clueless, sweaty-palmed homeowners on the fateful day when you're handed the keys. Gosh, that feels like yesterday.

Without further ado (well, there might be a bit more ado, but sooner or later we'll get on with it), we're excited to share a smattering of the crazy thoughts, tips, and ideas that swirl around in our project-lovin' minds. You know, the ones that get us excited to pick up the ol' hammer slash paintbrush slash staple gun slash glue gun slash something else in our toolbox or craft drawer. So you're cordially invited to join us in DIY adventureland and learn as you go, right along with us, because we always say that it's just as much about the journey as it is the destination, and figuring things out as you go is more than half the fun. Heck, we're still doing that every day, and we'll be right there with you on this little road trip through DIYville. So hop in the car. We'll even let you have shotgun.

xo,

Sherry + John

INTRODUCTION

Think of this book as a thought starter, a springboard, a jumping-off point, an inspiration rabbit hole. A kernel of something that could be the key to the whole house-love puzzle. Because everything starts with an idea.

Our goal for this book was to compile hundreds of fun, deceptively simple, budget-friendly ideas (both classic and unexpected—because the best homes have a little of both). To pass on a slew of projects, suggestions, tidbits, and lessons that we've learned to get people excited and give them the confidence to DIY their way to a happier, more functional, more inviting place to call home—aka a house you want to kiss (and we're not talking about the peck you give your aunt).

As you read through our little collection of house-sprucing suggestions, you might have some I've-never-thought-of-that moments or I've-thought-of-that-and-just-might-give-it-a-try-now moments or I've-already-done-that-where's-my-high-five moments. Hopefully you'll have all three. The point is to flip through the pages and pick and choose the projects that call your name. This is a good old-fashioned idea book. Nothing too serious. Because anyone who knows us knows that we try not to take things too seriously. Which is probably why we haven't abandoned home

improvement in the first place. (You gotta have a sense of humor when you're painting cabinets at eleven o'clock on Christmas Eve . . . and yes, we're talking from experience here.)

This book is for renters and homeowners alike. For people who have just moved in and for people who are almost done decorating but don't know what's missing. For people who love a good DIY project and for people who might sweat a little at the idea of trying to be handy. It's for people who've never cracked a decorating book or drawn a floor plan, but also for those of you who have seen it all and heard it all ten times but haven't actually picked up a hammer or a paintbrush lately. Perhaps seeing something here for the eleventh time might just get you to finally take a crack at it. And maybe knowing that we were once novice renters-turned-homeowners with zero experience will give you the confidence to say, "What the hey, I'll give it a whirl."

Picture us next to you giving you an encouraging (and not at all violent) push to take your house to the next level. Are you rolling your eyes because you think there's no way a book can help a gun-shy (or nail-gun-shy) individual like yourself? Listen, even if you're using this book with absolutely no knowledge on the subject (or a terrible track record of taking years to choose a paint color or breaking everything you touch)—relax. We were right there with you. Less than six short years ago, actually. And we remember it well.

So if you're stuck, doomed, indecisive, or whatever else you think is holding you back, remember that you have to start somewhere. This is just the beginning of something awesome: a blossoming lovefest between you and your home. We once didn't know how to pick a paint color without hyperventilating (or paint trim or load a caulk gun or make pretty much any other home-improvement or decorating decision out there). But thanks to good old-fashioned research, trial and error, and starting-from-nothing hunger (you know, that yearning to figure things the heck out), we got there. All without any formal training or boundless loot to pour into fancy upgrades. Dude, now we're writing a book about the stuff. Who would've thought?

We always joke that if we can do it, anyone can. We're not special. (Our moms will now call us after reading that sentence to argue, but they have to say that because, well, they're our moms.) The point is that even if you know as much as we did when we began renovating our home (as in: diddly squat), just take it one idea/day/project at a time and you'll get there too. We've labeled many of our tutorials with cost, work, and time details to help you pick out the cheapest, easiest, and fastest ones (so you can tackle those first if you'd like to ease your way into things). At least 75 of the ideas

in this book should cost under twenty-five dollars, and 60 of them can be completed in under an hour.

HOW TO USE THIS BOOK

This book doesn't include a lot of don'ts. It's more like a do anthem. Rules are limiting, and we find that in making a house a home there shouldn't be too many of those since it's a very personal experience and it's going to be a different journey with a different outcome for each person who takes the plunge. There are probably fifteen ways to skin a cat (gross expression, sorry) when it comes to tackling a task like hanging curtains or accomplishing something like adding color. And that's a good thing! In fact, we've found that there's something really freeing about tossing out the idea that your house has to please everyone who walks in the door. Make your house work for *you*. Make it make you smile from ear to ear. It's not about catering to the masses or playing it safe; it's about creating an amazing little love shack to call your own. In short: Do what makes you happy. Take it one day at a time. And most of all, have fun. We'd say follow your heart, but a tiny violin might start playing in the distance.

As for the 243 ideas that you'll find here, some are big and general while others are small and specific. Transforming your house definitely calls for taking a little from column A and a little from column B—and if you're anything like us, you'll work in fits and starts. Sometimes your energy will be up and you'll want to do something major, like paint your cabinets or refinish a dresser. And sometimes you'll just want a ten-minute art project to gussy up the loo. (Who doesn't enjoy a gussied loo?)

So feel free to flip around and slip in and out of this book depending on your mood and the amount of time or money you have on hand. The entries are numbered just to keep track of things, but you certainly don't have to go in order, and we've made sure that each tip can stand on its own, so you can literally put on a blindfold and point to something (anything!) and do it. Just not with the blindfold on. That could get messy.

The photos and illustrations in this book definitely reflect our aesthetic and our sense of style, but nothing would give us more joy than for you to adapt things to feel like yours. There's not one idea in here that can't be interpreted or executed in a range of styles and colors, so just do your own thing.

Oh, and for those who read our blog (high five!), we want to mention up front that we've done our best to keep all the ideas in this book as fresh and not-blogged-about as possible, which was actually really hard for two over-sharers like us. Some of the suggestions or tutorials here might also be something we've mentioned on our blog (e.g., "paint a piece of furniture" or "reupholster a headboard"), but those general concepts had to be included, so we tried to execute them in a different way when we photographed or illustrated them. For example, instead of the same picture of a bench that we painted from our blog, you might see a dresser painted in a completely different way that we secretly whipped up just for this book. So consider those new photos and fresh takes on those classic DIY ideas to be a little extra "sauce" along with all the new "meat" that we shoved into this metaphorical sandwich of a book.

A FEW WARNINGS

1. We can be annoyingly enthusiastic. No question about it. Sometimes even we want to smack ourselves for the whole you-can-do-it refrain. So feel free to read our book in a jaded teenage voice if it ever gets to be too much. Or alternate between this book and something fantastically serious and un-singsongy to balance things out. Like *War and Peace* or *The Grapes of Wrath.* Whatever you do, don't read this while watching a Disney movie. Yikes.

2. Some projects that you tackle might not work out. Heck, they might be tell-all-your-friends-about-it ugly. Do not let this get you down. You win some, you lose some. And you can't get the house you want without working it (and sometimes bombing it). Goodness knows we've had our share of epic failures, but you get back on the horse and you live to ride another day. A royal screwup can even be a learning experience. (Figuring out what you don't like is just as valuable as pinning down what you love.)

3. There's not one "right" decorating answer. It's hopefully both comforting and freeing to hear that our interpretations of the ideas and projects in this book are not the only way to go. Feel free to tweak the colors and materials and use your own sensibilities to end up with something that screams "your name here" and not "Sherry and John." Perhaps you'd prefer black frames where we've used white ones, or you like your books with the spine facing out (sometimes we randomly turn ours the other way). Maybe you prefer less boldness (or more!). Or you'd rather stain something that we painted. It's all good. The only real rule is to trust your instincts. If it looks good to you, you're onto something.

4. **These ideas aren't ours to own.** Just as a chef's cookbook might include a filet mignon recipe (his version of a tried-and-true dish), many of the ideas in this book have been around for generations, being freshened and reinvented by designers and regular folks alike. Our goal was just to smash a range of tips and ideas into one easy-to-reference place with lots of info, photos, and illustrations. You know, in the hopes of lighting a metaphorical fire under those home-sprucing buns of yours.

5. **Your hands will get dirty.** Again, we contend that this is a great thing. Nothing gets the serotonin pumping like good old-fashioned grunt work. From sanding and painting to staple-gunning and hammering, you might just surprise yourself with how accomplished and hard-core you feel. Caution: It's addictive.

6. **Momentum is a funny thing.** Sometimes you're humming along, checking things off your home-improvement to-do list like a bat out of h-e-double-hockey-sticks, and sometimes you're as slow as molasses. This isn't just normal, it's the DIY way. Progress seems to ebb and flow. So embrace the whole who-knows-how-we'll-get-there-but-we'll-probably-get-there-someday concept. Have

faith. Enjoy the journey. And try to have a little fun along the way.

7. **A home-decorating decision is not going to save the world.** Conversely, it won't be the end of it either. If something goes wrong, like you pick the wrong paint color or end up hating your new curtains, it's all going to be okay. This is comforting, because the human race doesn't depend on your never making a decorating mistake. This stuff is meant to be fun, and the goal is to end up with a house that makes you smile. So if any project that you take on (or this darn book in general) gets you grumpy, put the book down and step away from the hammer/paintbrush/etc. Then have a cookie and search for "baby Chihuahua" on YouTube. That usually works for us.

PRODUCT PICKS

You may notice that some of the tips or ideas in this book have specific product recommendations or suggestions within the description. We've always loved providing details about products that work for us on our blog, and we didn't want our book to be any different. So we want to make it clear that these mentions aren't paid product placements; they're just things that we've had luck using. You know we love to over-share!

SPEAKING OF OVER-SHARING

The difference between blogging and book writing is that we don't have the luxury of devoting ten paragraphs to each tutorial or sharing fifteen photos for every project here (as much as we would like to). Our solution? We created a landing page on our blog with 24/7 access to bonus photos, videos, and info that might come in handy for anyone with additional questions or a hankering for more juicy details. You can find it all at younghouselove.com/book. Hope to see you there!

PROJECT KEY

Since this book is full of a range of house-sprucing suggestions, many of the ideas are just thought starters to get you going, while others are a lot more detailed, and may even include a step-by-

step tutorial. For these more involved projects, we've included a rundown of info so you can quickly see the cost, the level of difficulty, and about how long they'll take to complete.

PHOTO FRENZY

Over the course of three sleepless but oddly fun weeks, we shot hundreds of photos for this book in our own house (after a mad dash to complete and style each one so that Kip, the photographer, could snap away, which even included repainting rooms and ceilings late at night before Kip returned the

THE PROJECT KEY BREAKDOWN

COST $

WORK SOME SWEAT

TIME DONE IN A DAY

1. **Cost** denotes how cheap or expensive each project might be. Of course, this depends on where you find your materials (certain types or brands of fabrics, frames, or furnishings are pricier than others) and what items you already have on hand—so we give a general range that may vary from person to person.

- "Free" obviously means that it's a zero-dollar project

- "$" means it's nice and cheap (most likely under twenty-five dollars)

- "$$" means it's moderately priced (probably twenty-five to a hundred beans)

- "$$$" means it's something you might want to save up for (usually well over a hundred big ones)

2. **Work** descriptions range from super easy to a bit more involved. There's "no sweat," which is extra simple; "some sweat," which involves a

bit of effort but nothing too challenging; and "lots of sweat," which marks the more labor-intensive suggestions in the book.

3. **Time** info includes a ballpark description of the length of time it could take to tackle each project. This usually ranges from "done in ten minutes" to "done in a weekend"—and there's even "done in a week" for those especially lengthy undertakings (like painting your kitchen cabinets). We generally note the amount of "active working time" that things take, so drying time or the time it takes to order something and wait for it be delivered isn't included. Everyone moves at a different pace and can encounter an unexpected obstacle or a lucky break along the way, so don't be discouraged if your project takes longer (but feel free to do a victory dance if you get 'er done in less time).

next morning). So this isn't your typical home book shot across multiple high-end residences. And this grassroots approach meant that some of the concepts we wanted to touch on couldn't be demonstrated in our house—like a project with stairs, since we live in a one-story ranch. So a handful of room shots in this book (along with some silhouetted accessories and furnishings) are photos that we got permission to use to help demonstrate some of the projects that we didn't want to leave sans photo. They can be found credited in the back of the book on page 336. Just didn't want you guys trying to figure out what-the-heck part of our house these photos were shot in!

TOOLS TO HAVE AROUND

You can do almost every project in this book with just the tools listed below. If you already own them, give yourself a gold star for the day. If not, this isn't your cue to raid the hardware store. Just buy what you need as you go, and over time you'll rack up a pretty nice collection.

- Hammer
- Flat-head screwdriver
- Phillips-head screwdriver
- Tape measure
- Yardstick
- Level
- Painter's tape
- Glue gun
- Staple gun
- Paintbrush
- Paint roller and tray
- Palm sander and sandpaper
- Power drill/driver

If you're the extra-credit type, here are some additional tools that we love to have around: nail punch, crowbar, clamps, razor or box cutter, needle-nose pliers, caulk gun, putty knives, saws (of various types), and wrenches.

KEEP IT SAFE

DIY is fun, but it's not worth risking important things like your health (or your fingers), so here are some tips for earning your Captain Careful badge.

- When in doubt, wear safety goggles. Also consider closed-toe shoes, long-sleeved shirts, pants, and work gloves to further protect yourself.

- Use low- or no-VOC products (which contain fewer or no volatile organic compounds) whenever possible. Why breathe in fumes when you don't have to?

- Keep your work area well ventilated when dealing with stinky or dusty stuff. Throwing on a dust mask helps too.

- Spray paint has yet to go VOC-free, so use it outside while wearing a mask and try to let items dry completely before bringing them in.

- Always unplug power tools when they're not in use. You don't want yourself (or your child or pet) bumping into a saw that's been left on.

- When taking on electrical projects, be sure the power is turned off. We often turn off our home's master breaker just to be sure.

- Test paint for lead in old homes and on old furniture before sanding. You can find inexpensive test kits at home-improvement stores.

- Always consult the directions and warning labels on any products, tools, or materials before diving into a project.

ONE LAST THING

This is just a little note about momentum, expectations, and self-defeating thoughts. We shared a few photos of our first home's transformation in the preface, but sometimes before and afters can be dangerous. Why? Well, they can make it seem like those rooms instantly came together and the makeover happened at warp speed just because you saw the before and the after in such rapid succession. But it's a lie! A big, fat one. And since we're all about keeping it real, we're here with encouraging news: Our room makeovers weren't quick. At all.

We know it can be more than a little disheartening if your house-to-home journey isn't moving quite as rapidly as you'd hoped. And dark, dated before pics next to "is that even the same room?" after photos can cause defeating thoughts like "I could never do that"; "It's pretty, but completely unattainable for me"; or "Ouch, rub it in. My house will never look like this."

But those thoughts are also a lie. Your house can blossom from the ugliest of caterpillars into the purtiest butterfly you ever did see. And you don't have to spend an arm and a leg. It just won't happen overnight.

We actually contend that in-the-blink-of-an-eye makeovers only exist in TV-land (where they edit out the months of planning/labor/snafus and just show the beautiful after, so it appears as if it was done within four commercial breaks). Our first home's transformation didn't happen in a day or a month or even a year. It took us four and a half years to take that old brick ranch from dated to done. And it's not like we always knew where we were going or made zero mistakes. Oh man, did we make our fair share of mistakes.

So with that in mind, we thought it might be helpful to put some pictures where our mouths are, and include some less-than-flattering photos of our first house after we'd lived there eight whole months. Spoiler alert: We were miiiles away from the "afters" that we shared on pages 6 and 7. Yup, things were looking a little . . . rough.

Progress isn't always pretty.

Our living room definitely didn't come together overnight, as demonstrated by this sad shot.

We painted the original cabinets, but the dated blue counters stuck around for a while.

See what we mean? The beauty of these in-progress pics is that they're a good reminder that homes take time. And sometimes they look crazy. Which is probably why some of the completely unfinished rooms in our current house don't make us want to cry as much as they did in our first house (back when we thought homes were supposed to be done a week after you moved in).

Now we know better than to think that way or put that sort of unnecessary and unrealistic pressure on ourselves. We've even grown to be suspicious of rooms that come together too quickly: Can they really be as thought out, functional, and meaningful as a beautiful, evolved, and collected-over-time space?

So this little diatribe is not included to discourage you in that "You're saying my house won't look awesome for four years? Why bother!" way. It's meant to encourage you in an "I'm inching toward my dream home, and every project gets me closer" way.

These things just take time. They have to percolate. Great rooms are put together layer by layer, project by project, with mistakes and small victories and speed bumps and happy dances along the way. So give yourself time to find the right pieces, breathing room to make mistakes, permission to save up and go slowly, and opportunities to learn as you go. It's okay to live in an unfinished room; heck, it's par for the course when it comes to finding your way to the most amazing "after."

We've been in our "new" house since the end of 2010, and some of our rooms have grown so much since then.

Our current living room,
then and now.

Our office, then and now.

Our kitchen, then and now.

Our laundry room, then and now.

Meanwhile, other rooms are woefully untouched, and a before and after of those rooms would basically just be printing the same photo twice. But that's okay with us. It's kind of how it seems to go when you take things one day and one project at a time. So rejoice if your house is only a shadow of what you long for it to be. That stuff takes years. Or at least it does for us. And getting there is just as fun as sitting on your finished couch in your finished room. A room's never really done anyway. (I bet you'll be looking around for something to tweak. . . .) So be sure to soak up all that good stuff in the middle.

01

CHILL

LIVING IDEAS

Back when we lived in Manhattan as twenty-something advertising drones, the term "living room" was quite literal. You did all of your living in one room, and it usually wasn't a very big one. In fact, when John and I met, I was living in a tiny 14-by-13-foot studio in SoHo, and John was sleeping on a futon in the living room of a one-bedroom apartment in Long Island City that he shared with two other guys. He wooed me by showing me how he kept his entire wardrobe on a rolling rack at the foot of his bed. (Yes, ladies, he's taken.)

John clearly needed a woman's touch. And a door. Definitely a door.

I wonder if Vanna White ever rocked a kitchen this tiny?

So it's no surprise that a few years later when we moved to Richmond, Virginia, and purchased our first home, the 1,300-square-foot layout felt like a palace by comparison. We hardly knew where to begin. But since living areas are, well, where we do most of our living, they were a natural place to start. Beyond relaxing and watching TV in our den, we were known to fall asleep on the sofa and log some pretty serious computer time at our desk in the corner. We even ate the occasional dinner on the couch. (We'd put a blanket on our laps first; we're not animals.)

It definitely wasn't an overnight transformation, but the slow and steady evolution of our den and living room were two of the biggest makeovers we accomplished in the four and a half years that we lived in that house. And those gradual changes are so interesting to look back on because they single-handedly taught us a ton about what we liked (and didn't like!), along with important things like blogging from a chair is more comfortable than blogging from a backless wooden stool. (Yes, we actually had to learn that lesson.)

So embrace your living areas for the amazing teachers that they can become. And go ahead, enjoy the occasional meal on the sofa. Just don't forget the blanket to catch any rogue meatballs.

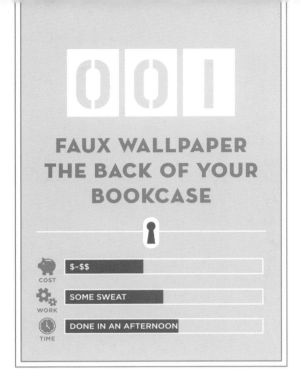

001

FAUX WALLPAPER THE BACK OF YOUR BOOKCASE

COST	$-$$	
WORK	SOME SWEAT	
TIME	DONE IN AN AFTERNOON	

Too scared to paint or wallpaper the back of your bookcase? Here's a less permanent option. Cover foam core or cardboard (cut to the size of the back of your bookcase) with wallpaper or fabric for an instant no-commitment makeover. You can even use sheets of wrapping paper for an overhaul that costs under ten dollars. It's crazy how much of an impact a new backdrop can have.

1   Measure the space on the back of the **bookcase** between each shelf.

2   Cut **foam core** or **cardboard** rectangles to rest against the back wall of each shelf.

3   Wrap them with **wallpaper, fabric,** or **wrapping paper,** taping or stapling it firmly around the back of the foam core or cardboard so it's held in place from behind. You can also use spray adhesive to secure wrapping paper or wallpaper to foam core or cardboard backing.

THE COLORFUL ROLL OF GIFT WRAP WE USED WAS JUST SIX BUCKS!

OUTLIERS   MALCOLM GLADWELL

The Guinea Pig Diaries   A. J. Jacobs

SLOW DEATH
BY RUBBER DUCK

Cabinet of
Natural Curiosities

THE LIGHT OF NEW YORK   ASSOULINE

TASCHEN

002

STENCIL A SISAL OR JUTE RUG

COST	$-$$$
WORK	SOME SWEAT
TIME	DONE IN A DAY

Rugs can make the room, and adding some bold pattern to an already texture-rich jute rug can be just the thing to wake up your space.

1 Find a relatively low-pile **jute rug.** (Nubby is okay, but something super raised and shaggy might be harder to stencil than something with a tighter weave.) We found this runner at Ikea.

2 Grab satin-finish **latex paint** in the color of your choice (we used Vintage Vogue by Benjamin Moore) and a **stencil** that you love (something large scale can look especially striking).

3 Lay down your stencil, centering it if you'd like, and gently dab on your paint using a **sea sponge** or a **foam stenciling brush** with a flat head like the one pictured below.

4 Slowly work your way around the rug until the entire surface has been stenciled. Or just stencil a border.

5 Let things dry for a while (forty-eight hours can't hurt) and enjoy!

NOTE: Painted areas can become a little worn over time (like a painted doormat might), but that subtle patina can actually look pretty amazing—like a well-worn antique rug.

GOOD, NOW I CAN SPRAWL OUT IN STYLE.

003

INVENTORY ALL THE TEXTURES IN YOUR ROOM

If everything feels a bit flat (all smooth and shiny, all worn and rustic), try to find an object with a contrasting texture to liven things up and refresh the whole room. If your space seems to be lacking texture in general, it's a prime opportunity to add some: like a fluffy faux sheepskin over a chair, a few rough woven baskets for storage, some natural bamboo blinds and airy curtain panels, or a sleek stainless-steel side table.

1   Breezy sheers add softness.

2   A faux-fur pillow is always fun.

3   A woven basket brings in a natural element.

4   Worn leather feels cozy.

5   A clean-lined lamp is sleek and modern.

Treat wood tones as neutrals. They can be layered to look intentional so you don't end up with cookie-cutter spaces. You can actually have a few dark pieces and a few light or even painted pieces. As long as there are at least two or three of each type in the same space, they'll look intentional and layered, as opposed to crazy and dorm room–esque (which can happen if everything is one tone but there's an odd man out, or if you have ten different wood tones or painted pieces going on instead of just repeating a few). Using accessories can further tie things together, like adding dark wood frames above a light wood table and a light wood bowl above a dark buffet to balance things out.

004

DODGE THE MATCHY-MATCHY TRAP

005

MAKE OVER A BAR CART WITH CHALKBOARD PAINT

COST	$-$$	
WORK	SOME SWEAT	
TIME	DONE IN A DAY	

This thrift-store bar cart was just ten bucks, and we dressed it up in a day.

1 Use a **table** or **bar cart** that you already have or pick one up (check secondhand stores or places like Target and HomeGoods).

2 Paint every surface except the top using the tutorial on page 278 (we used Dragonfly by Benjamin Moore).

3 Apply a few thin coats of **chalkboard paint** to the top, following the directions on the can.

4 As soon as it's dry, get your doodle on.

START HERE

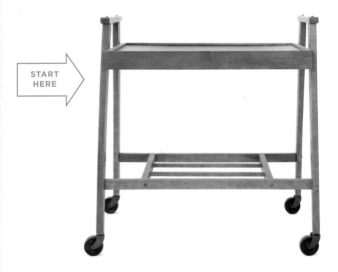

006

BRING HIGH CEILINGS DOWN SO THEY'RE COZY (AND EASIER TO PAINT)

COST $-$$

WORK SOME SWEAT

TIME DONE IN A DAY

When you have a big white room with a high ceiling, creating a horizontal stopping point for paint makes for a great two-tone effect around the room. Just by leaving the upper portion of the wall white (perhaps about 18 inches) and painting the area under this "horizon line," you'll create a cozy effect because the deeper color that's under the horizontal boundary feels enveloping. You won't need to break out a ladder or scaffold to paint extra-tall rooms, and it creates a nice boundary for art, so it feels more contained and no longer needs to be hung as high. Use painter's tape to mark the line and tear it down as soon as you're done with your last coat of paint to help keep the line extra clean.

007

CASUALLY SKIRT A TABLE

We draped an old duvet cover over a white pedestal table to add color and pattern (and create some great concealed storage). Any spare fabric can work, like a sheet, a shower curtain, a tablecloth, or a large fabric remnant.

DONE IN A MINUTE

008

CONSIDER A DAYBED

Can't find the perfect couch? Try a daybed instead. It not only earns you a space to lounge, relax, and watch TV, but you can also host an overnight guest more comfortably than by offering up a sofa or an air mattress.

009

MAKE SIMPLE
NO-SEW CURTAINS

COST	$-$$$
WORK	SOME SWEAT
TIME	DONE IN A DAY

3 Lay one end of your cut fabric on your ironing board and roll out a length of hem tape across it, placing it right at the edge. Follow the hem-tape instructions for which side to iron first, when to peel off the backing, and when to fold over your fabric.

4 Then use another strip of hem tape to fold the hem over one more time, and iron it to create a finished-looking hem.

5 Do the same with the other three sides of your fabric.

6 Celebrate. You've completed your curtain panels. Now just hang your rod and clip the panels in place using **clip-on curtain rings** from places like Target or Home Depot. Not only are they swanky, but they also mean you don't have to worry about rod pockets or tab tops. Huzzah!

NOTE: For more detailed steps and photos, visit younghouselove.com/book.

No curtains? No sewing machine? No problem. All you need is some iron-on hem tape and these easy steps and you'll have your favorite fabric canoodling with your windows, pronto.

1 Determine the desired height and width of your final curtain panels, add 1 inch to every side, and cut your fabric panels to that size. We usually make our finished panels 90 inches long, and we find that long bolts of **upholstery-grade fabric** are often the perfect width for one panel, so you may be able to save yourself two cuts by leaving the sides alone.

2 While the iron is heating up, break out the **iron-on hem tape.** (We used heavy-duty HeatnBond, which is available at most fabric or craft stores, like Michaels.)

BONUS TIP
Rug Ruler

Got a 5-foot-by-8-foot rug? It can be a handy guide to help keep your lines straight while you cut your fabric panels. Just roll the fabric out over the rug and use the edge of the rug as a cutting guide.

CURTAIN BASICS

Curtains can be confounding, and there are certainly a million ways to approach them. Here are a few of our favorite tips:

■ **You can make your windows** look twice as big by hanging curtain rods extra high and wide (usually around 4 inches below ceiling height and 18 inches wider than the window trim on each side). Then add breezy floor-length curtains. Doing this brings tons of height and softness to a room, plus the panels won't block nearly as much light as they would if they were hanging in front of the window (they'll rest mostly in front of the wall instead).

■ **If you have two rooms** that are very open to each other, you may want to keep the curtains consistent in both spaces so there's a nice effortless flow between the two rooms. This isn't a hard-and-fast rule, but if you're on the fence it's certainly not boring to keep your curtains the same and let other items (like furniture, rugs, accessories, and art) add variety and define each space.

■ **If you have a room with windows** that aren't all the same height, consider "cheating the rods" by hanging them all at the same height anyway. It can give the room a feeling of balance that it might have been lacking, and most people won't even notice that the windows themselves are slightly varied.

■ **If you have a row of windows** with a slice of wall between each one (maybe less than 20 inches), you might want to consider hanging one long rod above the entire row of windows and just adding curtain panels to each side of the rod and between each window. This can give the illusion of an entire wall of glass and really open things up. Places like JC Penney sell extra-long rods and rod extenders, or you can buy two rods that you can butt against each other (without finials) to create the effect of one long one.

■ **We don't use our curtains** for privacy, typically; we just like the added height and softness that they can bring to a room. So we like to use white inside-mount faux wood blinds for actual light-blocking and privacy (they layer in nicely with curtains and can be purchased inexpensively at big-box stores—where they'll even cut them to a custom size for free).

■ **Beyond curtains, a few other** window-treatment solutions that we love are frosting film (it adds privacy without blocking too much light), bamboo shades (great for adding texture), and roman shades (in white or a favorite fabric full of color or pattern).

I'M PARTIAL TO CURTAINS WITH CRUMBS UNDER THEM.

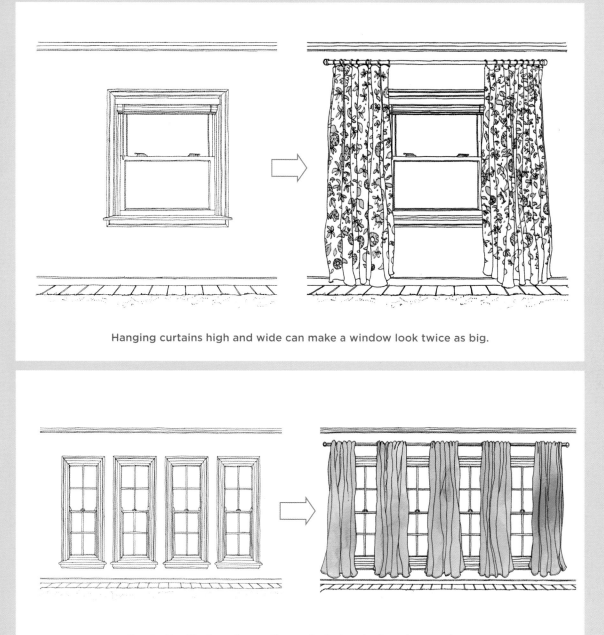

Hanging curtains high and wide can make a window look twice as big.

Create the illusion of an entire wall of glass by hanging one long
curtain rod over a group of windows.

ONE IKEA LACK TABLE THREE WAYS

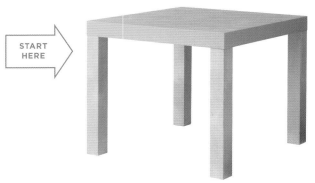

START HERE

This iconic and affordable table is always fun to tweak, especially since it comes in a bunch of colors. Here are three ways to take one über-cheap table (or a few of them) from so very Ikea to one of a kind.

ONE TABLE AS A SHELF

Use the tabletop as the backdrop for a series of shallow floating shelves made from the legs (we used one Lack table in the black-brown finish). We held each leg in place and screwed them in from the back of the tabletop. Try drilling pilot holes to make this process easier, and be sure to check that each shelf is level as you go. Use the existing holes on the back to hang your new shelf over a couple of screws drilled into studs or heavy-duty anchors in the wall. Total spent: less than $10!

TWO TABLES AS A HEADBOARD

Arrange two tabletops and four legs side by side and staggered to create a headboard for a full-sized bed (we used two high-gloss red Lack tables). We flipped our design over and laid three 1-inch-by-3-inch boards across them—across the top, the middle, and the bottom. Once we screwed the boards tightly to the table pieces to hold them together (through pilot holes that we drilled first), not only was our headboard secure, but the boards also created a small ledge for hanging it on the wall. You can use three Lack tables to create a queen-sized headboard (and attach two-by-four legs for added stability). Total spent: less than $30!

THREE TABLES AS A CUBE BOOKCASE

Assemble two tables and have a third tabletop on hand for the base (we used three high-gloss white Lack tables). Use a drill (try a ¼-inch bit) to make centered holes in the bottom of all eight legs and insert a 2-inch wooden dowel into each hole (you can pick up eight extra dowels from the Ikea spare parts area or at a craft store). Use the same drill bit to make matching holes in your spare tabletop and in the top of one of the constructed tables (our trick was to drill up through the existing holes Ikea made for the legs to be sure they were perfectly placed). Stack your tables, lining up your dowels with the holes in the tabletops for a secure fit. Total spent: less than $45!

SIMPLE WOODEN DOWELS HOLD IT ALL TOGETHER.

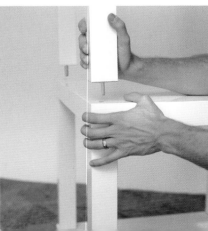

011

MAKE A DESK, HEADBOARD, OR SCREEN WITH AN OLD DOOR

Maybe you've removed an interior door (like a random one that ruined the flow between your kitchen and dining room) or you've come across one at a garage sale or salvage yard. Why not do something fun with it?

1 It can become a **desktop.** Just add store-bought legs (home-improvement stores sell them) and use the hole from the doorknob to wrangle computer cords.

2 Make it a **headboard** by hanging it on the wall. (Try screwing right through it into a few studs in the wall to secure it.)

3 Louvered doors can even be hinged together and painted a bright color to create a cool **free-standing screen** to hide clutter or divide a room. We splashed some emerald-green paint on a DIY bifold screen of our own and used it to hide the water heater in our first house's basement.

NOTE: Find more details on these projects at younghouselove.com/book.

0 1 2
REARRANGE YOUR LIVING ROOM

Nothing freshens a room (for zero dollars) like rearranging some furniture.

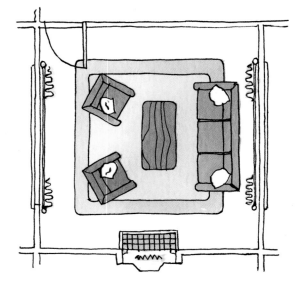

Here are some ideas for a square space.

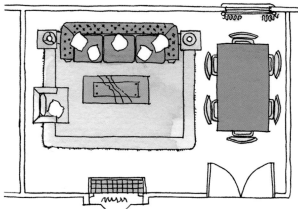

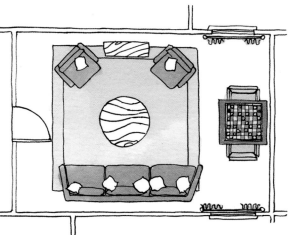

And a few more for rectangular rooms.

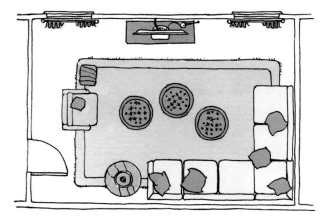

O13

DYE YOUR CURTAINS

COST	$
WORK	SOME SWEAT
TIME	DONE IN AN AFTERNOON

If you already have curtains but don't love them, you can always try to revive them before giving up hope. White panels can be gorgeous, but if they're too stark for your space (or old and yellowed), why not dye them a warm cream, sand, or honey color? Or go navy, plum, gray, or brown if you're looking for richer and deeper tones. Of course sunny yellow, teal, orange, or emerald can be stunning choices too. The sky is pretty much the limit thanks to the tons of dye colors that are available these days. (We like iDye from Jo-Ann Fabric, which you can toss into a front-loading or top-loading washer.) You can even dip-dye your curtains for a banded effect on the bottom (just dip the bottom of the panels into a dye bath in a bucket or tub instead of submerging the whole curtain). What's the worst that can happen? If you hate 'em, you can cut up those old curtains that you didn't like in the first place and use them as rags. Totally worth a shot.

BONUS TIP
Negotiating with Furniture Vendors and Contractors

Whether you're walking around a furniture showroom or getting an estimate from a contractor, our favorite question is "Is that your best price?" It's a great way to score 10 to 15 percent off with one simple question that's not hard to remember or potentially insulting. Negotiating at its finest is short and sweet.

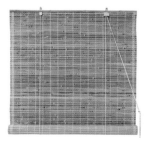

Texture-rich bamboo blinds

A Parsons desk

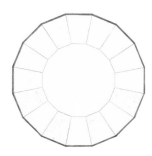

A round mirror

014

GET ONE (OR ALL SEVEN) OF THESE CLASSICS

These all seem to fit into nearly every room and every style—you almost can't go wrong by investing in them over time.

A clean-lined neutral slipper chair

A dark wood console table

A leather pouf or ottoman

A neutral-toned jute or wool rug

Three colorful pillows

╬

a throw

═

a charming
tossed-together look

015

ONE SOFA
THREE WAYS

It's funny how different the same
sofa looks when it's sporting
different outfits.

Five bright   ╬   a textured   ═   a happy-casual
pillows   throw   effect

IF CLOTHES MAKE THE MAN,
PILLOWS MAKE THE COUCH.

Two intricate pillows

╬

a bolster

═

a balanced graphic vibe

016

DON'T FORGET
THE HALLWAY

You can paint your hallway a color or hang a gallery of frames. You can even add or replace the hall light if you have one. Or introduce architectural details like crown molding, a chair rail, beadboard, wainscoting, etc. Since a hallway is a transitional space, you might not want to pick a color that won't go with all the rooms that attach to it, so bring home swatches and hold them up to see which ones relate well to the adjoining rooms while adding some interest to your former snoozefest-worthy hall.

Walk around your house at night, and if you see a corner or a table that needs more illumination, add a table lamp or a floor lamp for ambiance, warmth, and more of a balanced feeling (so there are no dark corners). If the space doesn't accommodate a table lamp or a floor lamp, you can hang a plug-in wall sconce, swag from the ceiling an overhead fixture that plugs in, or even hire an electrician to hardwire a ceiling fixture for you (which could start at around eighty to a hundred dollars).

017

KEEP AN EYE OUT
FOR DARK SPOTS

DO SOMETHING WITH A NICHE

We're the first to admit it: Niches can be challenging. But they're also a great opportunity to create a sweet little nook that can be both functional and inviting. So go show that nook who's boss.

1 Stick a bench in it and hang a piece of art above it.

2 Add a cozy chair and a lamp for a reading nook.

3 Hang a tension rod with fabric/a sheet/ a shower curtain draped over it to create a puppet show/stage nook in a kid's room.

4 Slide an armoire in there.

5 Hang horizontal shelving for a built-in bookcase effect.

019

SPICE UP YOUR STAIRS

There are so many things you can do to add interest to a staircase.

- Paint the risers a contrasting color.

- Stencil the risers with numbers or a meaningful quote.

- Use patterned wallpaper on each riser (adding clear water-based polyurethane makes it more durable).

- Stencil each riser with a pattern.

- Paint the handrail of the banister white but stain or paint the vertical rails deep brown or black for contrast.

- Add an interesting runner for more texture or to keep things kid-safe.

020

GUSSY UP A THRIFT-STORE MIRROR

COST: $-$$

WORK: SOME SWEAT

TIME: DONE IN AN AFTERNOON

WE FOUND THIS GUY FOR EIGHT DOLLARS AT A THRIFT STORE!

Hunt down the ugliest, saddest secondhand mirror that you can find. Bonus points for something sponge painted. Look beyond that terrifying exterior and remember that mirrors are so easy to transform. (Just find a size/shape that you love and ignore the color completely.) Once you get it home, here's how to fancy it up.

1 Tape off the mirror so just the frame is exposed. You can use **cardboard** or even a **plastic bag** and some painter's tape to keep paint off the mirror pane.

2 **Spray paint** the frame with a few thin and even coats of a fun color like lime or eggplant (we used Aubergine by Rust-Oleum's Painter's Touch). Tip: Using a **spray primer** first can help things stick for the long haul. Check out more spray-painting basics on page 87.

Voilà! Not so sad anymore. And if you're a bit gun-shy about using a bright, saturated color, you can always go with glossy white, chocolate, navy, light gray, dark gray, or black. Those colors are so classic they're practically error proof.

BONUS TIP
Reflect for a Moment

Remember to place mirrors so they reflect something positive, like a window or a pretty piece of art (as opposed to something like a big, hulking black TV screen or an ugly wall vent).

021

REFINISH WOOD FURNITURE

COST	$
WORK	LOTS OF SWEAT
TIME	DONE IN A WEEKEND

START HERE

THIS MOROCCAN-ISH TABLE WAS TEN DOLLARS AT A THRIFT STORE.

This is one of those projects that takes some time but is totally worth the trouble. Once you've mastered the art of refinishing, there's no end to what you can transform. (We've even seen people refinish ornate items—like a piano!)

1   Move your piece of furniture to a spot where you can be a bit messy (a garage, driveway, or cleared-out side of a room covered with a **drop cloth**) and wipe the piece down with a damp rag to remove any dirt, grease, or cobwebs—especially if this is a rescued thrift-store piece. You can also use a **deglosser** to get it clean.

2   Start with a **low-grit sandpaper** (the rougher kind, like 80-grit) and go over everything with a **palm sander,** sanding in the direction of the grain of the wood. Keep a spare sheet handy to get into those nooks and crannies by hand. This removes the existing finish and stain. The goal is to get your glossy piece closer to its raw wood form (although it doesn't have to look 100 percent stripped, just roughed up enough so new stain can penetrate). We then like to go over it again with a **high-grit sandpaper** (like 200-grit) to smooth things out.

3   Bust out your damp rag again and go over the piece one more time to remove any leftover sanding dust. Then, once you're certain the piece is dry, use a **paintbrush** to apply a thin and even coat of **stain** on all surfaces.

4   Let the stain sit. The length of time you leave it on depends on how dark you want your finished color to be. Refer to the directions on your stain (which can vary depending on the manufacturer) and try testing the stain color in an inconspicuous area if you're uncertain how long you'll need to wait to achieve your desired look.

5   When the wait is over and you think you've let the stain soak in enough, use a **clean rag** (old T-shirts work great) to wipe off all of the excess. Try using long, smooth strokes and applying a decent amount of pressure. You don't want stain to remain sitting on top of the wood, so whatever didn't soak in needs to be wiped off.

6   If the stain isn't as dark as you'd like, apply another coat, wait, and wipe away the excess until you're happy with the result.

7 If you haven't used a stain with a built-in polyurethane sealant, you'll need to seal your piece with separate coats of a **sealer.** We use a low-VOC version from Safecoat called Acrylacq or Minwax Water-Based Polycrylic Protective Finish in clear gloss, which shouldn't yellow. As with the stain, you'll want to apply thin and even coats using a **small paintbrush.** We recommend two or three coats; just be sure to let each coat dry before starting the next one for a not-sticky-forever result.

BONUS TIP

Got Veneer?

This method also works on wood veneer—just be sure not to sand too deeply, which can result in pitted or splintered veneer (you don't want to go right through it!).

022

STAIN OR PAINT INTERIOR DOORS

COST $-$$

WORK SOME SWEAT

TIME DONE IN A DAY

Weathered gray, rich navy, moody charcoal, soft platinum, light mocha, deep chocolate—there are lots of classic/neutral choices that you can use throughout your house for a dose of instant sophistication. As for how to stain or paint a door, we actually update ours right on the hinges, so you don't have to remove them to get great results.

1 Tape off the hinges with **painter's tape** if you don't have a steady hand or the experience to keep from gunking them up with paint or stain.

2 Remove the knob and any other hardware that doesn't keep the door suspended just so it's not in your way.

3 If you're staining, use **low-grit sandpaper** (like 80-grit) to sand any sealer completely off, so the **stain** can penetrate evenly for a nice seamless finish. Resand things with a higher-grit sandpaper (like 200-grit) to smooth them out. Then follow the instructions on the stain can. (We like Minwax Deep Walnut for a rich brown color.)

4 If you're painting, wipe the doors down with a **liquid deglosser** and prime them, using a **small foam roller** and a **2-inch angled brush** (to get into the cracks), with a **high-quality low-VOC primer** to block any bleeding and to add durability. (We like Zinsser Smart Prime.) Allow that to dry according to the instructions and then apply two or three thin and even coats of **semigloss paint** (also with a small foam roller and a 2-inch angled brush).

5 Reinstall the doorknob and any other hardware you removed after everything is dry, and rejoice—you've lived to tell the tale.

Misty Gray

Hazy Skies

Creekside Green

Smoke Gray

THESE OPTIONS BY BENJAMIN MOORE ALWAYS WORK.

Adding bold geometric shapes, carefree hearts, or even something splattery and Pollock inspired could be fun and lead to a lot less generic look than the white lantern you started with. We used teal watercolor paint to make soft painterly stripes that spiral around a five-dollar lantern from World Market.

CAPTAIN CAREFUL ALERT: Paper lanterns shouldn't be a fire hazard as long as heat can escape out the top and bottom of the shade, and the bulb has ample clearance (i.e., isn't super close to the paper). Using a CFL or an LED bulb is always a good idea, since they put out significantly less heat than incandescent bulbs.

023
PAINT A CHEAPO PAPER LANTERN

SIMPLE & CHEAP, CHEAP, CHEAP

024

TRY WALLPAPER

COST	$$–$$$
WORK	LOTS OF SWEAT
TIME	DONE IN A WEEKEND

So many people think wallpaper sounds . . . dated. But we're not talking about borders with chickens or grapes—there are so many graphic and cool wallpapers these days! It's a great way to add interest to a closet, an entryway, or a focal wall, and sites like diynetwork.com and youtube.com have great tutorials to walk you through it. So get on with your bad self.

MY UNCLE WAS A BOOKEND.

025

MIX HARDWARE FINISHES

Break free of matchy-matchy hardware. Here we've layered an oil-rubbed bronze mirror, pig, and paperweight with a silver lamp, tray, and nail-head detail on the chair. As long as each metal appears more than once, it looks layered and intentional as opposed to mismatched.

026

ADD INTEREST TO A DECORATIVE SHELF

COST: $

WORK: SOME SWEAT

TIME: DONE IN AN HOUR

Sure, a shelf is cool without any extra flounce, but sometimes a little somethin' somethin' can make you smile.

1 Hunt down **ribbon, fabric, decorative paper,** or even **pom-pom fringe** with some personality.

2 Run it along the front edge of a floating or bracketed **wall shelf** (securing it with **clear hot glue** or **craft glue** behind the ribbon, fabric, paper, or pom-pom fringe).

3 You may be able to do this with the shelf in place, or it might make for better results if you remove it and apply things while the shelf is resting on the floor (so the trim isn't fighting gravity while it dries).

4 If you can't, try to pull the trim behind the back lip of the shelf and secure it there for the most seamless look. (When you hang the shelf back on the wall, the ends will be hidden.)

It's always better when there's a story behind the things you use to decorate your home. Hold out for something that feels special or has sentimental value. Even something with personality found on Craigslist or a hand-me-down with serious character can end up making the room. So our main rule is to just say no to placeholder stuff. Why buy a light that you feel meh about when you can wait it out, save up, and get the light you really want. Any interim item just gets between you and the real thing you want—so it's worth resisting the urge for instant gratification if you can't find or afford The One right off the bat.

027

DON'T FILL SPACE— ADD MEANINGFUL THINGS

028

COLLAGE YOUR WALL

Use removable poster putty to arrange a giant collection of postcards or photos on the wall. You can place them randomly for a casual collage or space them evenly in a gridlike pattern.

029

ADD A PAINTED DETAIL TO YOUR PANELED DOORS

COST	FREE–$
WORK	SOME SWEAT
TIME	DONE IN AN AFTERNOON

WE USED MOONSHINE AND SILHOUETTE BY BENJAMIN MOORE TO GUSSY UP OUR BLAND BEDROOM DOOR.

Moonshine

Silhouette

Painting just the inset frames on a paneled door can accentuate the architecture. Try a light-gray accent on a white door, or go for more contrast by using a dark chocolate or a slate blue, if that ties in to your color scheme. You can even add a second color for extra dimension, like we did here. And using test pots of paint can get it done for under ten dollars. If you don't have a steady hand, taping things off works well.

BONUS TIP
Don't Have Paneled Doors?

Using painter's tape to create faux panels and painting those can add interest and dimension to a flat hollow-core door.

030

MAKE THE SHELF THE STAR

Add pattern to the top of a shelf with a regular ol' Sharpie. They come in metallic tones as well as nearly every color of the rainbow. Here are a few design ideas.

- Fish scales or scallops
- Irregular pinstripes (we used painter's tape to space ours)
- Polka dots (or use dot stickers from an office-supply store instead of a Sharpie)
- Leafy branches
- Teardrops
- Zigzags or chevrons
- Tiled diamonds or hexagons for a honeycombish look
- A woodsy faux-bois pattern

love life

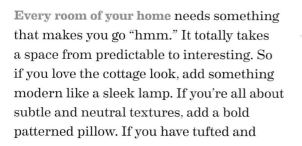

031

ADD ONE UNEXPECTED THING

Every room of your home needs something that makes you go "hmm." It totally takes a space from predictable to interesting. So if you love the cottage look, add something modern like a sleek lamp. If you're all about subtle and neutral textures, add a bold patterned pillow. If you have tufted and tailored sensibilities, try adding a casual ottoman. If all of your furnishings are tall, lower your frames 6 inches. Keeping your spaces from feeling too formulaic is the key to creating rooms with je ne sais quoi. Plus, it's fun to deviate from your own norm.

Got naked windows? Grab a curtain rod and clip-on curtain rings (places like Target and Home Depot sell 'em) and use the rings to clip anything up on the rod. No rod pocket or tab tops needed! Try items like:

- Bedsheets or even a duvet

- Tablecloths

- Rustic-looking drop cloths from a home-improvement store

- Fabric shower curtains

- Vintage tapestries (for a worldly look)

- Fabric remnants. (You can hem them with no-sew hem tape—more on that on page 34—or leave them raw for a cool casual vibe.)

032

MAKE INSTANT CURTAINS

033

MAKE A DRIFTWOOD-ESQUE TWIG MIRROR

COST $-$$

WORK SOME SWEAT

TIME DONE IN AN AFTERNOON

Bringing the outdoors in with a twiggy branch mirror can add texture and rugged charm to a room. It's a great way to spice up a bland mirror that you already have by raiding your yard for sticks. Or you can grab an inexpensive mirror at a thrift store and go to town.

1 Find a **mirror** with a wide, flat-ish frame.

2 Use **construction adhesive** that dries clear to secure similarly sized twigs to the frame.

3 **OPTIONAL:** Paint it all soft gray for a beachy, driftwood-esque effect—we used Fossil by Rust-Oleum's Painter's Touch. (If this is the plan, tape off the mirror before glueing the branches on, like we did in the picture below.)

START HERE

034

HANG TEXTURED WALLPAPER FOR A TIN-CEILING EFFECT

COST $-$$$

WORK LOTS OF SWEAT

TIME DONE IN A DAY OR A WEEKEND

You can find textured wallpaper at your local home-improvement center or online, and it's extremely affordable when compared to squares of actual tin. Bonus: wallpaper is lighter and easier to hang too (just follow the directions on the roll or the adhesive that you buy since they can vary). Once the wallpaper is up, paint it any color you'd like for a pretty darn convincing riff on a gorgeously detailed tin ceiling.

SNAG A DEAL

We always run down this mental checklist before we pay full price for anything.

- Do I have a coupon or can I find one online and print it out?

- Will the store take a competitor's coupon that I have?

- Will the store price-match?

- Is there a coupon code I can Google around for if I'm ordering online?

- Can I buy the item through a cash-back program like eBates?

- Can I use credit card points to purchase the item?

- Will using my store credit card snag me a discount? (Some stores like Target give you 5 percent off every purchase.)

- Does the vendor offer free return shipping if I don't like the item (or can I return it to a local store to avoid shipping fees)?

035

SHOP AT GARDEN CENTERS

Furnishings and accessories that are meant to be outside can add tons of texture and authenticity to a room. We've had a giant concrete greyhound hanging out in our dining room for years, and we love the cheeky industrial vibe that he adds. So the next time you're at a garden center, look around. Anything from a concrete creature to an outdoor side table or chair is fair game to bring in. It's touches like these that can take a room from generic to majorly memorable.

SURE, THIS PLANTER COULD LIVE OUTSIDE, BUT WE LOVE IT INSIDE FILLED WITH FESTIVE GIFT WRAP.

SEE HOW WE USED THIS ON PAGE 24.

An oil-rubbed bronze or sleek silver chandelier can swank up a dining area.

Something sculptural, fun, and kinda crazy adds interest to a living room or bedroom.

An airy glass pendant won't obscure views (great for over a sink with a window behind it).

036

REPLACE "BLAH" LIGHT FIXTURES

If the light fixtures in your space aren't doing you any favors, try one of these.

A large drum pendant hung about 32 inches above an island or a table can create a clean and traditional-meets-modern look.

A medium drum pendant is great when hung flush or almost flush to the ceiling in a bedroom, a hallway, or a bathroom.

037

JESSICA'S FABRIC DOOR

GUEST BLOGGER IDEA

BLOGGER:
JESSICA JONES

BLOG:
HOW ABOUT ORANGE
(WWW.HOWABOUTORANGE.BLOGSPOT.COM)

LOCATION:
EVANSTON, ILLINOIS

FAVORITE COLOR COMBO:
ORANGE + GRAY

FAVORITE PATTERN:
ANYTHING LARGE, CONTRASTY, BOLD, AND
ORDERLY

FAVORITE WAY TO FINISH A ROOM:
COOL ART PRINTS AND POSTERS

The plain front door of our apartment was completely un-fun, so one afternoon my husband and I wallpapered it with fabric to give it a graphic punch.

SUPPLIES

- Fabric
- Water
- Cornstarch
- Big paintbrush
  (or a paint roller if you want to do a larger wall)
- Scissors
- A craft knife
  (if you have obstacles like we did)

1 **CHOOSE A FABRIC.** I chose a lightweight cotton print from Ikea. Bedsheets would work really well too. If using brightly colored fabric, it's a good idea to machine wash it first and make sure the dyes won't bleed onto the wall or door when the fabric is moistened with paste; try a small test area first.

2 **MIX UP YOUR PASTE.** My paste recipe is ¼ cup of cornstarch with just enough water to dissolve it. Bring 2¼ cups of water to a boil in a pan on the stove. Then slowly add the cornstarch mixture and boil until it's thickened, whisking constantly. The ideal consistency is similar to that of really thick gravy.

3 **MEASURE.** While the paste cools, measure the door and trim the fabric down to size. Ripping it can work well since most fabric tears along the grain.

4 **APPLY THE PASTE AND FABRIC.** Brush paste over the entire door and begin applying fabric from the top down, adjusting and smoothing out wrinkles with your fingers as you go. In dry or stubborn spots, we glopped on more paste.

5 **CUT AROUND OBSTACLES.** Make a few quick slits with scissors where the lock and doorknob are located to fit the fabric over them.

6 TRIM THE EXCESS AND PASTE THE EDGES. After smoothing out the rest of the door, go back and carefully trim the fabric away from the hardware with a craft knife, applying more paste as needed. In addition to sticking the fabric down, paste also keeps the raw ends from fraying, so add a little extra around the four edges of the door for good measure.

7 REST EASY. When the fabric dries, it should be perfectly smooth and the paste should be invisible (ours was). And if you decide to remove the design, the fabric should pull off and leave the door unharmed.

We love the look, and it's useful too—there are four doors in this corner of our house, and departing guests sometimes get confused about which way they came in. Now we just direct them to exit through the village.

NOSH

KITCHEN AND DINING IDEAS

JOHN
SAYS

Our entire blog started because of a kitchen renovation that we tackled back in 2007 right after we got married and about a year into owning our first house. It was actually my idea. Sherry thought blogging sounded weird and lame and time waste-y, which is more than a little ironic since she soon fell in love with it and a few years later it became her full-time job well before it became mine.

I thought blogging was a great way to keep our family and friends updated on all of our kitchen changes without shoving photos down everyone's throat in annoyingly frequent e-mails. That way we could just share the URL once and people could drop in to see what we were doing whenever they wanted. Our friends and family members checked in on us periodically and cheered us on (which was a nice morale boost along the way), and soon strangers began to drop in on us too, which was funny and weird and awesome all at the same time. And so it began.

But back to that first kitchen makeover that we tackled in 2007. After 113 days without a kitchen (I wish I was kidding), we finally had the room put back together, and words can't describe how glorious it was to have modern-day conveniences like a working sink and fridge again (no more Hot Pockets for dinner and washing dishes in the bathtub—hallelujah!). So being the not-stellar chefs that we are, we invited some culinarily blessed friends over to celebrate by cooking a big three-course meal together in our new kitchen, which was going great until we somehow clogged the disposal during the first course. Yup, the homemade hummus did us in. Giant vegetable chunks slipped down the drain because no one was paying enough attention to flip on the disposal as they went.

So apart came the just-connected pipes mere hours after we sent our friends home with full bellies. The kicker? The blockage was so far back into the wall that taking the pipes apart and using a snake didn't get us anywhere. So we Googled around for unclogging tips and learned that boiling water can bust up deep, unreachable clogs. (It literally cooks vegetables and meat so they shrink up and water can rush through.) We put the pipes back together and gave that a try, and a few gallons of boiling water later . . . victory!

Let's just say we learned right then and there that we should never take small things like running water for granted. And that sometimes ~~road~~ veggie blocks can rear their ugly heads, but a little bit of effort (and Google!) can usually get 'er done.

Coming together...

...and coming back apart. Womp womp.

038

THREE EASY DIY BACKSPLASH IDEAS

COST $-$$

WORK SOME SWEAT

TIME DONE IN A DAY

There's no mortar and trowel necessary if you have an inexplicably ugly tile backsplash; just try one of these cover-ups.

1   **Tin ceiling tiles** can add a sleek yet charming feeling while bringing in lots of texture, and can even be painted for a totally different look. They can be hung with construction adhesive (just ask the store clerk what he recommends for the type of tile you're going to cover) or, if you're a renter, you can use removable methods like 3M Command strips for a temporary hold.

2   **Beadboard,** like tin, can be hung right over an existing backsplash with construction adhesive or 3M strips for a quick face-lift. It can also be painted for an easy upgrade.

3   **A slew of frames** full of anything from black-and-white photos to colorful fabric (like we've used here) can either be leaned up against the backsplash or secured in place with removable 3M Command strips. Not only can they add tons of personality (and hide an ugly backsplash), many European kitchens actually have glass backsplashes! So feel free to celebrate with a croissant.

BONUS TIP
Think Beyond a Piece of Furniture's Traditional Use

A dresser can work really well in a living room or foyer, while a bookcase can easily become a bar. An old library card catalog cabinet can be used as a kitchen island. A buffet can be retrofitted with a counter and a sink to become a bathroom vanity. We actually turned a night table into a vanity in our old bathroom by adding a sink and a faucet (see it on page 129). So go find one piece of furniture in your house and completely reimagine it as something else, whether you're hard-core DIYing it or just moving it from one room to another.

039

MAKE HAPPY HERB POTS FOR YOUR KITCHEN

COST $

WORK SOME SWEAT

TIME DONE IN AN HOUR

Planting fresh herbs in pots to place on a sunny sill is always charming (and functional). And upgrading those pots with decorative tape can take them from yawn to yes, please.

1 Find a few **small terra-cotta pots** at a home-improvement store, a garden center, or even a thrift store or yard sale.

2 Hunt down some **thick decorative tape** (we used one called Trim Accents from Michaels).

3 Create a paper template with **card stock** to wrap around your pot.

4 Stick decorative tape over your entire template and trim off any overhanging tape.

5 Wrap your template covered in decorative tape around the pot and secure it in the back with a small piece of **clear tape.**

START HERE

4

040

A FRUIT BOWL FIVE WAYS

So many options, so little time (and so much fruit).

1. A faux clamshell has been our fruit bowl of choice for years.

2. A white metal basket with geometric cutouts is modern and fun.

3. A wire basket can add tons of charm.

4. A rustic wood bowl brings natural texture to any counter.

5. A large footed bowl is always elegant (this was just three dollars at Goodwill).

041

THREE WAYS TO SET THE TABLE

Fifty percent of this duo (Sherry, in this case) loves to play with place settings. And 100 percent of this duo loves to eat. So here are a few ideas. . . .

1. Try rolling your silverware in a cloth napkin for a casual bistro vibe.

2. A clementine adds modern pop to a white and navy place setting (and tastes good too).

3. This eighty-cent thrift-store jar full of pistachios is a sweet surprise for guests.

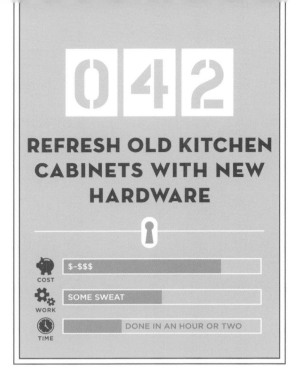

042

REFRESH OLD KITCHEN CABINETS WITH NEW HARDWARE

COST	$-$$$
WORK	SOME SWEAT
TIME	DONE IN AN HOUR OR TWO

You'd be surprised by how much new cabinet hardware can update things. And assuming your new hardware can go into the old hardware holes (for example, if they're both 3-inch handles), there's no wood filler, stain, or paint necessary, so you should be done with the project in an hour or two.

This chipper blue knob adds a pop of playful color.

A sweet ceramic flower runneth over with charm.

This modern stripe-fest feels cool and linear.

A chic gilded geometric knob oozes elegance.

Something clean and utilitarian is sleek and understated.

A bubbly blue glass knob looks dreamy and ethereal.

This stainless and glass knob looks fun and futuristic.

A dark octagonal knob is moody and sophisticated.

Something scalloped and full of detail is always charming.

This sweet owl knob is a hoot. (Can't. stop. the. pun.)

PUT ON YOUR BRAVE PANTS
AND SHAKE THINGS UP.

043

MIX AND MATCH YOUR TABLE AND CHAIRS

Your dining table and chairs don't have to match perfectly to "go"— and might just look a lot more layered and interesting if they're different. Here are a few pairings we love.

- Modern glass table + dark upholstered chairs
- Chunky wood table + sleek acrylic chairs
- Round white table + textured woven chairs
- Dark wood table + white upholstered chairs

044

PAINT YOUR KITCHEN CABINETS

🐷 COST — $-$$

⚙️ WORK — LOTS OF SWEAT

🕐 TIME — DONE IN A WEEK (OR TWO)

Both of our homes came with outdated dark wood kitchens, so we're no strangers to using this technique to give the room a totally new look (on a pretty awesome under-a-hundred-dollar budget).

1 Select your **paint color** and new **cabinet hardware** (if you've decided not to reuse what you've got). The best way to evaluate colors is to tape paint swatches on a vertical plane (in this case, your cabinet doors). Also, note whether your new hardware will use the existing holes or call for new ones to be drilled.

2 Remove all your cabinet doors and drawer fronts, as well as the hardware. (Be sure to set hardware aside carefully if you're reusing it.) Spread out your doors and drawers in a large, clean work area.

3 If you aren't using the existing hardware holes, fill them with **wood filler** using a **spackle knife.** Let the filler dry and sand until smooth. Repeat if needed until things feel flush. Do the same for any cracks or deep scratches in the doors or frames that you'd like to eliminate.

4 Using a **palm sander** and **150-grit sandpaper,** go over every inch of your cabinet boxes, doors, and drawer fronts (including the backs of the doors and the insides of your cabinets if you plan to paint them too). You don't need to remove all the existing stain, but sand enough that the glossy finish has been roughed up and is ready for primer.

5 Wipe down the doors and frames with a rag moistened with **liquid deglosser.**

6 After allowing the deglosser to dry completely, apply a thin and even coat of **primer** on all surfaces that will be painted. Use a **brush** to get into tight spots, but before the primer dries, make sure every surface gets a pass with a **small foam roller** to minimize brushstrokes. Consult your favorite paint store for primer recommendations (we've had good experiences with Zinsser Smart Prime), and remember to get it tinted if you're going dark.

7 Once your primer is fully dry, repeat the above step with **paint.** You will likely need two or three coats, depending on your color choice. There are great paint options specifically made for cabinets that go on smoothly and resist drips (we use Benjamin Moore's Advance paint, which is self-leveling and low-VOC), so rely on those to minimize coats and frustration.

8 As excited as you'll be to put your kitchen back together, be sure to follow the paint manufacturer's recommended drying time. You don't want your freshly painted doors getting dinged up because you jumped the gun.

9 Once everything is dry, attach your knobs or pulls to the cabinet doors and drawer fronts—drilling new holes from the front of your cabinets toward the back (with a smaller pilot hole if necessary). We always rely on an inexpensive **template** from the hardware store to speed up this process. Once the knobs and pulls are on, reinstall the hinges and drawers.

10 Rehang your cabinet doors, slide drawers back into place, put everything back in your kitchen, and call it a job well done.

NOTE: You can find more info and photos for the entire cabinet painting process at younghouselove .com/book.

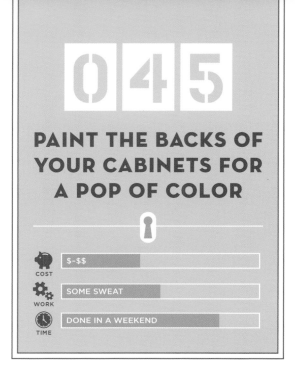

045

PAINT THE BACKS OF YOUR CABINETS FOR A POP OF COLOR

COST $-$$

WORK SOME SWEAT

TIME DONE IN A WEEKEND

Painting the back walls of your cabinets can look especially amazing if they're doorless or of the glass-door variety. When it comes to picking a color, something soft like robin's-egg blue, celery, taupe, or light gray is always pretty. Or something bolder like chocolate, lime, turquoise, red, or yellow can wake up your whole kitchen. You can use a satin or semigloss paint, which is easily wipeable (since the insides of your cabinets see some pretty major action), and the cabinet painting method on pages 82–83 works for the backs of your cabinets as well. One quick tip would be that if you tape off the sides of your cabinets (so you're just applying color to the back wall), peel that tape off as soon as you finish the last coat for the cleanest line. Then just wait for things to dry, load in your prettiest dishes, and grin like a fool.

Using a contrasting color on your island (or on your upper and lower cabinets) can add depth and style. A few classic combinations are dark chocolate stain and crisp white paint, moody gray-green and softer gray-green, sandy mocha and soft cream, deep navy and glossy white. See pages 82–83 for a step-by-step cabinet painting tutorial.

046

PAINT YOUR ISLAND A DIFFERENT COLOR THAN YOUR CABINETS

047

REMOVE YOUR CABINET DOORS FOR AN OPEN FEELING

It can vary by door, but most kitchen cabinets have hinges on the side that you can simply unscrew to remove the door and hinge to create an open-shelf look. It can visually be a lot lighter, and it's a great way to show off the dishes and glassware you use frequently (so it doesn't have time to get dusty).

You can usually find old brass chandeliers for ten dollars or less at local thrift stores like Goodwill or the Habitat for Humanity ReStore. And they'll definitely look like you spent a lot more by the time you're done making them over.

1 Head to the home-improvement store and grab a can of **spray primer** and a can of bold fruit-colored **spray paint,** like plum, watermelon, lemon yellow, clementine, or lime green (the list goes on). A color that's a little more subdued, like deep indigo, eggplant, dark emerald, or charcoal, could be awesome too. And of course glossy (or matte) black or white always works.

2 Wipe down the chandelier with a damp rag. Remove the bulbs and cover the sockets where the bulbs go with **painter's tape** to protect them. You don't want those getting all gunked up with spray paint.

3 Apply two or three super-thin and even coats of spray primer followed by three or four just as thin and even coats of spray paint (we used Gloss Purple by Rust-Oleum's Painter's Touch). If you know how to use a can of Aquanet (point, shoot, and always keep that can moving), you can use spray paint (same exact premise—just keep that can in motion, baby).

4 After the paint dries fully, bribe an electrically savvy friend to come hang it for you or look up a nice video tutorial on YouTube. (You're basically just turning off the power and connecting the wires in the same way that you disconnected them from the previous light fixture.) You can also always hire an electrician to do the work for an additional fifty to one hundred dollars.

A FEW SPRAY-PAINTING BASICS

Spray painting something can yield perfect results or a drippy mucked-up mess. Here are a few of our favorite tips.

■ Skip the cheap two-dollar stuff in favor of the six- to seven-dollar quality stuff. (We like Rust-Oleum's trigger spray nozzle because it allows the paint to go on thin and even and prevents it from getting all over your fingers.)

■ Keep the nozzle 8 to 10 inches away from whatever you're spray painting.

■ Always keep the can moving. If you're a-sprayin', your arm better be a-swayin'.

■ Three thin and even coats are better than one thick and gooey one. You really want to create a mist, not a heavy, wet coating. If you see drips forming, you're applying it waaaaay too thick.

■ Spray paint has yet to go no-VOC, so try to apply it outside while wearing a mask, and let it cure as long as the instructions recommend (usually twenty-four hours, but we try to double that when we can).

■ You can "seal" any spray paint (to limit off-gassing once you bring it inside) by applying two thin coats of a product like Safecoat Acrylacq, which is low-VOC and nontoxic.

■ We generally like to spray paint smaller items (chandeliers, frames, lamp bases, small stools, and metal side tables) but prefer to use a small foam roller and a paintbrush to tackle larger items (desks, tables, and dressers).

0 4 9

STASH YOUR KNIVES

COST $

WORK NO SWEAT

TIME DONE IN UNDER AN HOUR

We have two or three knives that we use all the time, and they usually just loiter around the kitchen—you know, sitting out on the cutting board or on a windowsill—which looks messy at best and serial killer–ish at worst (we do love *Dexter* . . .). This handy little knife-stashing system definitely looks better. Plus, the coffee version smells delicious— and we're not even coffee drinkers!

1 Grab a **vase** that's taller than all the blades of your knives. (It doesn't have to be taller than the handles.)

2 Fill the vase with **uncooked pasta, uncooked rice,** or **coffee beans.**

3 Shove your knives in blade-first (it's best to towel- or air-dry them before you do, so they don't get rice or coffee beans stuck to them).

4 You may occasionally want to rinse and fully dry your coffee beans/rice/pasta over months of use.

REMOVE SOME
UPPER CABINETS

In a cabinet-riddled room, ditching some lesser-used upper cabinets can instantly create a more airy and spacious feeling (they're usually just screwed into the wall and each other, so taking them down is as easy as removing a few screws). In their place you could hang floating shelves, your favorite piece of art, or even a mirror to expand the space and add interest.

051

MAKE ETCHED-GLASS CONTAINERS FOR YOUR COUNTER

COST — $

WORK — SOME SWEAT

TIME — DONE IN AN HOUR

We went for a nerd-tastic riff on the periodic table when it came to labeling our flour and sugar, but you can etch any simple-ish words or icons that you'd like with some sticker paper, a knife, and some etching cream. No lab coat required.

1 Print out any design or wording that you'd like on **sticker paper** from an office-supply store.

2 Stick your design onto your clean glass container and use an **X-Acto knife** to cut out your pattern or text (don't worry, it shouldn't hurt the glass).

3 Peel away the sticker to expose the area that you want to etch.

4 Grab your **etching cream** (found online or in craft stores), and follow the instructions to complete your design. We found that leaving it on for the longest time advisable made for a more uniform etched result (see how our flour etching looks a bit crisper than our sugar one?). Live and learn!

BONUS TIP
Perfect Schmerfect

Homemade DIY projects are often sweetly imperfect, but that's kind of what makes them so charming. They're not mass-produced or created by a machine, so there's likely to be a sign or two that they're personal projects that were made with love. Embrace imperfections and quirks and remember that many high-end shops actually charge top dollar for that homemade feeling (machines are frequently used to distress things so they look more worn or inconsistent). We wouldn't call any of the items and projects that we DIYed for this book perfect. So remember that a thrift-store dresser that you painted (who's going to notice that drip in the back corner?) or a headboard or chair seat that you upholstered (so what if the pattern is a quarter of an inch off?) is still a lot more of an upgrade than doing nothing at all.

MIGHT I SUGGEST AN ETCHED DOG TREAT JAR?

THESE JARS WERE $5.99 A POP AT TARGET.

052

UPGRADE YOUR COUNTERS AFFORDABLY

If you aren't loving your countertops, changing them doesn't mean you have to splurge for granite or marble. More and more designer kitchens are now including less expensive (and just as gorgeous) materials like butcher block, poured concrete slabs (there are some good online tutorials on diynetwork.com, instructables .com, and concreteexchange.com), and even solid-surface options like Corian (in classic and inexpensive colors like white). The great thing is that all these materials are not only budget friendly, they're also pretty neutral, so they shouldn't look dated or be hard to decorate around in a decade or two.

You generally want to ground your dining table with a rug that's large enough for you to pull out all the chairs without worrying that they'll fall off the rug. Not only is this functional, it won't make the table look cramped, and the whole dining space will have a more open quality. It's always nice to let things breathe a little.

053

FIND THE RIGHT-SIZED RUG FOR YOUR DINING ROOM

START HERE

054

REUPHOLSTER A DINING CHAIR

COST $-$$

WORK SOME SWEAT

TIME DONE IN AN HOUR

We know, we know, it's all fine and dandy to toss out ideas like "upholster a chair," but if you've never done it, it can sound like quite an undertaking. How do we know this? Because there was a time that we had never tackled jobs like these either. But now that we've done it (and lived to tell the tale) we can assure you that it's not brain surgery or rocket science. So here's how to add some new swagger to an old chair in the form of fresh upholstery.

1 First, remove the seat cushion. There are usually just a few screws to undo on the underside of the chair to free up the seat.

2 Place the cushion on top of your new **fabric** (if it has a pattern, make sure it's straight and centered) and cut out a piece that's the size and shape of the cushion with an extra 2 inches on all sides.

3 Place the cut fabric over the seat cushion and turn the whole thing facedown on the floor so you can pull the fabric tightly around to the underside of the seat and staple it into place with a **staple gun.** Be sure to pull the fabric so it's taut and keep it straight as you work your way around, adding a staple every 2 inches or so for a secure hold.

4 Periodically check that the front of the cushion looks tight, centered, and wrinkle-free by peeking as you go. You don't want a big surprise when you flip it over forty staples later. Remember that if the fabric looks loose or crooked, it's easy to pop out a few staples with a flat-head screwdriver and redo them.

5 When it comes to stapling the corners, pretend you're wrapping a present. Tuck the fabric to create folds that are hidden on the underside of the seat so that the top of the cushion looks snugly wrapped. It can help to flip the cushion over before stapling each corner to be sure you like how it looks before pulling the trigger.

6 Once you've finished stapling and you're left with a freshly covered seat cushion, screw the cushion back into the chair from the underside the same way it was originally secured.

7 Hot diggity; you're done. That is, unless you want to go the extra mile and paint or stain the chair too (which is best done before reattaching the cushion).

NOTE: You can find more info and photos for chair reupholstery at younghouselove.com/book.

THIS CHAIR WAS JUST **$7** AT A THRIFT STORE.

055

MAKE QUIRKY SHADOW-BOX ART FOR THE KITCHEN

COST $

WORK SOME SWEAT

TIME DONE IN AN HOUR

This is your chance to collect kitchen-related "curiosities" and display them in a science-y way. For example, an array of dried pasta that's labeled like "specimens" and framed in a shadow box can look really cool. Unless you think we're crazy. (We just might be. . . .) Seriously, though, you can also display a variety of tea bags, dried beans, or coffee beans. The key to keeping it interesting is trying to evoke that science-lab feel. Geek is the new black.

rotini

farfalle

marcaroni

angel hair

tri-color rotini

penne

fettuccine

Here's super-simple tip number one. If you're nervous about floral arrangement, use all of the same type of bloom in the same color. It always looks sophisticated and is a lot easier than wrestling with baby's breath and other variables.

Splitting up a bouquet and spreading it out across a few smaller vases is error proof—just snip off a few stems and drop them in. (Water! Don't forget to add the water!)

Fluted vases are your friends. They help stems splay out in a natural way without much effort. Sometimes the vase you'll find yourself grabbing again and again is just a simple fluted glass vase that lets the flowers be the star.

056

DON'T BE SCARED OF FLOWERS

Confession time. Flowers used to confuse us. Until we cracked the code. We're hardly master florists, but these few quick tips might simplify things and help you bring blooms home without any flower freakouts.

Isn't this tip about flowers? Where are they? Well, some vases are awesomesauce without them, so when flower money is low, a gleaming silver statement vase like this will still make you smile.

This happy little lady-vase can do no wrong—with or without flowers. If we were going to load her up, we'd choose simple white blooms to let the vase be the star, or go with something in the same tone (like yellow tulips) for a cool monochromatic effect.

Like his fine vase-friends before him, this dude can get by on his looks (read: flowers are optional), but a ball-like cluster of all the same bloom (like red carnations, yellow roses, or white mums) would look pretty dapper.

057

THINK BEYOND POTPOURRI FOR VASE FILLERS

Everything from wine corks to uncooked brown rice to coffee beans or unshelled walnuts can look elegant and cost next to nothing when placed in a vase. Heck, you might even have something growing out back you can use. One of the prettiest centerpieces we've seen is a simple bowl full of floating flowers from the garden. Other stuff to consider:

- Ribbons
- Pennies
- Shells
- Dried pasta
- Dice
- Marbles
- Dominoes
- Rocks or stones

058

STENCIL A TABLE RUNNER

COST	$-$$	
WORK	SOME SWEAT	
TIME	DONE IN AN AFTERNOON	

Sometimes it's easier to find boring old basic table runners than something in the pattern and color that you have in mind, which is where making one yourself can really come in handy.

1 Lay a lovely **patterned lace remnant** over a **plain fabric runner.** It's best to do this outside on a drop cloth.

2 Lightly mist the whole runner with **spray fabric paint** in the color of your choice, being careful to follow the application instructions and to not apply it too heavily (we used Stencil Spray in copper from Jo-Ann Fabric).

3 Once the runner looks well covered with paint, carefully remove the lace on top of it to reveal the lacelike design that you've created.

4 Allow ample drying time and then use/wash according to the fabric paint directions.

059

STEFANIE'S WORLDLY SIDEBOARD

GUEST BLOGGER IDEA

BLOGGER:
STEFANIE SCHIADA

BLOG:
BROOKLYN LIMESTONE
(WWW.BROOKLYNLIMESTONE.COM)

LOCATION:
BROOKLYN, NEW YORK

FAVORITE COLOR COMBO:
SILVER + GOLD (OR SOMETIMES
NICKEL + BRASS)

FAVORITE GO-TO TOOL:
STAPLE GUN

FAVORITE WAY TO FINISH A ROOM:
WITH SOMETHING OLD

While browsing in a local flea market, I stumbled upon a damaged but affordable dining-room sideboard. I loved its shape, the extra storage would be fabulous, and the dimensions were ideal to substitute as a sofa table. The finish wasn't in great shape and the look was far too traditional for what I had in mind, but I knew that could be remedied with a little imagination. This would be the perfect canvas to add some personality to my very neutral living room.

SUPPLIES

- Sideboard
  (a dresser, buffet, or table would work too)
- TSP solution
  (a cleanser sold at home-improvement stores)
- Palm sander and sandpaper
- Semigloss paint
- Metallic craft paint
- Paintbrush, foam roller, and small craft brush
- Projector *(try renting one or borrowing one from a local school or office)*
- Transparency paper
- Polyurethane sealant *(optional)*

1 **CLEAN.** After removing the hardware, I started my sideboard's makeover by washing the whole thing down in a solution of TSP and water to clean off the decades of dirt that had accumulated on it.

2 **SAND.** When it was dry, out came the palm sander to rough up its lacquered surface. The top was in particularly bad shape with several large gouges, so I gave it some extra sanding time to wear down the wood until it was smooth.

3 **PAINT THE BASE.** Once my sideboard was sanded, out came brushes and rollers to give it new life in peacock blue. (I used Plumage by Martha Stewart.) I loved the color, but it needed something more.

4 PICK SOME PUNCH. I realized that some gold paint could pick up on the metallic accents in the rest of the room and add a little sparkle. I wrestled with lots of different options (chevron? faux bois? stripes?) before realizing that my love of travel, in the form of a world map, was the perfect way to accentuate this piece.

5 PROJECT A PATTERN. I found a map that I could transfer onto a transparency and pulled out my overhead projector. (Yes, the very same kind that you heard humming in school all those years ago!) I drew the shades and turned down the lights to let the shadow of the map light the way.

6 PAINT AGAIN. With a small brush and an inexact hand, I got the outline of the world onto the top of the sideboard and then just filled that in. It took a few coats to get a nice, solid cover, but almost no skill or artistic ability was required.

I planned to let the sideboard cure for thirty days and then cover it with a coat of polyurethane to protect the finish, but amazingly it's been quite durable without it. So it was even easier to complete than I imagined. Voilà! The world right in my living room!

STUCK? FRUSTRATED? OVERWHELMED? THAT'S PAR FOR THE DIY COURSE

- **Everyone makes mistakes.** For example, we painted our trim with flat paint and had to redo it all. And it sucked. But we course-corrected (and learned a lesson or two along the way). Look at mistakes as a sign that you're moving forward, not stagnating. If you're doing something, even if it turns out to be the wrong something, it's still teaching you how to get there faster next time.

- **Tastes change.** Don't beat yourself up if you have a few things that no longer suit your style. You can always put them on Craigslist or paint them or otherwise adapt them. It's a lot more frustrating to force yourself to embrace something that you can't stand than to allow your rooms to grow.

- **Relax; it's only decorating.** We like to say this when we're fired up about something going wrong or how long something takes. Things happen, and sometimes the budget or the time line can get you down, but it's nice to take a few deep breaths and remember that no one's life is on the line.

- **Keep at it.** Hang art. If you hate it, you can caulk those holes in ten minutes. Paint. If you hate it, you can repaint. Nearly every design decision can be undone pretty easily. And chances are you'll like most of what you do, so there's only a marginal amount of true error in the whole trial-and-error method.

- **In the end, it's all worth it.** Trust us.

060
MAKE A BRANCH CANDLEHOLDER

COST	FREE–$
WORK	SOME SWEAT
TIME	DONE IN AN HOUR

Here's a great way to bring the outdoors inside—especially because branches are *f-r-e-e*.

1 Find an interesting-looking **branch** or fallen **tree limb** that's at least 3 inches thick at a few points.

2 Make sure it's dry and free of bugs by leaving it in the garage for a few days or even popping it into the freezer for a day or two (if it fits).

3 Use a **drill** and a **large circular drill bit** (a 1¾-inch bit will run you about six dollars at a hardware store) to carve out three to four little round cubbies to hold glass votive candle holders about 5 inches apart.

4 Pop **glass-encased votive candles** into the holes that you just drilled. Glass votive holders with small votive candles inside are safer than bare votive candles without any glass to contain the flame. We found these at Target.

5 Light 'em up and bask in the glow.

WE DID THIS
WHOLE PROJECT
FOR UNDER NINE
DOLLARS.

DOZE

BEDROOM IDEAS

The one room that you have a pretty decent amount of influence over as a kid is your bedroom. You can hang New Kids on the Block posters or fill a pet hammock with stuffed animals. (Yes, I was guilty of both—along with wearing airbrushed jeans that winked.) Sometimes you're even allowed to select the wall color or add some other customized detail. I actually painted clouds on my closet doors, and John admits to decorating with more than one Garfield accessory. (He had a weird thing for that grouchy lasagna-eating cat.) John also made an "artistic" collage of the cast of various seasons of *The Real World*. And I may or may not have had one of those wildlife posters with a baby seal on it. Oh yeah, we had a grand ol' time making our rooms into our own little hideouts, since we definitely didn't have much decorating "say" outside of those spaces. (I wonder why.)

Don't look now, but my jeans are winking at you.

John still had this sheep blanket when I met him.

Even for adults, the bedroom is one of those rooms that's usually seen only by you and your immediate family. So it's a place that you can really have freedom and fun with since you don't need to cater to guests or entertain friends there.

Take our first house's master bedroom, which was completely lacking in closet space (there was only one minuscule half-sized closet that we desperately struggled to share). After some time spent living with it (and thinking about possible solutions) we decided to do something pretty unorthodox. We introduced a curtained ceiling-height wardrobe on each side of our bed and added a header to make it all look built in. This created a cozy sleeping nook with tons of hidden storage. It's

definitely not something you see every day—and probably isn't the right choice for everyone—but it worked like a charm for us.

When we were selling our house, we learned that the new owners were planning to bring in a king-sized bed, which would mean completely dismantling our built-in closets. At first we were so sad and confused as to why anyone wouldn't want triple the closet space in exchange for a still-spacious-by-our-standards queen-sized bed. But in the end we realized that bedrooms really are personal spaces, so just like our New Kids on the Block and *Real World* posters of yore, everyone has different ideas when it comes to making a bedroom feel like home.

061

MAKE AN UPHOLSTERED HEADBOARD

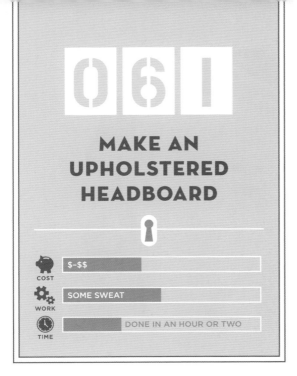

COST $-$$

WORK SOME SWEAT

TIME DONE IN AN HOUR OR TWO

START HERE

Nothing screams "unfinished bedroom" like a missing headboard. So why not make one?

1 Instead of cutting a frame from plywood, one of our favorite cheap and easy options is to go to an art-supply store and buy a wooden frame called a **canvas stretcher.** It's nice and light and easy to hang directly on a wall, unlike a piece of plywood. The stretchers also come in so many sizes, you can usually find one that's perfect without having to cut any wood yourself—just build a frame to meet your desired size (ours for this full-sized bed was 24 by 54 inches).

2 Roll out some **extra-loft batting** on the floor and lay your stretcher frame on top of it. Cut your batting, leaving a few extra inches on all sides so it can be pulled and stapled around the stretcher frame.

3 Wrap the batting around each edge of your frame and use a **staple gun** to secure it. We like to put staples in at twelve, three, six, and nine

o'clock first, keeping the batting pulled tight to prevent bunching. Finish by stapling every 3 to 4 inches around the entire perimeter, wrapping and stapling the corners just like you'd wrap a present (folding it around to the back so the front looks nice and clean at the corners). If your headboard isn't as plush as you'd hoped, apply another layer or two of batting.

4 Just like you did with your batting, cut your **fabric** a few inches larger than the frame on all sides. Just pay special attention to keeping any fabric pattern straight and centered before stapling. Then staple your fabric in the same manner that you did the batting, double-checking every few staples to be sure your pattern hasn't skewed or gotten off center. Be sure to pull things tight so you don't end up with a droopy result.

5 With your headboard done, you just gotta get it on the wall. The stretcher frame should be light enough to hang on a couple of **screws.**

NOTE: You can find more info and photos for making an upholstered headboard at younghouselove.com/book.

4

5

THIS TOOK
UNDER AN
HOUR TO MAKE!

062
ONE BED
THREE WAYS

1. Dark bedding feels luxe and enveloping, and a leafy bolster adds interest.

2. A white duvet + color + pattern = a lively look.

3. Moody colors like slate blue and gray are serene, while geometrics add sophistication.

063

ADD LIGHTS YOU CAN REACH FROM BED

COST $-$$$

WORK SOME SWEAT

TIME DONE IN A DAY

It's such a luxury to have a light that you can switch off from bed. Here are a few options.

• Table lamps on bedside tables

• Sconces

• Swing-arm lamps

• Hanging pendants

They can all be found as plug-in versions so you don't need a professional, but it could cost as little as a hundred dollars to hire a pro to hardwire something (which might be a nice birthday present to yourself or your other half). Or you can try an inexpensive light remote from the hardware store. Seriously, life is better when you don't have to pretend you're sleeping to avoid getting out of bed to turn off the light.

064

"SLIPCOVER" YOUR EXISTING HEADBOARD

Drape a tapestry or a blanket over your headboard for a whole new look. That's it.

065

HAND-STAMP A DUVET

If you've got a plain duvet around that's begging for a bit more excitement, it may just be time to break out the fabric paint and get your stamp on.

1 Choose a **fabric paint** (we used Met Olive Green from Lumiere by Jacquard) and a **stencil** that you like at a craft store or online.

2 On a sheet of paper or scrap of fabric, test your stencil to figure out how to get the cleanest print. We prefer dabbing paint on lightly with a **sponge-tipped craft brush.**

3 Once you're happy with the test stencil, start stenciling your duvet. Try staggered rows or even just a border around the edge.

4 Follow the instructions provided with the fabric paint for washing and setting your stamp before using the duvet.

TURN THE PAGE TO SEE THE FINISHED PROJECT!

ADD A COZY FAUX FIREPLACE

COST $-$$$

WORK SOME SWEAT

TIME DONE IN A DAY

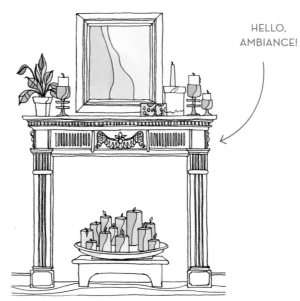

HELLO, AMBIANCE!

Here's an easy way to warm up a dull corner of the bedroom.

1   Buy a secondhand mantel (many architectural salvage stores sell them; we've also seen them at thrift stores, as well as on Craigslist).

2   You might want to prime and paint the mantel to give it a fresh look. (Semigloss white **paint** on a mantel in a room with trim of the same color can look great, but go with whatever calls your name, like a rich wood **stain.**)

3   Secure it to the wall by driving **screws** into the studs or using **anchors.** You may need to remove a small section of your baseboard or cut a small notch out of the mantel so it will sit flush against your wall.

4   Help "authenticate" the fireplace effect by adding a slew of glowing candles to the firebox or placing some art above the mantel.

CONSIDER A NIGHTSTAND ALTERNATIVE

If you have no space in your bedroom for a proper nightstand, try hanging a floating shelf with room for a small task lamp. Or you can add a long console table or a bookcase behind the bed for a modern take on a headboard. Bam: a place to put your alarm clock, retainer, and Harry Potter books.

068

PAINT A HEADBOARD ON THE WALL

COST: FREE-$

WORK: SOME SWEAT

TIME: DONE IN AN AFTERNOON

If you can't afford a proper headboard, this is a quick way to add presence, ground a bed, and bring in color. It's a win-win-win.

1 If you have leftover **paint** from another room that you'd like to use, go for it. Or pick up a quart of paint at the store. We used Hale Navy by Benjamin Moore.

2 Use **painter's tape** and a **level** to tape off a simple rectangle on the wall behind your bed. (Make it the same width as your mattress, so it feels balanced, and about 32 inches tall for a standard look.)

3 Fill in the rectangle with your new hue using a **paintbrush** or a **small foam roller.** Two or three coats should do the trick.

4 Remove the tape right away (before the last coat of paint dries for the cleanest result) and celebrate your faux headboard with a nap on the sofa while it dries.

NOTE: You can sketch a more ornate headboard shape on a giant piece of cardboard (or a template created by taping card stock or poster board together). Then trace that curvy or geometric shape onto the wall and carefully outline it with painter's tape or paint the edge with a small paintbrush. Then just fill it in. Here are a few shape ideas.

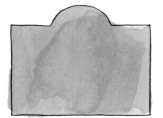

WE MADE OUR HEADBOARD WITH A PAPER TEMPLATE THAT WE TRACED ONTO THE WALL AND FILLED IN WITH PAINT.

069

SWITCH OUT A CLOSET DOOR FOR SOMETHING ELSE

If you just hate hate hate the closet door you have, you can switch it out for something else. Like . . .

- Curtains
- A barn door on a cool industrial track
- Strips of ribbon to create a breezy and playful curtain
- Blinds
- A fabric panel that slides to the side

You can also go with no door at all. (Painting the inside of the closet and adding glossy white shelves with baskets or other eye-pleasing storage can totally work.) You can even shove a dresser in there to make the closet feel like an open nook. Door removal is great for making things easily accessible, and the room can feel larger since there are more nooks and crannies for the eyes to peruse.

Your dresser drawers don't have to be boring. It's like a secret shot of happy to pull open a drawer and see cheerful graphic drawer liners. Patterned paper from a craft store or gorgeous sheets of gift wrap can work too. Putting away laundry might even be—*gasp*—fun.

1   Cut sheets of **gift wrap** or **decorative paper** to the size of each drawer's bottom. (You can use a template made of printer paper taped together.)

2   Affix the patterned paper to the drawer with double-sided tape in each corner and in the middle.

3   For extra durability, you can break out the big guns and apply **decoupage medium** (like matte Mod Podge). If you do, let it fully dry before putting away your clothes.

070

LINE YOUR DRAWERS WITH PATTERNED PAPER

071

MAKE DRAWER SHELVES

COST	$-$$
WORK	SOME SWEAT
TIME	DONE IN A DAY

This is sort of a riff on a bookcase, but it's more free-form and fun.

1 Find three nonrickety **drawers** at a thrift store or yard sale.

2 **Stain, paint, decoupage, stencil,** or **wallpaper** them to your heart's content.

3 Use **heavy-duty anchors** and **screws** (or long screws into wall studs) to securely hang them.

4 Fill them with stuff that you love, as you would any shelf or bookcase (except they're cooler, because they're *drawers!*).

072

ONE NIGHTSTAND THREE WAYS

It's amazing how many looks you can achieve with a basic wooden nightstand, thanks to paint, new hardware, and a few other tweaks. (See page 278 for a full furniture painting tutorial.)

1. A stainless handle + a craft-store roll of cork (glued in place) + inexpensive casters = an industrial effect.

2. Glossy white paint + a natural wood drawer = a cool mod look.

3. A bright color + playful hardware = a bold and cheerful vibe.

073

MAKE A WEATHERED-WOOD HEADBOARD

COST $$

WORK LOTS OF SWEAT

TIME DONE IN A WEEKEND

If tufted or fabric headboards aren't your thing, you can DIY a handsome and rustic version instead. We made this one for just thirty bucks.

1 If you're lucky enough to have some reclaimed weathered wood around, skip ahead to step 3. If not, pick up some **wood planks** at a lumber yard or home-improvement store and have them cut to your desired headboard width. A home-improvement store can usually cut wood for you right there (which makes it easier to haul and simpler to assemble once you get home). You'll also need **two bracing pieces** of wood, cut to the height of your headboard or a bit shorter (we used two 1-inch-by-3-inch boards). See step 3 for more details.

2 Our favorite trick for aging new wood is to rough it up a bit (try scraping it with a screw or smacking a bag of nails against it). Then sand it smooth with 150-grit **sandpaper** and stain it using a nice, rich **stain** color, following the application instructions on the can. We used Dark Walnut by Minwax on ours.

3 Once the stained boards are dry, lay them side by side facedown on the floor, to create your final headboard arrangement. Take the two bracing pieces that have been cut to the height of your headboard and lay them perpendicular to either end of your boards. Secure them to each board with a couple of wood screws to hold everything in place.

NOTE: If you don't want these bracing pieces to show, cut them slightly shorter than the height of your headboard and place them a few centimeters in from the edge. You may want to add a third or fourth brace depending on the length of your headboard.

4 Your headboard will be heavy, so find a few studs in the wall behind your bed to screw it into. Or add **heavy-duty wire hooks** (screwed into the back) and some strong **hanging wire** that you can hook over **heavy-duty anchors** (or screws that go into a stud). Or you can use two-by-fours cut to size to add legs to your headboard so that it stands between your bed and the wall.

NOTE: See more info and photos for making this project at younghouselove.com/book.

LEARN HOW
WE MADE THIS
YELLOW MIRROR
ON THE NEXT
PAGE!

074

MAKE A SPIKY BRANCH MIRROR

COST $

WORK SOME SWEAT

TIME DONE IN AN AFTERNOON

This finished project will look like a sunburst mirror, but a bit less common and full of natural texture. Plus, bringing the outside in never fails to make a statement. We found this branchy wreath at Michaels for twelve dollars, covered it with a couple coats of sun yellow spray paint, and used heavy-duty adhesive to attach it to an 8-inch mirror from Hobby Lobby that cost three dollars. The result? A cool 25-inch mirror for under eighteen bucks!

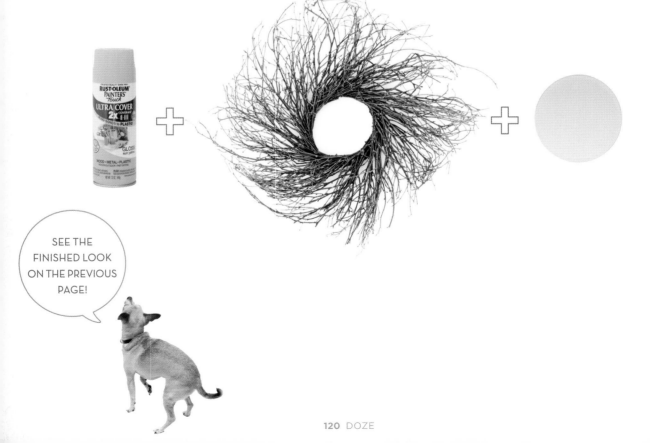

SEE THE FINISHED LOOK ON THE PREVIOUS PAGE!

This is such a fun and easy project. When it comes to the color, white shelves with a matching white cloud painted behind them obviously work best on a nonwhite wall (ours was Moroccan Spice by Benjamin Moore), but you can also paint a shelf any color (sky blue? silver? turquoise?) and make the painted cloud behind it that color too.

1   Hang your **floating shelf** on the wall in the desired spot (Ikea, Bed Bath & Beyond, and Target sell cheap ones).

2   Lightly trace the shape of a cloud above the shelf with a pencil and run the pencil along the top of the shelf so you know where your paint should stop.

3   Remove the shelf or, if you can't easily remove it, use **painter's tape** to tape off the shelf to avoid getting paint on it and fill in your cloud outline with **white paint** using a **small paintbrush.** (A three-dollar jar of white test paint in the same finish as your wall should do the trick.) **Tip:** You might want to bring home a bunch of white paint swatches and pick the one that looks the closest to your shelf color so things blend well.

4   Apply a second coat of paint if necessary to get good coverage.

5   Let it dry, and you're done! Load up the shelf with a few cute things and enjoy the view.

BONUS TIP
Change It Up

You definitely don't have to be limited by a cloud shape. You could add a giant sail over the shelf and a semicircle under it to create the look of a sailboat. Or you can chic it up for an adult space by painting a quatrefoil or a curvy bracketed shape behind the shelf.

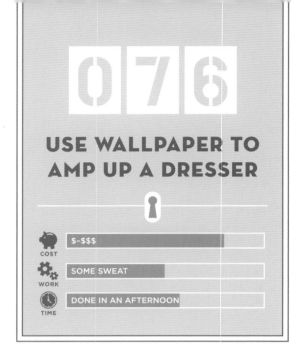

076

USE WALLPAPER TO AMP UP A DRESSER

COST $-$$$

WORK SOME SWEAT

TIME DONE IN AN AFTERNOON

This is one of those things that just might be your favorite project when you get 'er done. So take your time finding some wallpaper that you're in love with and have fun!

1 Find an inexpensive **dresser** with flat-front drawers.

2 Track down some **wallpaper** that tickles your fancy. Cut rectangles of wallpaper the exact size of the front of each drawer by placing the drawers facedown on the wallpaper and carefully tracing them.

3 Use **wallpaper paste** or **heavy-duty spray adhesive** to attach the wallpaper to the fronts of the drawers, following the directions on the container.

4 You can also paint the dresser a new color before wallpapering the drawer fronts if you'd like.

START HERE

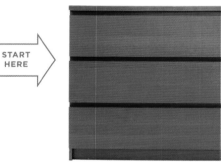

ONE BEDROOM TWO WAYS

There are lots of ways you can go with a bedroom: cool and calm, warm and enveloping, energizing and bold— there really are a ton of possibilities. So here are two takes on the same bedroom, one done up with a clean and modern vibe and the other with an ornate traditional look.

1 Clean-lined furniture paired with sleek sconces and crisp roman shades makes for a modern hotel-chic vibe.

2 A curvy oversized headboard paired with plush bed linens and oversized lamps creates an elegant traditional effect.

078

KATE'S DRESSER MAKEOVER

GUEST BLOGGER IDEA

BLOGGER:
KATE RILEY

BLOG:
CENTSATIONAL GIRL
(WWW.CENTSATIONALGIRL.COM)

LOCATION:
NORTHERN CALIFORNIA

FAVORITE COLOR COMBO:
GRAY + WHITE WITH ANY OTHER
ACCENT (PINK, BLUE, ETC.)

FAVORITE PATTERN:
SUBTLE GEOMETRIC OR IKAT

FAVORITE DIY SIDEKICK:
MY SUPER-HANDY HUSBAND, MATT

When I began to transition my son's nursery into a space for a bigger boy, the first thing I knew he needed was a really good dresser—one that provided plenty of storage and complemented the style of his room. I'd had my eye on the Ikea Hemnes dresser for a long time and finally tracked one down on Craigslist for half the retail price. It was a great buy since it was in perfect condition, but the black finish was too dark for the coastal-inspired space I had planned. No worries! Just a little primer and paint was all it took to reinvent this piece.

SUPPLIES

- Dresser
- Painter's tape
- Primer *(try Zinsser's oil-based Cover Stain primer)*
- Small foam roller
- Paintbrush
- Sandpaper and power sander
- Paint
- Spray paint (for knobs)

1   **PREPARE THE DRESSER.** To begin, I removed the hardware and taped off the inside of the drawers with painter's tape to protect them from primer and paint.

2   **PRIME.** When you go from extreme dark to extreme light, it's best to use primer. A good bonding primer (like Zinsser's Cover Stain) covers any dark coloring that can seep through and ensures a lasting paint job that will stand up to daily use and the wear and tear of a little kid. I used a foam roller for even application of the primer, then followed it up with a paintbrush. With the oil-based primer I also used an additive called Penetrol to condition the primer and minimize brushstrokes.

3   **SAND.** After giving the top of the dresser and drawer fronts two coats of primer for added durability, I sanded them smooth with a power sander.

4 PAINT YOUR BASE COLOR. I gave the dresser two coats of white paint (Calming Sensation by True Value) and allowed it to cure for forty-eight hours.

5 ADD YOUR STRIPES. To create the stripes, I carefully taped off all the edges with painter's tape and then painted the first slate-blue stripe (try Artistic by True Value) with a small artist's paintbrush, then the second about ten minutes later. I found the key to creating a perfect line is peeling the tape off while the paint is still wet.

6 DON'T FORGET THE DETAILS. I spray painted the existing knobs on the dresser a rich chocolate brown to coordinate with the retro-inspired blue and brown geometric print on the window panels in the space.

The crisp, clean blue lines on the drawers now provide a rich contrast to the white paint, and that boxy blue trim adds a great boyish stripe to an otherwise plain dresser.

079

MAKE A TWINE HEADBOARD

START HERE

COST $-$$

WORK SOME SWEAT

TIME DONE IN AN AFTERNOON

The rough texture of twine will look amazing next to soft, welcoming bedding. There are lots of woven headboards on the market for over two hundred bucks, and you can always sit up and read with pillows propped behind you, so you won't get roughed up by the added interest.

1 Use a headboard that you already have but don't love, or find an **old wood or metal headboard** that fits your bed. Look in thrift stores, at yard sales, or on Craigslist. We found ours for ten dollars at a thrift store.

2 Grab **thick twine** from a home-improvement store and tie or nail it on one end to secure it to the back (you can see the nail in the back of ours in the photo at left). Then densely wind the twine around the headboard over and over again to create an entirely woven look.

3 When you're finished weaving, tie or nail the twine again (in the back) to keep it secure so the vertical pattern stays tight.

This is a great solution for a guest room that's missing some key furnishings (like a nightstand).

1. Find a chair in your house or track one down at a yard sale, thrift store, or decor store.

2. Paint it a fun color or reupholster the seat if you so desire. (See pages 278 and 94 for tutorials on furniture painting and upholstering.)

3. Pop a stack of books or magazines and an alarm clock on top of the seat and you're good to go.

080

USE A CHAIR AS A CASUAL NIGHT TABLE

THIS CHAIR WAS SITTING ALL ALONE ON THE CURB FOR TRASH PICKUP, SO IT WAS FREE.

RINSE

BATHROOM IDEAS

SHERRY SAYS

Back when we took on our first bathroom gut-job in late 2009, I was dying to swing the ol' sledgehammer and tell that loathsome cracked and stained tile who was boss. But alas, I was cooking a tiny human.

So John got to do all the backbreaking demolition (even renting a mini jackhammer to tear through some intensely thick mortar that was reinforced with metal mesh). All while I wistfully stood on the other side of the sealed-off doorway and lived vicariously through my better half. You know that scene in *Armageddon* when there's a hand up to the glass screen? That was pretty much me, except I was resting my hand on the plastic drop cloth sealing off the bathroom door.

John emerged later (much later . . . about ten hours later, to be exact) covered in dust and moaning about various aches and pains. To which I replied, "Um, remember when I tossed my cookies for a hundred days straight thanks to this sweet baby of ours?" I took great joy in reminding John just how heroic I was for the whole child-baking thing.

Of course we both reveled in the fact that we had a completely blank canvas of a room to rebuild from the studs up, but I was more than a little jealous that John got to do all the heavy lifting . . . and John was probably more than a little jealous that I didn't have to swing that sledgehammer.

But I did get to help after all the drywall dust had settled when it came time to use no-VOC paint to help coat the freshly hung drywall. And after being in the room no more than ninety seconds, I bent over to re-dip my brush into the can of paint on the floor and my larger-than-I-was-used-to pregnant posterior hit the exposed plumbing pipes (we had yet to hook them up to the vanity) and somehow turned the shutoff valve, causing ice-cold water to shoot out so forcefully that it actually splashed up onto the ceiling. The thing was like a fire hose.

I ran out of the room screaming and John braved the flood long enough to knock the valve back into the closed position. Then came the impromptu wipe-down phase, which we completed while singing a certain caboose-related song by Sir Mix-a-Lot. Oh man, those were the days. But we cleaned up and I got my arse right back in the game. Literally. Although I was a bit more careful where I was pointing that thing. Eventually we got the room primed and painted and I even got to help turn a nightstand into a sink vanity.

So in the end, Momma got to get her hands dirty, and only flooded the place once.

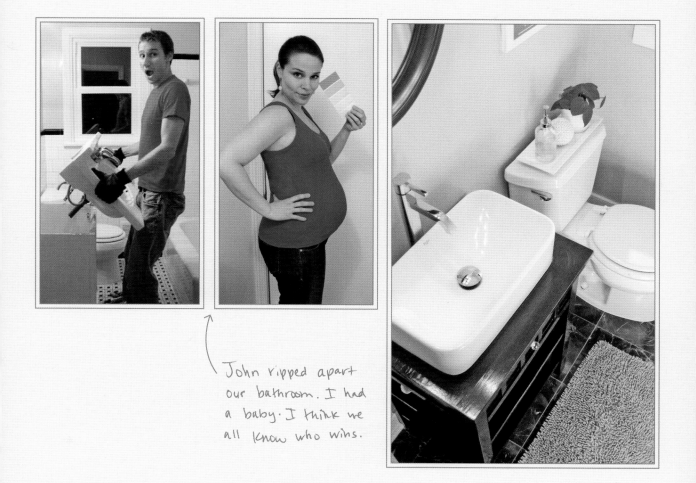

John ripped apart our bathroom. I had a baby. I think we all know who wins.

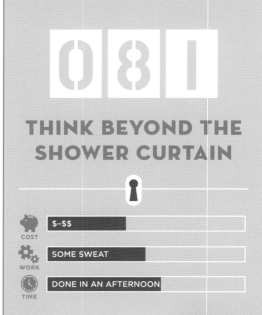

081

THINK BEYOND THE SHOWER CURTAIN

COST	$-$$	
WORK	SOME SWEAT	
TIME	DONE IN AN AFTERNOON	

Two regular curtain panels (made for windows, not showers) can be hung up with ring clips on a shower rod—and hemmed if necessary—to create an amazing focal point in the bathroom. And the shower liners that will keep them from getting wet can be hidden behind each panel, out of view (right on the same rod, thanks to those ring clips).

BONUS TIP
Anything Goes

Bedsheets or fabric that you've hemmed on four sides can work for your shower curtain panels too. Heck, you can even use two canvas-like drop cloths from the home-improvement store. Just use ring clips (usually meant for curtain rods) to hold up anything that doesn't have tabs or grommets. You can clip your shower curtain liner up there on the same rings, so it all moves as one unit.

GET INSPIRED BY YOUR FAVORITE GEMSTONE

Emerald? Turquoise? Ruby? Aquamarine?
Bring that color into the bathroom with a few gleaming accessories like a shower curtain, a soap dispenser, and a storage basket. Functional everyday items like these (along with bath towels and charming countertop containers full of necessities) can really change the vibe of a bathroom, and they might cost only a few bucks a pop if you're on a budget. You definitely don't have to replace everything at once. Try slowly upgrading one item at a time (maybe springing for one thing on the list each month). You'll be amazed by how much those small things can amp up the enjoyment factor while brushing your teeth.

GET YOUR OWN BASKET.

AQUAMARINE & SAPPHIRE			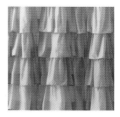
AMBER & RUBY			
EMERALD & CITRINE			

083

ALTER BASIC BATHROOM BULB COVERS WITH PAINT

COST $

WORK NO SWEAT

TIME DONE IN TEN MINUTES

START HERE

BONUS TIP
Move On

You can also alter basic bathroom fixtures by spray painting the metal part (see page 87 for some general spray-painting tips) and even by replacing the glass shades with something that's more your style. They sell replacement shades pretty cheaply at home-improvement stores, and you can swap out something fluted or frosted for a clear glass—or even a seeded glass—option.

So many bathrooms have basic metal light fixtures with glass bulb covers of all types. Instead of scrapping the fixture entirely, you might be able to work with it (and save some dough) just by swanking up the glass shades with a posh ring of paint. It's just one of those small details that can give a seen-it-a-million-times fixture a little something extra. And speaking of something extra, check out Abby Larson's use of this technique on vases (page 268).

1 Any removable **glass bulb cover** should work for this project—just make sure yours comes out (usually by removing the lightbulb or unscrewing some small screws that hold the cover in around the base).

2 Buy some inexpensive **acrylic craft paint** in the color of your choice. We used Limeade by Apple Barrel, but something metallic or deeper in tone (like gold or navy) could look great too.

3 Pour some of the paint into a bowl. (Don't load too much in there: A puddle of paint about as thick as a pencil is recommended.)

4 Dip the edge of the bulb cover into the paint to gently coat just that rim with color. You don't want the bulb to come into contact with the painted part of the glass cover after everything is reassembled, but the bulb cover's edge is usually a fair distance away from the actual bulb, so you should be good.

5 Repeat to coat each bulb cover with a thin rim of paint around the edge.

6 Allow your bulb covers to dry completely and rehang them on your fixture.

7 Bask in the glory of your charming ten-minute upgrade for under three dollars (seriously, a tube of acrylic paint is that cheap).

084

THE PALMERS' TILED SINK BACKSPLASH

GUEST BLOGGER IDEA

BLOGGERS:
LAYLA AND KEVIN PALMER

BLOG:
THE LETTERED COTTAGE
(WWW.THELETTEREDCOTTAGE.NET)

LOCATION:
PRATTVILLE, ALABAMA

FAVORITE COLOR COMBO:
BLUE + WHITE (BUT ASK AGAIN IN AN HOUR; WE MAY ANSWER DIFFERENTLY!)

FAVORITE GO-TO TOOL:
OUR PNEUMATIC NAILER

FAVORITE WAY TO FINISH A ROOM:
PATTERNED PILLOWS AND FRESH FLOWERS

Our goal with this project was to create the look of a wall full of beautiful tile, without actually having to purchase a *wall full of beautiful tile*. To save money, we decided to tile only the wall space around our bathroom mirror, and we were stoked when we found our 1-inch blue-gray marble tile at a local builder-supply warehouse for just $4.97 a square foot.

SUPPLIES

- Pencil
- Notched plastic trowel
- Premixed tile adhesive
- Sheets of tile
- Rubber gloves
- Rubber float
- Premixed grout
- Large sponge
- Plastic tub

1   **MARK THE AREA TO BE TILED.** We started by holding up our mirror and tracing the shape of it onto the wall. We used that pencil line as our guide, knowing that we'd only have to tile around and just inside of it so that our "secret" would be safe!

2   **APPLY ADHESIVE.** We used our notched trowel to spread a layer of tile adhesive onto the wall and another layer onto the back of one sheet of tile.

3   **STICK THE TILE TO THE WALL.** When we pushed the sheet of tile into place, we were sort of worried that it wouldn't stay secure because we were laying the tiles on a vertical surface; but it did, so we continued attaching sheets until the wall around and just inside our pencil line was completely covered.

4   **WAIT.** We waited twenty-four hours for the tile adhesive to dry.

5   **APPLY GROUT.** We put on our rubber gloves and used a rubber float to smear a generous amount of premixed grout into all the spaces around each tile.

6 WIPE OFF EXCESS GROUT. After waiting the recommended amount of time outlined on our grout bucket, we used a damp sponge to wipe off the excess grout. It helped to have a plastic tub of water nearby for this step because we could re-wet the sponge and wring it out as needed. A few hours after that, everything was dry and the project was complete!

You'd never know there isn't really a full wall of tile now that our mirror is back in place. And we saved about eighty dollars by not tiling the hidden part of the wall. Yahoo!

085

ADD STYLISH BATHROOM STORAGE

Looking for a more aesthetically pleasing way to corral things like Q-tips and dental floss? Scalloped dishes or monogrammed mugs (sold for around six dollars a pop at places like Anthropologie or Sur La Table) can create a personalized and charming look on any floating shelf or vanity in the bathroom. Here are some other wouldn't-that-look-cool-stuffed-with-cotton-balls-or-nail-polish ideas.

These could be filled with lotions, salt scrubs, or bubble bath.

A few favorite bottles of nail polish could hang out in here.

Each drawer could hold makeup, cotton balls, Q-tips, or other small items that are better off corralled.

Q-tips and cotton balls are an obvious choice for this guy, but even small perfume bottles or small white boxes of floss could work.

A pile of fluffy washcloths, pretty bar soaps wrapped in decorative paper, or even loofahs or sea sponges could live here.

A lidded basket is great for hiding clutter or other stuff without pretty packaging.

086

REPLACE YOUR BATHROOM FAUCET

COST $-$$$

WORK SOME SWEAT

TIME DONE IN AN AFTERNOON

Swapping out a faucet is a quick way to update the whole bathroom. There are some detailed videos on YouTube to walk you through how to do this, if you'd like more deets, but here's a general rundown.

1 Turn off the water to the sink by closing the shutoff valves, which are usually located in the base of the vanity.

2 Remove the hoses and screws that kept the old faucet in place beneath the counter (paying careful attention to what was attached to what).

3 Attach your new faucet in the same way (referring to the directions that came with it).

4 Turn the water back on and check for leaks.

BONUS TIP
Skip the Store

Checking out sources like eBay or Craigslist or even a local Habitat for Humanity ReStore can yield great like-new faucets for less loot.

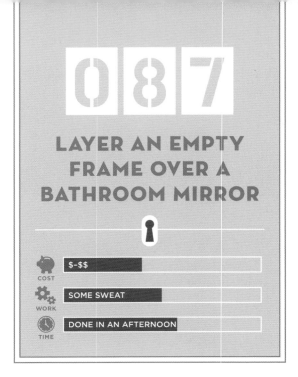

087

LAYER AN EMPTY FRAME OVER A BATHROOM MIRROR

COST	$-$$
WORK	SOME SWEAT
TIME	DONE IN AN AFTERNOON

Hanging an empty frame or two can be a great way to define certain areas and break up a big builder-basic mirror.

1 Locate a **frame** (or two) that will help you define the area over your sink(s).

2 Remove the backing and the glass, leaving just the empty frame(s).

3 Use removable products like **3M Command strips** or a **mirror-safe adhesive** (which can later be removed) to secure your frame(s) directly onto the mirror.

4 Wink at that clever person staring back at you.

Here are some things you can easily hang in a bathroom without worrying so much about moisture issues.

• A collection of mirrors in a variety of colors and finishes

• Wall-mounted vases (CB2 makes the ones in the photo on the right)

• Decorative plates (use plate hangers from the craft store to mount them)

• Wood signs or letters

• Floating shelves stocked with pretty glass cups, bowls, candles, and soaps

088

ADD MOISTURE-RESISTANT BATHROOM ART

089

GO AHEAD—CHIC UP A TOILET TANK

Decorating the ol' porcelain throne is usually a no-no (especially when it involves furry seat covers), but using the space on top of the tank can definitely be an upgrade. Here are a few ways to upgrade the top of your toilet.

• A long ceramic dish holding a candle, a small vase, and a shell ball (we love a good shell ball)

• A long, low basket filled with washcloths and pretty soaps wrapped in decorative paper

• A leaning frame or a potted plant

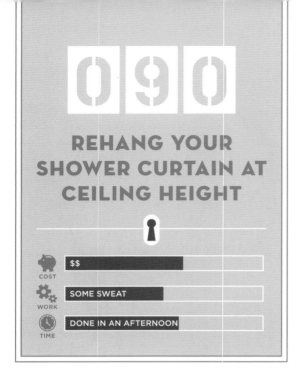

090

REHANG YOUR SHOWER CURTAIN AT CEILING HEIGHT

COST	$$
WORK	SOME SWEAT
TIME	DONE IN AN AFTERNOON

Raising your shower curtain adds instant drama to the bathroom and makes the whole place feel loftier. Don't groan. It sounds way harder than it is.

1 Remove your old shower curtain rod. (If it's not a tension rod, **spackle** and **paint** any old holes that it leaves behind; see page 174 for more on that.)

2 Rehang your existing rod at ceiling height if you've got the skills, or find a nice new **tension shower rod.** (We've had luck finding them at Home Depot.) We like tension shower rods because they don't involve any hanging hardware or holes in your wall. Oh yeah, and you'll need some **shower ring clips** too.

3 Track down a nice **floor-to-ceiling fabric shower curtain,** which isn't always as easy as finding one in a standard size—a little online searching usually does the trick. (Search things like "95-inch shower curtain" or "extra-long shower curtain" on a site like Amazon, or just Google it and see what pops up.) You can also hang fabric curtains meant for windows with a liner to keep them dry (see page 130 for more on that).

4 You don't have to worry about your fabric curtain getting wet if you use a store-bought **plastic or fabric liner** along with it (which can be found in extra-long lengths online and sometimes even in stores like Bed Bath & Beyond). We especially like fabric liners because they're machine washable and don't off-gas like some of the plastic ones. An 86-inch liner usually does the trick. (It doesn't have to be 95 inches like the curtain because it hangs on the inside of the tub.)

Buy pretty hand soap, lotion, shampoo, or conditioner, just for the gorgeous packaging. And if you can't afford to spring for it all the time, refill the ooh-la-la bottles with your usual budget-friendly stuff. Maybe no one but you will notice it, but the upscale bottles can make you feel like quite the high roller. Even when you know your own secret.

091

BUY THE FANCY STUFF AT LEAST ONCE

STOW

ORGANIZING IDEAS

JOHN SAYS

Uh-oh, here comes the chapter about organization.

Perhaps you're expecting tips about color-coded binders and arranging your closet by season, color, or "how thin it makes me look." Well—spoiler alert—we don't have any of that kind of advice in here. Why? Because we're not exactly organizing overachievers.

That's not to say that we don't admire those who give the Dewey Decimal System a run for its decimal-tastic money when it comes to sorting and storing every inch of their lives. But for us (and probably most of the world), it's not a realistic goal to keep life *that* buttoned-up at all times. Things get messy. Things get misplaced. Things get disorganized. Clutter happens.

That's why our preferred method of organization is the find-out-what-works-for-

you system. Figuring out how you can best contain and locate your junk—excuse me, precious belongings—while adding a bit of style can be key. In fact, Sherry and I had different organizing styles when we met, and we have managed to merge the two fairly well.

I'm a bit of a sentimental hoarder. I like to hang on to things for the memory of them or because they remind me of a place, time, or person. Meanwhile, Sherry doesn't get emotionally attached to objects very easily (and usually frames or somehow memorializes the few things that she loves) but is oddly dependent on paper. She writes lots of notes, tears out tons of magazine pages, and loves stuffing receipts in her purse. (Hmm; maybe she just loves shopping.)

This impulse to hang on to things is tough because in our hearts we both prefer to be minimalists, living the simple life with only the things we really need. So we've learned from each other. Sherry has taught me that there are other ways to keep a memory than by filling box after box with mementos that will just sit in the closet. For example, I don't need the whole newspaper that featured an article with my name in it—just the clipping of the actual article, maybe even stuck in a frame or an album instead of stashed away. Another one of Sherry's tricks is to photograph the object

and frame that (or put it in an album) rather than store the three-dimensional item. Did I mention she's got a thing for paper?

On the other hand, I've helped Sherry digitize her paper dependency. Slowly, her to-do lists have moved to her iPhone (although she does occasionally revert to Post-its), and more receipts are being ditched now that it's easier to check histories online and make returns with just the purchasing credit card.

By paring down both of our "collections," we're also finding interesting ways to corral—and even display—the things we want to keep around. So forgive us if you were hoping the following pages would teach you how to alphabetize your socks or color-coordinate your credit card bills. We're crazy. Just not *that* crazy.

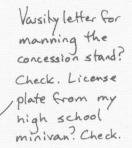

Varsity letter for manning the concession stand? Check. License plate from my high school minivan? Check.

Sherry's nicknames: Listy VonListenstein, Lady Lists-a-lot, Lista McListerpants, and Queen Listifa.

092

MAKE A WHOLE-HOUSE BINDER

COST	$
WORK	NO SWEAT
TIME	DONE IN AN HOUR

Create one place where you keep everything for your house, from fabric samples and paint colors to warranties, manuals, and product guides. Even handyman/contractor/ serviceman names and numbers should go in the binder. This way you have an easy reference guide on hand whenever you need it. Grab a three-ring binder with a bunch of plastic sleeves and add dividers to help you group certain things by category. (For example, "decor-related" is where you can slip fabric samples and paint swatches into the clear sleeves, and "manuals/warranties" is where you can slot in all that pesky paper.)

This versatile hook works well for hanging scarves in a coat closet.

This one's great for coats or backpacks in a mudroom or kid's room.

Hooks can also add color or "handmade" appeal.

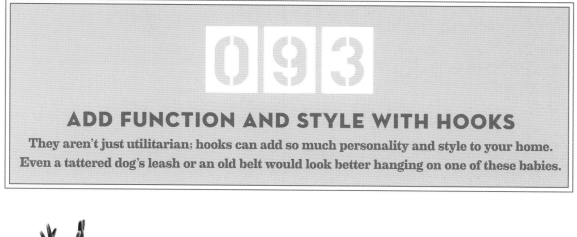

093

ADD FUNCTION AND STYLE WITH HOOKS

They aren't just utilitarian; hooks can add so much personality and style to your home. Even a tattered dog's leash or an old belt would look better hanging on one of these babies.

A rustic choice with personality can add character to any room.

This classic hook works in bathrooms, coat closets, and entryways alike.

This guy has vintage appeal and antique charm.

094

THREE WORDS: ADD STORAGE OTTOMANS

We have more than ten storage ottomans in our house (yes, ten) and not only do they hide clutter (from receipts and printer paper to dog toys and baby toys), they also provide extra seating in a pinch. Win-win. Here are a few places you can stash some.

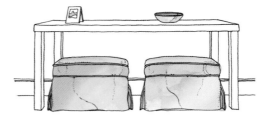

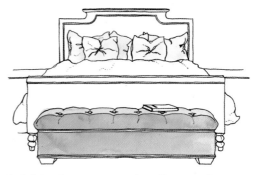

1. Slide two under a leggy console table to make use of the empty space beneath it.

2. Stick a long rectangular ottoman at the foot of a bed.

3. Swap out a coffee table for two smaller ottomans that work for putting your feet up and for extra seating.

4. Replace two of your kitchen chairs with one. The kids will fight to sit on it.

5. Use one in a kid's room or nursery for putting your feet up (if you have a rocker or a reading chair) and for stashing toys (which always seem to multiply).

BASKETS SOLVE (ALMOST) EVERYTHING

You already know we love storage ottomans, and when you add in baskets, well, we really get excited. They're just our organizing jam. It might sound like a "duh" suggestion, but sometimes the truth is simple. Baskets can be lidded, they can be round, they can be big, they can be small, and most of all, they can hide a multitude of ~~sins~~ stuff. So use them to your advantage, and rejoice at the blissfully contained life that you lead.

Storing towels or washcloths in baskets like this keeps them together (and from toppling over).

This can be a garbage pail or even a hamper in a nursery.

This basket could hold cleaning products under the sink. Take it with you from room to room as you clean.

From holding spare lightbulbs in a supply closet to boxes of pasta in a pantry, this gal is diverse.

This would make a cool industrial magazine or mail holder.

The lid means this basket can hide almost anything (and keep all of your secrets).

096

UPGRADE YOUR HANGING STORAGE

Coat hooks, **key hooks**, cubbies, and even drawers can be more functional when they're labeled for each user in the house. But you don't have to whip out the label maker and slap plastic stickers everywhere. Here's a simple and sweet way to identify things.

1. Grab small **metal** or **wooden letters** at a craft store (these hail from Hobby Lobby) and paint them any color (or leave them au naturel if you'd prefer).

2. Use **strong adhesive** like Liquid Nails to glue the letters onto a **small, boxy canvas** from an art supply store or craft store. Optional: Glue **decorative paper** to the canvas first—we used some gift wrap we had on hand.

3. Hang the canvas on a **nail** above a coat or key hook (or use a removable hook like the ones by 3M to secure it over a cubby or on the front of a drawer).

WE WHIPPED THESE OUT IN UNDER AN HOUR!

097

ONE CLOSET FOUR WAYS

Just because your closet has one measly hanging rod doesn't mean you have to keep it that way. Make it work for you! Here are a few ideas.

1. You can squeeze more function out of a typical closet by adding an extra hanging bar.

2. Shelves spaced 15 inches apart from floor to ceiling make for a great game or craft closet.

3. A single bar and two top shelves leave room on the floor for shoe storage.

4. A dresser in the closet with shelving above it works well for keeping things contained.

Instead of a big, ugly pile of shoes by the door, try tossing your footware into a shoe caddy or cabinet. Or place a big basket, a large bin, a storage ottoman, a toy chest, a low shelving system, or a dresser by the door (each drawer can house shoes!). These simple solutions can make all the difference. A steel boot tray can even "contain" things in plain sight, so footwear looks less like clutter and more like it's in its place.

TAME
YOUR MAIL

Piles of mail can be wrangled with a simple basket or box system (one for stuff to be shredded and one for stuff to be paid/responded to). Once the things in your must-respond-to box are attended to, file them away (if you want to keep a record of things like paid bills or medical paperwork) or move them into the shred pile and take care of that once a week or so. You also might want to have a calendar, a planner, or a bulletin board nearby to hang or record important events (so invitations don't sit forgotten in a stack with other mail and can be recorded or pinned up after you RSVP). The key to uncomplicated mail is a simple, easy system, so resist anything that seems too hard to stick to.

One bulletin board for invitations and other fun-to-look-at mail: $10

+

Two boxes or baskets for stuff to shred and stuff to deal with: $15

=

Total solution cost: $25

Gone are the days of prominently displaying your CD and DVD collections to show off how many you own. So many concealed baskets, bins, or entire cabinet systems to house them are now available, and they're attractive too. You can even go digital and store all of your music on your computer, if you dare. (It's free and means you don't lose an inch of space in your place.) Or you can stick all your DVDs into a clear-sleeved binder that you can tuck into a closet or slide slyly onto a shelf.

100
STASH THOSE CDs
AND DVDs

Closets are rooms too. Well, not really; they're more like little spaces full of stuff that you use all the time. So why not do something fun and create a smile-worthy nook behind that closed door? Here are some ideas.

- Paint the inside of your closet a bold color.

- Use decorative baskets to corral stuff.

- Hang eye-pleasing hooks and shelves.

- Cover cheap cardboard storage boxes or magazine bins with decorative paper or gift wrap for storage.

- Hang art or photos if the closet is particularly big (like a walk-in closet).

- If there's a ceiling light, switch that out for something more exciting like a small pendant or chandelier.

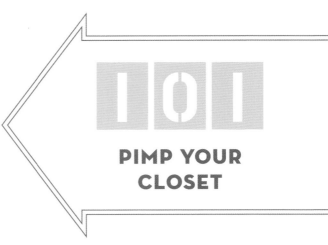

101
PIMP YOUR CLOSET

102
LOSE THOSE MISMATCHED HANGERS

Replace all the random wire and plastic hangers in your closet with matching wooden ones for a streamlined and boutique-ish effect. Many magazines and books suggest this because it works, and it's such a good idea that we're not above beating this dead horse ourselves. We bought a ton of wood hangers, and it's amazing how much better everything looks when it's not on random plastic and wire ones. Those can also stretch out your clothes, so this is a functional upgrade as well. And you know we're into that sort of thing.

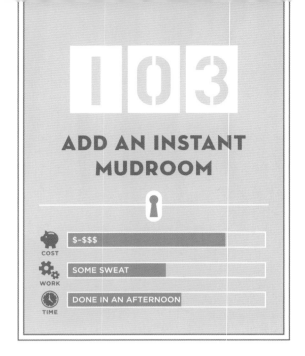

103

ADD AN INSTANT MUDROOM

COST $-$$$

WORK SOME SWEAT

TIME DONE IN AN AFTERNOON

A mudroom can be added in the corner of any room, like a den, a wide hallway, or a laundry room near the back or side door. Large mudroom systems can cost hundreds of dollars—even over a thousand—but you can bring in similar function without sacrificing form for a lot less. Here's how to create a low-cost version.

1 Get a shoe cubby/shelf or even a storage bench or ottoman for concealing your foot gear.

2 Create a place to hang coats, purses, and scarves, like a strip of wall hooks hanging above the shoe shelf or bench/ottoman.

3 Throw in some optional, extra-credit items like a boot tray or a wall shelf above the hooks for added storage with baskets for hats and scarves. (You can even label baskets or hooks with each family member's name or photo.)

104
DEAL WITH BOOKCASE CLUTTER
In need of some bookshelf beautification? Here are some ideas.

BONUS TIPS

- Add baskets or lacquered boxes to your shelves to break up all those books for a more balanced and decorative (but still super-functional) effect.

- Bring in some pretty pieces (like a few feathery potted ferns, glass vases, or other accessories) to keep things from looking all business.

- You can cover your books with white or tan craft paper (or even grass-cloth wallpaper or pretty gift wrap) for a sophisticated look. Then add the titles/authors in scripty black ink on the spine or print out labels and stick them on.

STEP 1
Start with some vertical groupings of books and other large vertical objects. Staggering them adds balance.

⬇

STEP 2
Add horizontal objects, like a few stacks of books and some storage boxes to contain clutter.

⬇

STEP 3
Add personality with a few accessories, like a frame, some decorative items, and even a picture taped to the back.

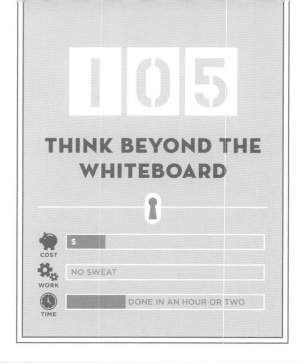

105

THINK BEYOND THE WHITEBOARD

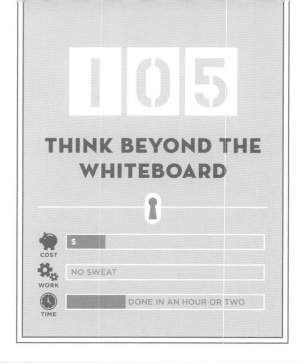

COST: $

WORK: NO SWEAT

TIME: DONE IN AN HOUR OR TWO

Frame a printed calendar and write over it with dry-erase markers or grease pencils. It's sort of like a souped-up whiteboard.

1 Track down a monthly **calendar.** (Make one by hand with markers and decorative paper, print a free one that you find online, order one from a site like Etsy, or even make one in Photoshop, like we did.)

2 Slap it into a **frame** (white, wood, metal, painted, simple, ornate—whatever ya like!).

3 Use a **dry-erase marker** or a **grease pencil** to jot down notes and dates on the glass. (You can even have an each-person-gets-a-different-color system to keep appointments straight.) At the end of each month, just wipe it down and start again.

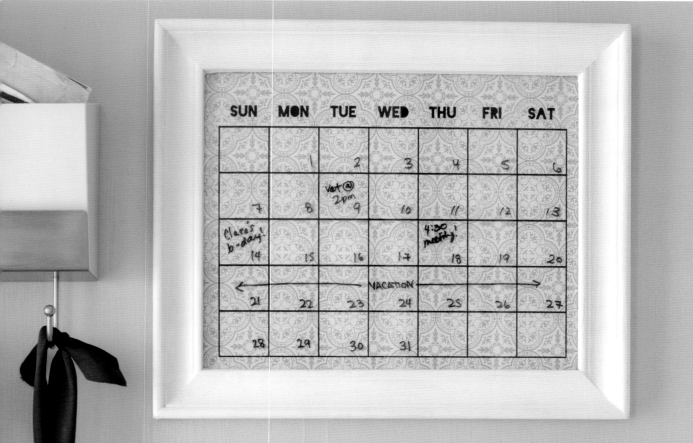

106

CLEAN AND ORGANIZE AS YOU GO

Who likes to clean/straighten/sort stuff? Not us. But we're big fans of doing these chores as we go instead of letting things pile up and then having to dedicate a whole weekend to it. So whenever we have a lull (like when we're waiting for water to boil or for the computer to unfreeze), we try to do one or two of these quick tasks. When they're done frequently enough, they make the whole house feel pretty darn clean without much big-block-of-time effort.

- Get everything out of the kitchen sink and either wash it and put it away or load it into the dishwasher.

- Run a hand vac along the baseboards and under tables and other large furnishings to grab the dust bunnies that threaten to tip off visitors that you haven't vacuumed in a while.

- Swipe a microfiber cloth over frames (or use a feather duster if you're feeling fancy).

- Swish the toilet brush around the toilet every week (it can prevent you from needing to scrub the toilet on your hands and knees every month).

Wondering what you should keep and what you should get rid of? Keep only what you need, love, or use regularly. If you're meh about something and don't use it a lot, donate that sucker ASAP (this means everything from clothes to decor items). Think about it this way: Space is a precious thing to waste. You don't want to fill your house with anything that doesn't directly add to your happiness. So what if you paid a lot for an item? You're paying for it again every single day that you give up valuable space in your home to store it (especially if something that you need or love more could be sitting in its place).

107

KNOW WHEN TO HOLD 'EM, KNOW WHEN TO ~~FOLD~~ TOSS 'EM

108

STAMP YOUR STORAGE BOXES

COST	$–$$	
WORK	SOME SWEAT	
TIME	DONE IN AN HOUR	

Got a bunch of yawn-inducing storage boxes? Just stamp your way to an upgraded look. You can even stamp manila folders the same way.

1 Grab simple **cardboard file boxes** at places like Ikea, OfficeMax, or a local office-supply shop.

2 Add interest to them with a **rubber stamp** and some bold-colored **ink** from a craft store. For example, a black fleur-de-lis pattern stamped on a white box would be *très* sophisticated, while antiquey gold quatrefoil or honeycomb shapes could add soft, layered style.

109

MAKE A TO-BE-DEALT-WITH BOWL

This bowl is basically a drop spot for anything you need to deal with (forms you have to fill out, receipts you have to file, a reminder card for a dental appointment you have to schedule, etc.). If you use a giant colorful bowl, it won't look half bad on a table or counter, and it'll function as a stash-everything-in-one-big-stack system (as opposed to spreading things out all over the house and losing them or forgetting to deal with them). Pick a bold color to make it especially fun to look at between sorting sessions (yes, you do have to eventually deal with the items inside).

WE HAPPIED UP THIS SILVER IKEA BOWL WITH A LITTLE RED SPRAY PAINT.

110

ACTUALLY GET RID OF THE STUFF IN YOUR TO-GO PILE

Sometimes after you've made a get-rid-of-this pile, the momentum stalls because you're not sure where it should go. We know this from experience. But putting your finger on a means of removal can be all you need to get that space-sucking stuff out of your life. Here are a few easy ways (without much heavy lifting on your part).

- Use sites like Craigslist and Freecycle to create a listing for anything you want to nix. You'll be surprised how quickly stuff will go if you list it as free.

- A lot of nonprofit thrift stores and places like the Habitat for Humanity ReStore are happy to come to you with a truck for a free pickup of whatever you're donating. (We got rid of a ton of old fans and bifold doors that way—it was even a tax write-off.)

- You can also try junk-hauling companies that you find on Craigslist or in the phone book.

- Some home-improvement stores offer Dumpster-in-a-bag contraptions that they drop off and pick up (for much less than a traditional Dumpster).

ANA'S RUSTIC SHELVES

GUEST BLOGGER IDEA

BLOGGER:
ANA WHITE

BLOG:
ANA WHITE: HOMEMAKER
(ANA-WHITE.COM)

LOCATION:
DELTA JUNCTION, ALASKA

FAVORITE GO-TO TOOL:
COMPOUND MITER SAW—I'D CUT STEAKS
WITH IT IF I COULD!

FAVORITE DIY SIDEKICK:
MY SWEET DAUGHTER, GRACIE

FAVORITE ROOM IN MY HOUSE:
THE GARAGE! THERE'S ALWAYS A PROJECT
GOING ON.

A blank off-white wall in our new home needed something with rustic appeal. Without enough space for a piece of furniture, I decided to make some wall shelves using reclaimed wood and inexpensive metal brackets.

SUPPLIES

- 2-foot long board(s), preferably scrap or reclaimed wood
- Four L brackets with screws for each board
- Drill
- Screws or drywall anchoring system
- Level

1 **RECLAIM YOUR WOOD.** Broken shipping pallets are my favorite reclaimed wood because they come with a story and character. But be careful when using pallets: Some are treated with harsh chemicals (mine come from an organic produce delivery service). I reclaim boards by using two hammers, pounding the claw end of the first hammer under the nail joints with the second hammer, and prying the boards loose. If reclaimed pallet boards are not an option, new pine boards left in the sun to bleach and then banged up with a hammer will give you a similar look. Or try soaking steel wool in vinegar for a few days, and painting this very stinky but effective concoction onto your new boards to give them an antiqued color.

2 **BUY YOUR BRACKETS.** Once you have the boards, purchase metal L brackets, at least two-thirds the width of your boards. For example, if you have a 6-inch-wide board, buy 4-inch brackets. For 12-inch boards, buy 8-inch brackets. Brackets are very cheap, and you can spray paint them black or bronze—just make sure to paint the screws to match.

3 **SCREW THE BRACKETS TO THE BOARDS.** Space your brackets 24 inches apart (measuring bracket screw hole to bracket screw hole). This way, if your wall has studs spaced 24 inches on center, you will be able to attach the shelves directly to the studs in the wall.

4 MOUNT YOUR SHELVES. Drill screw holes into the wall, directly into a stud if possible. Position the shelves on the wall and screw them in, using a level to keep them straight. If you can't find a stud, hang the shelves with a drywall anchoring system (like heavy-duty anchors and screws), screwing through the bracket holes into the wall.

I'm thrilled with the way these reclaimed-wood shelves turned out. They're beautiful and functional, and they add just the right amount of interest to a formerly bland wall.

112
ORGANIZE YOUR PAPER CLUTTER

Here are three easy and effective ways to organize bills, invoices, receipts, and other paper clutter.

1 **FILE FOLDERS.** At first it may seem too office-y and corporate to have a filing cabinet for your home, but it's a super-effective method that you can make feel more homey by choosing a less industrial style of cabinet (rich wood or even clean white ones can look pretty cool) or file-box options. Places like Target and Ikea also sell decorative file boxes that don't look boring and cubicle-ready.

2 **BINDERS.** Decorative printed or patterned binders can look great on a bookcase or can be tucked into a drawer or closet. They're ideal for flipping through to see everything that you have. (We're particularly happy with this method when it comes to keeping inspiring magazine tear sheets together or organizing our appliance manuals.)

3 **ACCORDION FOLDERS.** These combine the easy and quick organization of a hanging file folder with the portability of a binder. Plus they're easy to throw into a storage ottoman, a drawer, a closet, or even the backseat of your car if they're files that you need on the go.

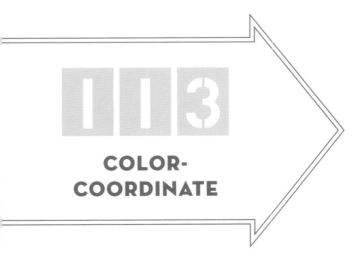

113
COLOR-COORDINATE

An easy way to designate a certain sibling's or spouse's personal items is to assign them a color. For example, gray bins, baskets, and other containers could store all of your son's or your husband's things, while yellow ones could house all of your things or your daughter's. And if you don't want to buy a bunch of bins in specific colors, adding stickers in each person's color to the storage containers that you already have can work too.

A deep canvas tote is awesome for housing anything from a big stack of magazines to toys or even blankets next to the couch.

A lacquered box in a bold color is one of our favorite things ever (we live on the edge, what can we say?). Boxes are great for stashing everything from toiletries to sewing supplies.

Sure, these are perfect for magazine storage, but they also work surprisingly well for holding those random manila folders that litter your desk. Really, they're like a mini desktop filing cabinet.

114

STORE STUFF STYLISHLY

Wanna see more ways to shove things inside of other things to keep them straight? Why the heck not?

Tall glass cylinder vases are sold for holding large wiggly sticks, but we love them for something else . . . toilet paper. Yup, a few stacked rolls can look downright elegant in a glass cylinder next to the porcelain throne. We've even smuggled a roll of TP into the store to be sure it would fit before buying the vase.

BONUS TIP
Boxed In

A small lidded box can be so useful for stashing your remote controls. It's amazing how civilized you'll feel when you have a designated spot for small things like this. It makes it easier to clean up if stuff has a drop spot. So if your house always feels like it's chaotic and completely un–company ready, adding systems (like lidded boxes) can be the key to straightening up on autopilot. Because knowing where to stash things in a split second before the doorbell rings is more than half the battle.

115

TRY SOME ALL-NATURAL PROBLEM SOLVERS

Here are a few household issues that can be resolved using items that you probably already have in the kitchen. Three cheers for working with what you have (and for walnuts, because they're delicious).

PROBLEM	SOLUTION
ANTS	**Cinnamon + bay leaves.** Use either or both of these natural deterrents on a counter, cabinet, table, or anywhere else you see ants marching by.
SCRATCHES IN A WOOD FLOOR OR ON A PIECE OF FURNITURE	**A walnut.** Rub a raw walnut on scratched wood to "oil" any scratches so they're less visible.
NASTY CLOGGED SHOWERHEAD	**White vinegar.** Unscrew the showerhead and soak it in white vinegar overnight. Or tie a plastic bag full of vinegar around it so it can soak while it's still attached.
CLOGGED DRAIN	**Baking soda + vinegar + boiling water + sink plunger.** Pour half a cup of baking soda followed by a cup of white vinegar into a clogged drain, and let it fizz/ sit for five minutes. Flush it out by pouring a gallon of boiling water down the drain. If the boiling water didn't do the trick, plunge the heck out of it (while blocking off any overflow openings with a rag) to break up the clog.
CARPET DENTS	**Ice + fork.** Let an entire ice cube melt on a wool or cotton carpet dent (go have fun doing something else for a few hours while it does its thing), then return after the ice has melted and gently fluff up the dent with a fork until it's gone. Natural fibers like cotton and wool are just fine with a smidge of water, so one melted ice cube shouldn't hurt a thing.

116

STREAMLINE YOUR PHOTOS

BONUS TIP

Make a Family Yearbook

Another idea for storing tons of photos without giving up a lot of space is to order a photo book from a company like Shutterfly or MyPublisher. They often have great discounts, and a hundred-page book can easily house a year's worth of photos with only about an inch of binding. So ten years of photos can be stacked to create just a 10-inch-high pile on a table, bookcase, or closet shelf. That's a lot of photos in a little space (waaaaay less than most albums take up due to their padding and binder rings).

The easiest way to organize your pictures is to get a ton of the exact same albums. (You can usually find them at Michaels or Marshall's on sale.) First, remove all your photos from the random albums and shoeboxes they're currently shoved into and get them in some semblance of chronological order. You can be as type A as you'd like here (a general guess from oldest to newest works well). This task could take an afternoon or a few days of work on and off, so laying everything out on a not frequently used dining table or guest bed might be a smart idea. Once you have the order down, insert all your photos from oldest to newest into your new stack of albums and glue or draw little numbers onto each one's spine to keep them in order (we used stickers). Warning: Completing this task will feel more amazing than you thought possible.

06

HANG

ARTSY IDEAS

JOHN SAYS

I don't think we had any "real" art in our house
for the first few years. That's not something we're proud of (I'm a huge art lover,
and Sherry actually went to art school in New York City, where she got her
BFA); it's just how it was. We were twenty-three-year-old kids without a lot of
extra income to hit the galleries, and Etsy wasn't even something we had heard
of back then. So we fell into a "let's just make our own paintings and prints until
we can afford the real stuff" routine. And it was actually a pretty great habit to
fall into, because although we now own some awesome prints and paintings that
we love from Etsy vendors and local artists, we still have such a soft spot for the
homemade items that we've framed. Like our little box o' keys, for example.

You know by now that we're sentimental folks (yes, I copped to that in the last chapter), so back in 2006 when Sherry saved a copy of all the keys that had meaning for us (one from my New York apartment, one from hers, one from our first apartment together in Richmond, and one from our first home) and framed them in a small shadow box with little handwritten labels under each one . . . well, it quickly became one of our favorite things. As in, it's probably in the top five on our "what we'd grab in a fire" list. It reminds us where we've been and how far we've come, and it's sort of like bottling a bunch of memories that otherwise might have somehow slipped away.

We've learned that art is one of those to-each-his-own things, so you'd probably be hard-pressed to find ten people who would all rank the same five pieces of art from favorite to least favorite in the same order. But that's what's so great about it. It can really set your place apart. You know, so it feels like you and not like Generic Home #489. There's this awesome turning point after you move when you suddenly feel a lot more settled and comfy, and it's usually right around the time you finally start hanging things up on those bare, echoing walls.

So our advice is to save your pennies for "real" art that you love, but also never to be too intimidated to DIY a little wall decor. There's a certain satisfaction when you bang in the last nail, hang your frame or canvas up on the wall, and step back to survey your latest masterpiece. At least give it the old college try. Heck, you can even don a beret, wear overalls covered in paint, or sport any other clichéd item that "the artistic one" in a movie might wear if it helps you get into character. Whatever it takes.

Keys to our old New York City apartments. I wonder if they still work....

It's true: We just might be addicted to white frames and homemade art.

A classic gridlike layout always works, and leaving 2 to 3 inches between each frame keeps them from looking too spacey.

007

MASTER A FEW FRAMING ARRANGEMENTS

From something a bit imperfect and asymmetrical to a balanced and gridlike layout, there's no limit to what you can do with arrangements on your walls. And using paper bags or wrapping paper to make frame-sized templates to tape up and move around can help you finalize your arrangement before picking up the hammer (and making too many holes).

This arrangement is vertically but not horizontally symmetrical, so it looks balanced but a bit less typical.

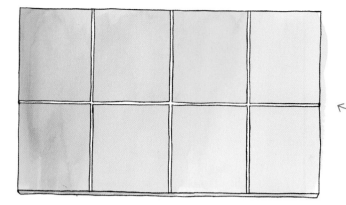

Who says frames can't touch? A grid of frames hung right next to one another can make for some great drama (especially if you cut one large image and display it across all of them).

An asymmetrical layout adds loads of casual style and interest. It helps if the frames are hung 1 to 2 inches apart so they all read as one unit.

Another casual way to display frames is to lean them up on a floating shelf. A wad of poster putty at the base can keep them from slipping.

WE MADE
THIS FOR
FOUR
BUCKS.

118

SEW A PATTERN INTO CARD STOCK

COST $

WORK NO SWEAT

TIME DONE IN AN HOUR

Sewing a design into card stock is one of those fun texture-rich things that anyone can do. And it's actually not too difficult. (Do we get points for resisting the urge to say it's "sew easy"?)

1 Choose a favorite shape, design, or word (you can spell it out in a cool typeface on the computer).

2 Get a large, sharp **darning needle** and **embroidery thread** for a few bucks at a craft store. (This is the cheap string that kids use to make friendship bracelets.)

3 Use heavy **card stock** in your color of choice. Trace your design or word on the back so you have a guide (remember to reverse it so it reads correctly from the front).

4 Pierce the card stock with the needle and thread from the back to create your design. That way it looks great from the front (and the knots are in the back).

5 It may also help to pre-pierce all of your holes to get the shape before using thread—then just connect the dots.

6 Pop that sucker into a **frame** (and brag to anyone who will listen that you sewed it yourself!).

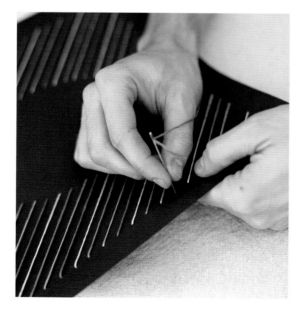

SILVER LEAF A SECONDHAND CANVAS

COST	$
WORK	SOME SWEAT
TIME	DONE IN AN HOUR

START HERE

Adding silver leaf or even rough and imperfectly applied metallic silver paint to a cheapo canvas from a thrift store or garage sale can transform that baby into a glammy metallic showstopper that's surprisingly neutral. (It can slip into nearly any room.) And you'll always laugh about the weird still life or portrait that's hidden beneath your top layer.

When we amassed a collection of leftover paint swatches from a few other projects, we figured we might as well recycle them to make something fun and colorful for the wall.

1 Cut gradational **paint chips** (the ones with a few paint colors in a row on them) into long thin strips.

2 Line them up in zigzag-y rows to create a chevron pattern.

3 Glue them in place on a piece of **card stock** (or thick decorative paper in the color of your choice) with inexpensive **craft glue.**

4 Frame that posh little paint-chip creation.

NOTE: Don't be that shady person who shoves a hundred paint swatches into your pockets! Paint chips won't always be free if folks hoard them for side projects, so we recommend reusing the chips that you already have or even buying a paint deck to grow your collection. (They're not that expensive, and can definitely come in handy for future painting projects too.)

MAKE PAINT-CHIP ART

USE WHAT YOU HAVE.

BUH-BYE,
FRUIT.
↓

1 2 1

HANG SOMETHING BY A RELATIVE

COST	FREE–$
WORK	NO SWEAT
TIME	DONE IN AN AFTERNOON

There has got to be a family memento tucked away in a box that belongs on display! I begged my dad to send me a little picture that he sketched of an owl ten years before I was born, and John asked our niece and nephew to each paint a small canvas for us—just so we'd think of them every time we walk by their masterpieces. Adding personal items like these to your walls is such a quick way to make a house feel like home. You can even ask your grandma for something your mom drew as a kid or have your sister write a meaningful quote in her handwriting and blow that up and frame it.

HOW TO SPACKLE NAIL HOLES

Don't worry about making mistakes. Those nail holes can be easily fixed. Just dab some spackle on the hole with a putty knife, drag the knife over the hole to pack the spackle in, wait as long as the package recommends, and then sand that area with a 150-grit sanding block until it's flush. This process can be repeated if the spackle isn't flush after the first pass—just add more spackle, wait, and sand again. Now there's no reason to be afraid to hang things anymore. (You can also try hanging stuff with products like Ook or 3M hooks, which involve little or no hole making at all.)

122

USE A PROJECTOR TO TRANSFER AN IMAGE ONTO A WALL

COST	$-$$
WORK	LOTS OF SWEAT
TIME	DONE IN AN AFTERNOON

Large-scale images can look especially great in an entryway, a hallway, or a small powder room. If you don't have access to an overhead projector, they can often be rented or borrowed from a school or the library. Then just trace or print any image that you like onto transparency paper (found at office-supply stores) and use the projector to cast the image onto your desired accent wall. Here's where it gets romantic. It helps to dim the lights for this part. Lightly trace the projected outline onto the wall with a pencil, and fill in the shape with latex wall paint in the color and finish of your choice.

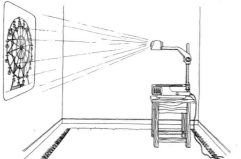

BONUS TIP
Project onto Other Surfaces

Things like stair risers, the top of a large desk or chest, a wood or metal headboard, a large piece of fabric, or even the back wall of a bookcase can also look amazing with something projected and painted on them. See pages 100–101 and 184–85 for a few examples.

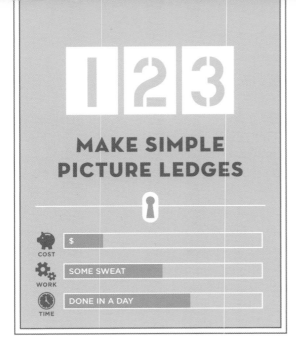

MAKE SIMPLE PICTURE LEDGES

COST	$
WORK	SOME SWEAT
TIME	DONE IN A DAY

Building your own shelves might sound intimidating, but the materials are inexpensive, and there are only a few steps. In short: You can totally do it. And then you can tell everyone all about how handy you are (preferably at length with lots of hand gestures).

1 Pick up a **1-inch-by-3-inch board** and a **1-inch-by-2-inch board** at a home-improvement store and have them both cut to the length that you want your ledge to be. (They can be cut for you right at the store for free.)

2 **Paint** or **stain** the boards (clean white shelves or rustic, stained ones always do it for us) and wait for them to dry.

3 Use a **stud finder** to locate each stud in your wall in the area that you'll be hanging the ledge, and mark its placement lightly with a pencil or some painter's tape.

4 Hold the 1-inch-by-2-inch board up right below those marks (with the 2-inch section against the

wall and a **level** resting on the board to be sure it stays straight). Use **2-inch self-sinking screws** to **drill** right through the 1-inch-by-2-inch piece and into the stud in the wall to securely hold it up. (Drilling a pilot hole with a smaller bit first will help keep the board from cracking when you drill through it.) Repeat along each stud mark that you made on the wall.

5 Lay the 1-inch-by-3-inch board on top of the support that you just created with the smaller board. You'll want the short part of the board against the wall (so it sticks out to create a 3-inch surface area for leaning art, votive candles, etc.).

6 With **1½-inch self-sinking wood screws,** drill down through the 1-inch-by-3-inch board and into the 1-inch-by-2-inch board below it to fasten them tightly together. (Be sure to push the 1-inch-by-3-inch board back against the wall as you go so it's nice and flush.)

7 If your shelves are white, you might want to paint your screws so they blend in. If you went with stained shelves, seeing a few screws can be cool and industrial (and items on the shelf can obscure many of them anyway); or you can use **wood putty** and **stain** to hide them.

124

WHIP UP CUSTOM STATE ART

Why not give a little hometown holla (or celebrate where you went to college or honeymooned) with some playful homemade state art? Just find an image of your state's outline online. Then print it and cut it out to make a template for tracing that shape onto decorative or patterned paper. Tape or glue the shape to paper with a different pattern or a contrasting color or even lay it over textured fabric like burlap or linen.

WE MADE THIS SHELF FOR LESS THAN SIX DOLLARS!

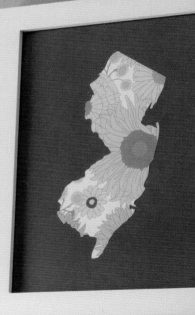

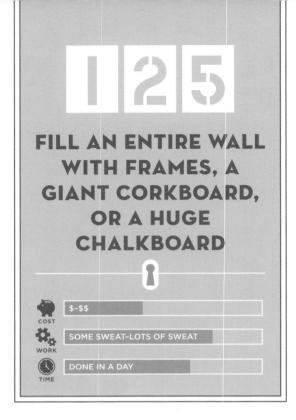

1 2 5

FILL AN ENTIRE WALL WITH FRAMES, A GIANT CORKBOARD, OR A HUGE CHALKBOARD

COST	$-$$
WORK	SOME SWEAT–LOTS OF SWEAT
TIME	DONE IN A DAY

Filling one wall or even an entire room can be interactive and ever-changing.

TO FILL A WALL WITH FRAMES

1. Cut up **brown paper bags** or **wrapping paper** to make paper templates to help you figure out the placement of all the **frames** that you want to hang.

2. Hang each frame with a **nail.** (A **3M hook** or an **Ook hook** also works if the frame is light.) Use an **anchor** and a **screw** for very heavy frames.

3. Frame anything from favorite greeting cards and family photos to meaningful notes, postcards, prints, keepsakes, and beyond.

TO MAKE A GIANT CORKBOARD WALL

1. Find **self-adhesive cork squares** at places like Target or a local craft store.

2. Grab a **heavy-duty adhesive** or a removable 3M product like their **picture-hanging Velcro** to hold the squares in place on the wall. (Lighter-weight Velcro or even the self-adhesive tabs that are included with the cork squares might pop off the wall, so the 3M picture-hanging stuff is a longer-lasting choice that's still removable later.)

3. Adhere each square one at a time, butting them up against one another for a nice seamless look (so when you step back it looks like a wall of cork).

4. You can cut squares to fit into certain places with a sharp **X-Acto knife** and a **metal ruler.**

5. Allow the adhesive (or the 3M Velcro) to set and then go nuts pinning things up.

TO MAKE A HUGE CHALKBOARD WALL

1. Get a can of **chalkboard paint** at the hardware store. Optional: Grab **magnet paint** and apply that first for a magnetized chalkboard.

2. Measure out the space you want to cover, then apply the chalkboard paint (following the directions on the can).

3. Let it dry, then chalk that baby up.

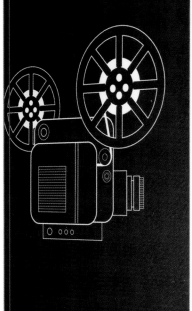

126

ADD A SURPRISE SLICE OF COLOR TO A FRAME

Painting just the outside edge of a frame in a bold color is the stuff of dreams. At least for people like us. Just remove the glass, art, and backing so you're left with an empty frame and lightly sand the side of the frame to rough it up. Tape off the front of the frame with painter's tape and use a paintbrush to apply two thin and even coats of latex paint to only the sides of the frame (we used Berry Fizz by Benjamin Moore). When it's dry, put everything back together, grin at it for a while (that's totally normal), and then hang it up.

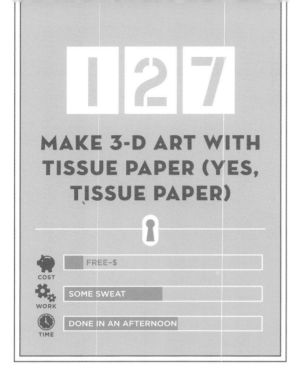

127

MAKE 3-D ART WITH TISSUE PAPER (YES, TISSUE PAPER)

COST	FREE–$
WORK	SOME SWEAT
TIME	DONE IN AN AFTERNOON

Here's a sneaky way to get the rich, painterly look of a textured oil painting by dipping into your stash of gift-wrapping supplies and leftover paint.

1   Slather your **canvas** with plain **craft glue** with a **small foam brush** and stick randomly torn sheets of **white tissue paper** onto the canvas in interesting, scrunched-up shapes. It shouldn't be totally flat, but don't let the tissue clump up too much or it could look crazytown.

2   Allow it to dry and then apply one or two coats of cheap **craft paint** or even some **leftover wall paint** if you have that around (we used Bunker Hill Green by Benjamin Moore). White always looks classic, dark colors like navy and chocolate are moody and elegant, and of course softer tones and bright, bold hues can work too.

3   After it's dry, hang it up. People will never guess it cost under five dollars, and the monochromatic, texture-rich effect is amazingly universal. (It can layer into almost any space.)

FLOAT AN EMPTY FRAME AROUND SOMETHING 3-D

BONUS TIP
Hanging Options

You might be able to use removable 3M picture-hanging Velcro to attach some of these objects directly to the wall, while others might look best threaded on twine or ribbon and hung from a simple nail or hook that floats inside the frame.

Take the glass and the backing out of a frame and hang just the empty frame on the wall (with two small finishing nails). Then hang something else inside of that rectangle to showcase it as if it's floating right there in the middle. Here are some things to try.

1   A key (tiny or oversized, spray painted a bright color or left as is)

2   An ornate spoon or other kitchen gadget from the flea market

3   A pretty beaded necklace (the bigger the better)

4   A vintage Barbie

5   An antique candy or cookie tin

6   An old wooden baby block with your initial on it (or the baby's or your sweetheart's)

These are just a handful of ideas, so get creative! Even some vintage Pez dispensers can look really fun floating in glassless frames in a kids' bathroom.

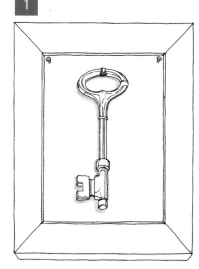

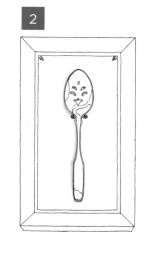

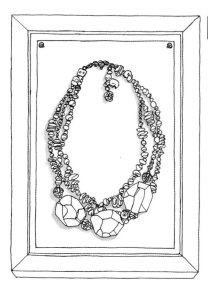

129

HANG FABRIC AS ART

Cool fabric can look striking when it's hung in a grid of frames on the wall, or even as one large tapestry. A frame (or several of them) can give the fabric a modern look, while draping it over a dowel or even pinning it up from each corner makes for a more rustic and natural vibe. Stapling fabric firmly around a canvas or even a large scrap of wood—which is what we did here—can be cool if you want a giant piece of art, and you usually only need a yard of the stuff. A small remnant of yellow coral fabric was also popped into the white frame for a layered look.

THE LIGHT OF NEW YORK ASSOULINE

130

FILL THE EMPTY SPACE ABOVE YOUR TV

Got blank space to fill above your tube? A nice round mirror can soften the sharp rectangular shape and bounce light around. Or you can opt for a floating shelf or two with anything from vases to leaning art to plants that can be switched out whenever your mood changes.

131

BEEF UP PUNY ART

Got a piece of art or a mirror that looks too small above something large like a sofa or a console? Hang candle sconces on either side of it to bulk up the look and add balance. Plus if they're meant for candles, there's no electrical work required.

132

FRAME SOMETHING THAT MAKES YOU SMILE

Your home should make you giddy. If it makes you grimace, yawn, or frown, you have to admit that's not the effect you're going for. The cure? Hang or display something sweet that makes you grin like a fool. Here are just a few ideas.

- A childhood sketch

- A note from your best friend in grade school

- A photo or postcard of a destination you adore

- A ticket to your favorite concert ever (ah, the memories)

- A collection of bottle caps (the ones that say something on the inside are always fun in a shadow box)

- A favorite fortune cookie message

- A greeting card that you can't seem to toss

- A treasured childhood item of yours, like a green kazoo or a timeworn *Velveteen Rabbit* book jacket (find the book on eBay if you don't still have it)

- A memento from something more recent that makes you feel all warm and fuzzy (like a quirky misspelled letter from your niece that says "You rok")

There will be many surprises: unexpected gains are likely.

133

DANA'S DROP-CLOTH ART

GUEST BLOGGER IDEA

BLOGGER:

DANA MILLER

BLOG:

*HOUSE*TWEAKING*

(WWW.HOUSETWEAKING.COM)

LOCATION:

SOUTHWEST OHIO

FAVORITE COLOR COMBO:

WHITE + OATMEAL + POP OF COLOR

FAVORITE PATTERN:

STRIPES OF ALL TYPES

FAVORITE GO-TO TOOL:

MY SEWING MACHINE

I had a blank wall in my foyer that was crying out for large-scale art. I knew I wanted something typographical in nature that held meaning for our family. Not wanting to spend a lot of money, I brainstormed a way to create an inexpensive yet personal piece of art.

SUPPLIES

- Transparency paper
- Large canvas drop cloth
- Needle and thread (or iron-on hem tape or a sewing machine)
- Grommet kit
- Wall hooks
- Twine
- Letter stencils or a projector (If you don't own one, try borrowing one from a local school, university, library, church, or business instead of buying one.)
- Pen
- Paint
- A few small foam brushes
- Slender PVC pipe or dowel

1 **PRINT YOUR QUOTE.** I had a transparency of a phrase from my son's favorite lullaby printed up at an office-supply store.

2 **HANG YOUR DROP CLOTH.** I laundered a drop cloth to preshrink it. Then I cut and hemmed it to my desired wall-art size, added grommets along the top, and hung it from wall hooks with twine.

3 **PROJECT AND TRACE.** Once the drop cloth was hung, I projected the lullaby phrase printed on my transparency onto the drop cloth (this works best in low light). I traced the phrase onto the drop cloth with an ink pen. You could also use letter stencils if you don't have access to a projector.

4 **PAINT.** Using small foam brushes, I painted each letter with one coat of black no-VOC paint that I already had on hand. I was careful not to saturate the fabric to keep the paint from soaking through the drop cloth and onto the wall behind it.

5 **ADD WEIGHT.** Once the paint dried, I stitched a slender PVC pipe into the bottom hem of the wall hanging to give it some weight and straighten it a bit. You can do this by hand, use a sewing machine, or even use iron-on hem tape.

The DIY wall hanging turned out great. It was large enough to give the wall in our foyer newfound visual impact, didn't take up any precious floor space, and cost me less than twenty-five dollars. The graphic typography contrasts nicely with the worn, textured canvas. It's not perfect—there are wrinkles and seams that run throughout the piece—but it means so much to our family. I can't help but smile every time I walk by it.

3

MAKE LIKE
MARIAH!

134

ADD A BUNCH OF 3-D BUTTERFLIES

COST FREE-$

WORK NO SWEAT

TIME DONE IN AN HOUR

BONUS TIP
Anti-Butterfly?

This idea works for a lot of small shapes, so you can go with dragonflies, birds, ginkgo leaves, or anything else you'd like.

You'd be hard-pressed to find a less expensive way to add serious three-dimensional interest to a wall. Use an old book or newspaper (that you've finished reading, of course) and some straight pins to make a little swarm to call your own.

1 Find a butterfly shape online and print it out on **card stock** to create a template (or use something like a butterfly-shaped cookie cutter or a paper punch).

2 Use your template to cut out a bunch of butterflies from a **newspaper,** an **old book,** or even a **road map.** We wrapped our template around a folded book page and traced its outline. Then we cut it out as seen below.

3 Pin the butterflies to the wall in a pretty little swarm with regular old sewing **straight pins** (use a hammer to tap them in). We love that the simple pin toughens it up so it doesn't look too cutesy. And this entire project was free since we had an old book and some pins on hand.

135

MAKE A FROSTED FRAME MAT

COST: $

WORK: SOME SWEAT

TIME: DONE IN AN HOUR

You can find frosting film at a hardware store (it's meant for windows and doors) and use it to frost the pane of glass in any frame, for a peekaboo effect. The art behind the pane of glass will show all the way through in the middle (where you've cut a rectangular window), but it'll also subtly peek through the frosted mat around the perimeter of the frame for a little something extra.

1. Carefully remove the **glass pane** from any **frame** and place it on your rolled-out piece of **frosting film.** Trace the pane's shape on the film with a **pencil** and cut out the traced rectangle.

2. Apply the rectangle of frosting film to the inside of your glass pane by following the frosting film directions on the package. Then dry the freshly frosted pane with a towel to remove any leftover moisture.

3. Find an item that you can use to create a smaller rectangular shape that's nested inside the frosted pane (for example, a shoebox, a piece of card stock, or a smaller frame). Center the item on the frosted side of the glass (check the measurements around it on all sides with a ruler) and trace the outline with a pencil.

4. Carefully use an **X-Acto knife** to cut along the lines you just traced (use a **ruler** to help keep your knife straight). Don't worry, it shouldn't hurt the glass.

5. Starting in one corner of the rectangle that you just cut out, slowly peel the frosting film away from the glass. Use **nail polish remover** to buff off any leftover adhesive on the clear part of the glass.

6. Let the glass fully dry for a day just to be sure it's not harboring any art-ruining moisture before adding your art and putting your frame back together with the film on the inside of the glass.

DID SOMEBODY SAY FROSTING?

4

5

Bulk Up

This technique can look pretty darn cool for a collection of frames that you want to subtly unify. Just adding frosted mats (of the same or varying thicknesses) and rehanging the collection can tie mismatched frames together or make random photos and prints relate a lot more as a group. There should be more than enough film in one package to do at least six decently sized frames (and maybe even twelve smaller ones).

THIS OLD FAUX-BRASS GUY WAS FIFTY CENTS AT A THRIFT STORE.

136

HANG AN OLD CORBEL OR SCONCE

Find a corbel or sconce at an architectural salvage yard or thrift store and either hang it as is or spray paint it a bold color (we used Raspberry Gloss by Krylon). Ah, ambiance. You can even hang two of them—one on either side of a mirror or work of art. A collection of sconces or corbels would also be great in a small hallway or nook, or even on the vertical wall space above a toilet in a bathroom.

One of the most common decor mistakes is hanging everything in a room way too high. How do we know? We've done it. Then we learned that bringing things down made rooms feel cozier and the ceilings feel taller all at the same time. As a general standard, the middle of most hanging art should be at average eye level, which is usually estimated to be 58 to 60 inches from the floor. But sometimes following that rule for something hanging over a sofa, buffet, or console will backfire, so try keeping the bottoms of any art that you place above furniture no more than 12 to 24 inches away from the item below, just so it doesn't look like it's riding too high instead of relating to what's under it.

137

HANG (OR REHANG) YOUR ART AT THE RIGHT HEIGHT

12 TO 24 INCHES HERE IS A GOOD RULE.

1. Turn it black-and-white and frame it for a classic look.

2. Crop it in an interesting way and enlarge it (200 to 300 percent can look awesome!).

138

ONE PHOTO FIVE WAYS

Here are five easy ways to make any photo that you've already taken more wall worthy.

3. Cut it into strips or a grid and frame each piece individually.

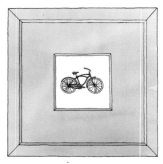

4. Pair it with a thick, colorful mat or frame for added personality.

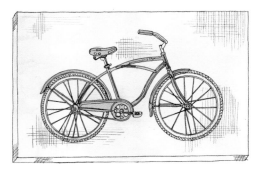

5. Get it printed on a large canvas for a gallery effect.

From old eyeglasses or skeleton keys to wood-block printing letters or white ceramic birds, there's got to be something out there that speaks to you. (Just don't tell people that your ceramic birds actually speak to you.) Collections always make a house feel more personalized and charming, and as they say in the business, grouping like objects (i.e., displaying them all together in one place) can have quite an impact. You know, as opposed to spreading them out all over the house, where they can't really be appreciated en masse. Try placing everything in a shadow box or on a floating shelf or in a bookcase to concentrate all the loveliness in one spot.

139

START A COLLECTION

140

MAKE DECAL ART

COST	$	
WORK	NO SWEAT	
TIME	DONE IN AN AFTERNOON	

Use a sticker to block off an image on canvas or a piece of wood and paint the rest of it. Remove the decal, and voilà! You have a crisp, two-tone piece of art that you didn't have to freehand.

1 Print out an image of something with an interesting shape (like an octopus or a favorite building or monument) on **sticker paper** from an office-supply store.

2 Cut your shape out and stick it on a **canvas.** (Press and rub it down firmly around all the edges so **paint** won't seep under it.) Or stick it on a stained **piece of wood** and cut it out in place with an **X-Acto knife** like we did below.

3 Paint the entire thing one solid color (we used Berry Fizz by Benjamin Moore), being sure to go over the edges of the sticker for a clean line.

4 Carefully remove the sticker to reveal your shape. Peeling the sticker off before the paint dries will make for the cleanest lines; but if you worry you'll muck everything up when the paint is still wet, it's okay to let it dry and just touch things up later if you have to.

5 High-five yourself. (Yes, this basically looks like a single clap in the air.)

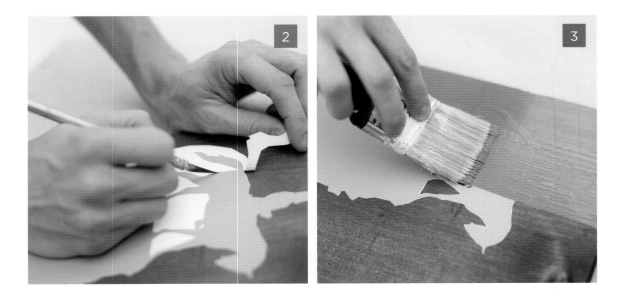

141

SKETCH EACH OTHER

Convince your significant other or BFF to play artiste, and take thirty minutes to sketch each other (with a thin black Sharpie on a small stretched canvas or on a plain old piece of paper with a pencil—whatever you'd like). Sit across from each other and crack a few jokes as you go. We admit that this could go terribly wrong, but you'll most likely LOL at least a little when you reveal your masterpieces. And no matter how horribly they turn out, commit to hanging/framing them for a week. Odds are they'll become lovably entertaining and you'll keep them up a lot longer. Or their "charm" will last only about an hour and they'll end up in the trash. But at least you tried.

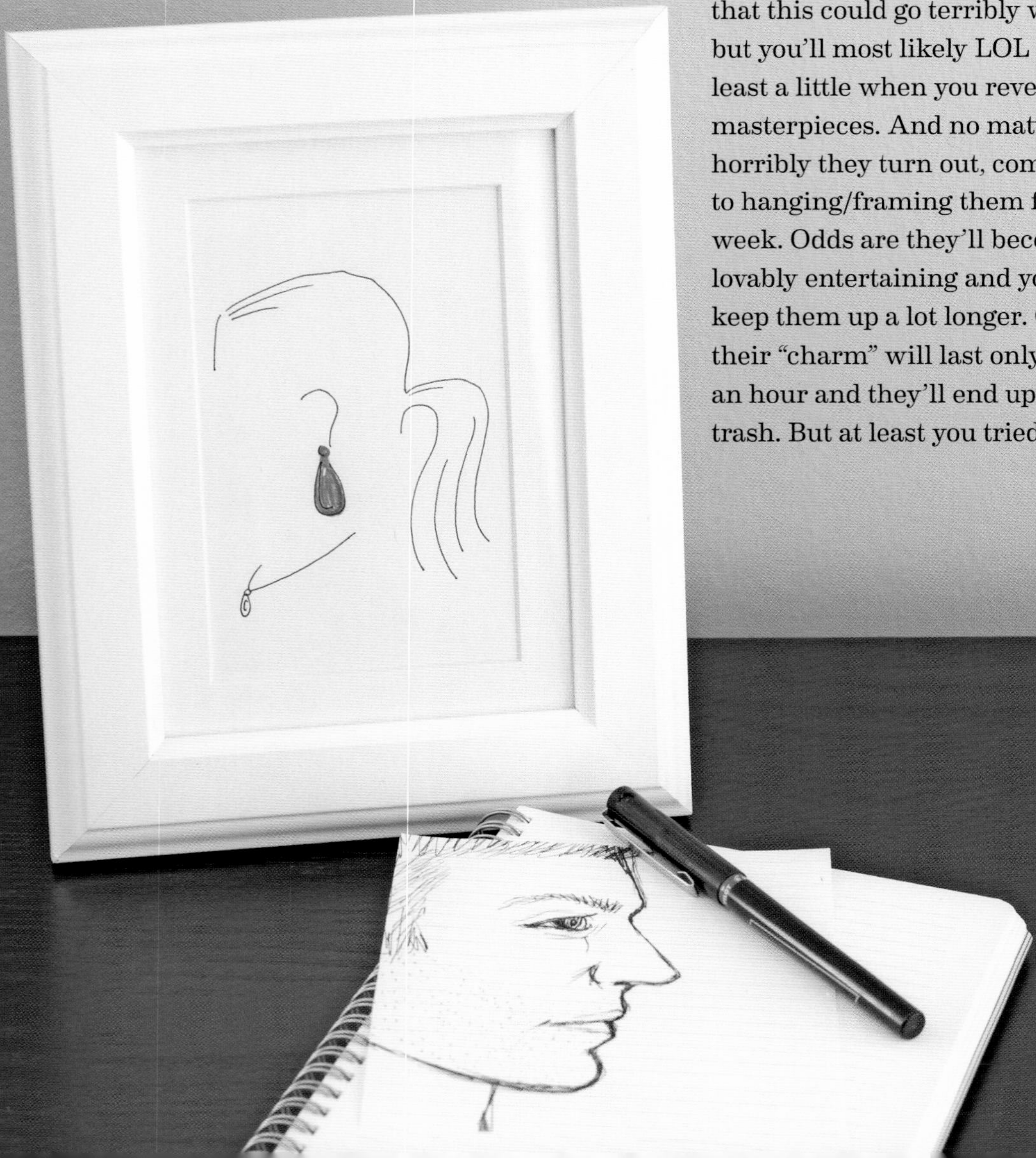

142

THINK BEYOND THE FRAME

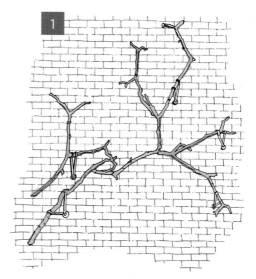

Here are some other things you can hang on the wall.

1 Found objects like branches

2 Vintage wood or metal signs

3 Candle sconces

4 Plates

5 Round baskets or woven plates

6 Shutters

7 Old windows

8 Floating vases

9 Floating shelves

10 Old wire bins

11 Large 3-D numbers or letters

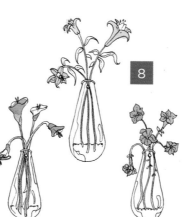

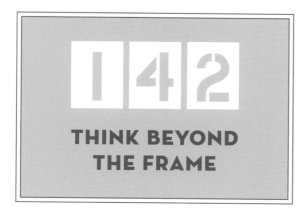

143
FIND FREE ART

It's amazing how many things can be popped into a frame. And once they're behind glass, everyday objects can look surprisingly legit. We've even framed especially scenic and creatively cropped magazine ads. Here are some other ideas.

1 A feather

2 Photos or illustrations from a calendar

3 A stencil of a letter

4 Book jackets (or interior pages)

5 Playing cards

6 A collage of ticket stubs

7 Old scarves

8 An old T-shirt

9 Small calendar pages (with a heart around a favorite date)

10 Flash cards

11 A horseshoe

12 Photo-booth strips

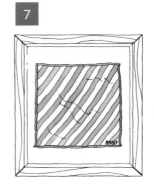

Just grab cheap frames in a variety of shapes, sizes, and styles at a thrift store or yard sale. They probably won't cost you more than a few bucks a piece. Spray paint them all the same color (tip: Choose a spray paint with built-in primer for the best coverage; see more spray-painting tips on page 87) and hang them in a grouping on your wall. No matter what you stick in each one, the coordinating frame color will tie everything together. And you'll probably save 80 percent off retail frame prices.

144
CREATE COORDINATING FRAMES

START HERE

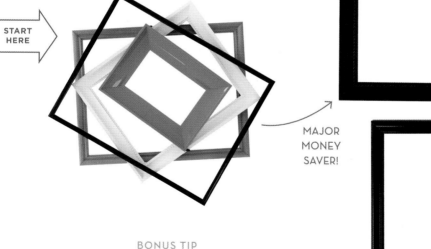

MAJOR MONEY SAVER!

BONUS TIP
Expand Your Frame Color Palette

Not only are black, chocolate, and white great classic color choices for frames, but soft gray, dark charcoal, navy, and even hues like emerald green, soft turquoise, ruby red, and cheerful yellow can also look amazing on the wall. Colored frames work especially well when paired with black-and-white images to keep things from looking too chaotic.

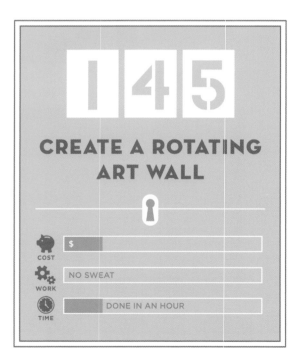

1|4|5

CREATE A ROTATING ART WALL

COST | $

WORK | NO SWEAT

TIME | DONE IN AN HOUR

Want a place to display easy-to-switch-out art without having to pay for a ton of frames or make a million holes? Jackpot. This solution can look surprisingly chic with black-and-white photos or Polaroids strung up with metal clips—or playful and cute with colorful kid drawings and bright clothespins.

1 Find a blank expanse of wall and run **wire** or **twine** between two decorative **wall hooks** or **nails**.

2 Clip up anything (like kids' drawings, a postcard collection, or photos) with industrial **binder clips** or even **clothespins** that you've spray painted a fun color.

146

PLAY PHOTOGRAPHER

COST	$-$$	
WORK	NO SWEAT	
TIME	DONE IN AN AFTERNOON	

Taking photos to create your own art doesn't have to be involved (no need to stalk a swan at the lake or anything). Just try snapping a few pictures of some of these beauties.

- A feather on top of a piece of burlap
- Eggs in a pretty bowl on a large white piece of paper
- A field with wildflowers
- A hand holding a balloon
- Old peeling paint on a fence or door
- Or anything else, really (go nuts)

Sometimes it's not even what you're shooting, but how you shoot it. So remember to try cropping your subjects in interesting ways (like getting really close or standing really far away) and to hunt for unusual angles that will make your photograph more interesting. Places like Costco or CVS will blow photos up inexpensively for you, or you can try an online service or a local print shop.

147

MAKE FUN GEOMETRIC ART

COST $

WORK NO SWEAT

TIME DONE IN AN HOUR

Tissue paper looks amazing on a canvas, thanks to the semi-sheer quality of the paper. You can cut out repeating shapes like triangles, circles, hexagons, or fish scales and play around until you find a pattern you like. Here's how we made ours.

1 Trace a mug or a cup to make a circle template out of **card stock.**

2 Use the template to cut circles out of **colored tissue paper** (in varying intensities of one color for a gradational effect or with a few complementary colors that you love). They don't have to be perfect (rough edges are part of the charm). Then cut them in half.

3 Arrange them in cascading rows on a **canvas**—sort of like an abstract take on fish scales. Use **Mod Podge** applied with a **sponge brush** both on the canvas and gently on top of them to attach them after they're positioned the way you want them.

148

MAKE A PHOTO WREATH

COST — $

WORK — NO SWEAT

TIME — DONE IN AN HOUR OR TWO

Just use poster putty (that blue stuff teens use to hang *Twilight* posters) or painter's tape and black-and-white photos (Polaroids or pictures printed with a white border look especially awesome) to make a no-nail-holes and no-commitment photo wreath on the wall. You can even crop your own photos into Polaroid-sized squares on the computer and then print them on photo paper. Then cut them out with a wide white border to get that signature Polaroid look.

NOT YOUR GRANDMA'S WREATH

149

MAKE FAUX ANTLER ART

COST: $

WORK: SOME SWEAT

TIME: DONE IN AN AFTERNOON

Making this cool graphic art with a plank of wood and some decorative paper is easy and inexpensive (ours was four dollars!). So go ahead, take a walk on the wild side.

1 Find **decorative paper** to make your antlers (we got this metallic gold poster paper at Michaels).

2 Look up antler shapes online and sketch one that you like on the back side of your paper. Cut it out and use that as a template (flipped the other way) to make your second antler.

3 Optional: **Stain** or **paint** your **wood plank.**

4 Use **craft glue** to secure your antlers to the wood plank and add a **picture hook** to the back of your plank for hanging.

EARN SOME HIPSTER STREET CRED.

150

A MODERN TAKE ON "BRONZED" BABY SHOES

COST $-$$

WORK NO SWEAT

TIME DONE IN AN AFTERNOON

START HERE

This is an updated spin on the traditional bronzed baby shoes (no melted metals necessary).

1   Cover the back of a **shadow box** with colorful **fabric** or **paper.** (If you can't find a shadow box that works, a regular frame with the glass removed can do the trick too.)

2   **Spray paint** a pair of **baby shoes.** (Colors like oil-rubbed bronze, dark indigo, hot pink, or glossy white could all look good—just choose whatever works best with your paper or fabric backdrop.)

3   Mount the fully dry spray-painted baby shoes in the middle of the paper or the fabric backdrop of the shadow box with a **heavy-duty adhesive** applied to the soles to secure them.

4   Allow them to fully dry while laying flat before hanging them.

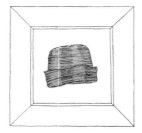

BONUS TIP
Other Frame-Worthy Baby Mementos

Things like tiny booties, an ID bracelet from the hospital, a newborn's blanket or hat, a coming-home outfit, footprints, and weight and length notes from doctor visits also look great in frames or shadow boxes.

clara
kenley

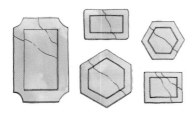

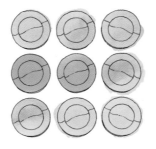

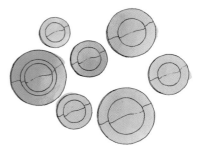

An asymmetrical option with angular plates can be graphic.

You can't go wrong with a nice symmetrical grid.

Something free-form and asymmetrical is always a crowd-pleaser.

1 5 1

HANG LOTS OF PLATES

A ton of plates hanging en masse can look really cool. Just mount them using plate hangers, which you can grab at a craft store or even order online in a number of styles (some are hidden, some peek out around the plates' edges). Here are a few possible plate layouts to get you going.

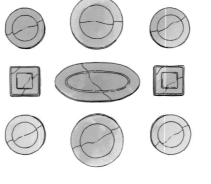

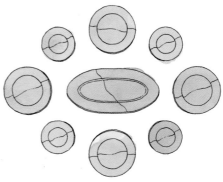

Working in some different shapes makes it more eclectic.

A balanced diamond pattern with larger plates at each point can be fun.

152

"COMMISSION" KID ART

Have fun while your wee one creates art by giving him or her specific colors that coordinate with a certain room's decor. You can even go with a sophisticated black-and-white palette or something really punchy like teal, lime, and tangerine. As for the painting surface, you can supply watercolor paper, card stock, or even a textured fabric like linen, muslin, or burlap. Heck, a cool old plank of wood could rock too.

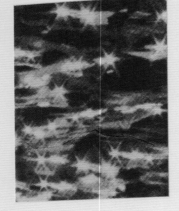

THIS WALLPAPER SAMPLE WAS JUST A FEW BUCKS.

153

FRAME WALLPAPER SAMPLES

Even if you can't afford anything for a hundred dollars a roll, you can probably still swing spending five dollars for a wallpaper sample that makes you happy every time you look at it. Just find an online vendor or a decor store that offers samples for a small fee, and pick the one you love most (or three of 'em for a little framed collection). Adding a nice thick mat can beef up your wallpaper sample (so it takes up more space and makes even more of a statement). Framing and art-supply stores sell all sorts of mats, and you can even paint them with a few thin coats of latex paint in any color you'd like to add interest. See page 215 for more on that subject.

SEE PAGE 188 FOR HOW WE MADE THIS FROSTED FRAME MAT.

The area over a door is so often overlooked, and it's a great place to add personality and interest for anyone passing through. Try hanging something small, like a tiny faux antler trophy, or something as wide as the doorway itself, like a long skinny painting from a thrift store.

154
HANG SOMETHING OVER A DOOR

DUCK!

155

MAKE SIMPLE SILHOUETTES

COST	$	
WORK	NO SWEAT	
TIME	DONE IN AN AFTERNOON	

Silhouettes can be classic black-on-white versions or bold colorful riffs that feel modern and playful. You can even use the methods described here to make silhouettes of pets or objects that you love. (Three different decorative chair silhouettes to hang in your dining room could be fun.)

A LOW-TECH OPTION

1   Take a picture of your subject that shows his or her whole head in full profile (and his or her body, if that's what you're silhouetting). Make your life easier by snapping it against a plain, light background like a wall or a sheet.

2   Print the image at home or at a photo center and then get it blown up at a copy shop. (Try 200 to 300 percent and inch up or down from there to reach your desired size.)

3   Once you have a nice-sized enlargement of your subject, carefully cut out his or her profile (or entire body). Use this cutout as a template and trace it lightly with a pencil onto **decorative paper** in any color of your choice.

4   Carefully cut out your paper silhouette (small nail scissors can be helpful) and use **craft glue** to attach it to another piece of **decorative paper in a contrasting color** to serve as a background.

5   Frame it and commence happy dance.

A HIGH-TECH OPTION

1   Take a picture of your subject that shows his or her whole head in full profile (and his or her body, if that's what you're silhouetting). Make your life easier by snapping it against a plain, light background like a wall or a sheet.

2   Open the photo in a graphics program like Photoshop, and trace the outline of the shape with a select tool (try Photoshop's Magnetic Lasso).

3   "Paint" or fill the selected shape with black for a classic look, or another color for something more playful.

4   Invert your selection and fill that with white or any other color that works well with the color of your silhouette.

5   Print and frame that baby.

WE USED A WEDDING
PICTURE OF OUR FIRST
"WE'RE MARRIED" KISS.

156

MAKE FINGERPRINT ART

We're not talking about *CSI* stuff here
(no arrest required). This fingerprint art
is more fun family tree meets geeky
science lab. Just use an ink pad and have
people sign their own scripty name under
their print).

157

MAKE FAMILY BOTANICALS

A symbolic little leaf family of sorts can
add "aww" to your walls.

1 Go outside and find **leaves** that represent
   your family (big ones for adults, smaller ones
   for kids). Place each leaf flat between **two
   thin rags** or in an **old T-shirt.**

2 With your **iron** on medium heat, iron each
   cloth-enclosed leaf for around eight minutes,
   always keeping the iron in motion, and
   periodically checking if the leaf feels crisp.

3 Once the leaves are dried out, lay them on
   a piece of **paper** and **stamp** each person's
   name next to each one with small letter
   stamps. (Stickers or printed labels work too.)
   Use **craft glue** to secure the leaves in place
   and frame the whole shebang.

158

MAKE A STAMP FAMILY TREE

We surprised Clara's stamp-lovin' grandpa by
making a stamp family tree to honor his family.
At a local stamp shop, we found postage stamps
from the birth years of the relatives we wanted
to represent—some going as far back as 1920!
You can try eBay or other online vendors if you
can't find stamps locally. Arrange the stamps in
a treelike order with rows for each generation
on white card stock. Before adhering the
stamps, use a thin black marker and a ruler to
draw the lines that will connect them. Then
use stamp hinges (sold at stamp shops or online)
or craft glue to secure your stamps in place on
the lines. This meaningful gift cost us less than
fifteen bucks (frame included).

159

PAINT YOUR MAT

Add major impact to any frame by simply
painting the mat with thin and even coats of
latex paint, using a brush or a small foam roller.
Turn your entire gallery wall into a major
showstopper with bright coral or soft green
mats (or any other color of the rainbow, really).

TWEAK

ACCESSORIZING IDEAS

SHERRY SAYS

As anyone who reads our blog knows, I have an unhealthy and completely odd attraction to certain ceramic animals. Back in 2006 I saw a handsome three-foot-tall white ceramic dog sitting obediently in HomeGoods and knew that for twenty-nine dollars I had to make him mine. And so it began. I love finding quirky, sort of masculine animals. (I also have a rhino and an octopus, just to name a few.) So it's not the sweet ceramic cat or the magical ceramic unicorn thing going on with me—I'm all about animals with edge. The ones that you wouldn't want to run into in a dark alley.

Why ceramic animals? I'm not sure. I'm just a sucker for surrounding myself with things I love (even if there's not much of an explanation for why I love them). So I picked my accessory poison, if you will. And I gotta say that ceramic animals are easier to work in than you might think. Many of them are white, which makes them fairly neutral and simple to slip into any room, and they certainly add personality and character. They're sort of like modern, cheeky, not-so-ordinary sculptures. Animals have always been something I love, so why not "adopt" as many as I can, right?

Let's not talk about how my first ceramic animal ever (my beloved dog from HomeGoods) met a sudden and tragic end when John was hanging some frames in our hallway and one came crashing down on the dog's stoic little face. The horror.

I stood there with my mouth open and fought back tears until John drew his depiction of the event to try to cheer me up. Which resulted in tears of laughter and 90 percent forgiveness.

Thankfully I have about twelve other ceramic friends in my menagerie to keep my mind off of that unthinkable day. And I'm not the only one with an accessory obsession. John's a little bit too into maps and typography. As in, they make him as giddy as Britney Spears did in 1998. (Yes, he loved her at least as much as the rest of the male population when she donned that schoolgirl outfit.) But back to the present. John likes collecting all sorts of vintage atlases and globes and even has a type map of Richmond (where his love of maps and type collide). So the whole idea here is to surround yourself with accessories that you love, and say buh-bye to anything blah. Life's too short for so-so accessories.

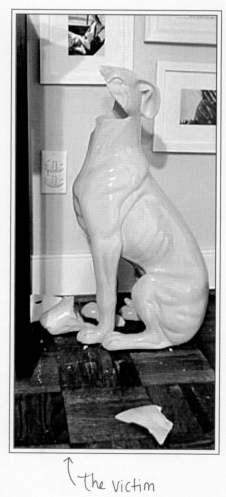

the victim

The sketch of the crime

Now these guys shudder every time John walks by.

160

ADD SOMETHING RED

Painting a basic metal chair or a wooden desk (see page 278 for a tutorial) red can add a ton of impact. Even if there's just one red thing in a room (like an inexpensive ruby-toned pillow or a red ceramic drum stool), it can wake up the entire space in a major way.

SEE HOW WE MADE THIS PILLOW ON PAGE 289!

BONUS TIP
Not Seeing Red?

No worries if you're anti-red. Try fiery orange, bright yellow, or hot pink. Bold, warm colors can set your whole room off in a similar way.

161

CREATE YOUR OWN DECOR STORE RIGHT AT HOME

It might sound like common sense, but keeping all of your decorative objects (vases, candles, spare pillow covers, etc.) in one place will allow you to more easily "shop" at your own house. You know, instead of dropping money on new stuff when you can't find something. So try not to have a cabinet for storing candles and another area for small frames and a third location for pillow covers and vases. Group it all in one spot if you can, like a spare cabinet in the kitchen, or a closet—even an under-bed storage bin can work. Then you can see virtually everything you have to work with in one pass.

EVALUATING PURCHASE-WORTHINESS

Here are some steps to evaluate whether something is worth buying. Just a good price or a deep discount isn't enough. You should be able to answer yes to at least four and ideally all six of the questions below.

1 Will it fit where I need it to go? And if I don't know where it'll go, will I be able to realistically find a spot for it?

2 Do I like the lines of it? (Lines and shape aren't something you can easily change like paint or fabric.)

3 Is it in good condition? If not, am I confident that I can make it so?

4 Will it work with other items that I already have and love? (There's no point in buying something that'll clash with the rest of your stuff.)

5 Is this a long-term item instead of an interim item? Sometimes it's better to just save you money toward the thing that you really want.

6 If the item is on sale, ask yourself: Would I buy it if it weren't on sale? (This is a true test of whether you love and need something or whether you're just buying it for the rush of a deal.)

162

PLAY MUSICAL CHAIRS WITH YOUR ACCENT PILLOWS

Move all your pillows one room over and see how they look in their new home. Or just try randomly mixing and matching your pillows in ways that you haven't before. Sometimes it takes your eyes a little while to adjust to small changes like this, so give the pillows a few days in their new spots before rushing to judgment. You can even take photos of a room with a few different pillow contenders and look at them to see what you like best. (Photos can make it easier to evaluate things like scale, shape, and color than standing there scratching your head in person.)

163

ADD A PLANT THAT (PROBABLY) WON'T DIE IMMEDIATELY

Some plants can make you feel like a real loser (or even worse—a murderer) if you kill them. But that shouldn't keep you from picking up an easy-care plant to add life (and fresher air) to each room of your house. Here are a few black-thumb-approved plants that you probably won't kill (fingers crossed).

Aloe vera (so cute in a clean white pot)

Burro tail (a simple succulent like aloe that's hard to murder)

Bamboo (cheap, easy, and Zen)

Philodendron (lots of syllables, not a lot of work)

Boston fern (feathery and chic)

Corn plant (we've had one for years)

English ivy (for proper Brits . . . and everyone else)

Pathos (always a crowd-pleaser)

164

MAKE NAPKIN PILLOW COVERS

COST	FREE–$
WORK	SOME SWEAT
TIME	DONE IN AN HOUR

If you can't find the perfect pillows for your sofa or bed, using fabric napkins or place mats to make them can be the answer—and they're usually nice and cheap.

1 Gather your supplies; you'll want two of the same-sized **fabric napkins** or **place mats** for each pillow, and you'll need a **needle** and **thread** (a sewing machine is optional).

2 Place your napkins on top of each other. If they have a "good side," make sure those sides are facing each other. Use your sewing machine (or needle and thread) to sew the napkins together along three of the four edges.

3 Now turn your pillowcase-in-the-making right side out and stuff **a pillow that's the same size** as your new cover inside (anything too small will make the pillowcase look baggy). You can also fill it with the **stuffing from an old bed pillow** if you can't find a pillow that's the right size.

4 Use your needle and thread to sew the fourth and final side closed. Try to use tiny stitches and thread that matches the color of the fabric so it's not too noticeable along that edge.

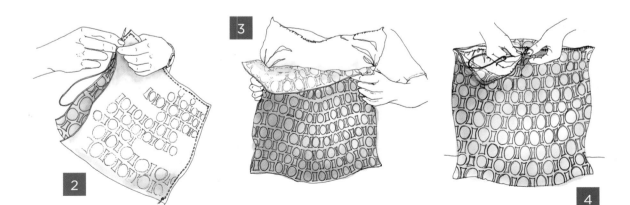

"Recycling" old bottles with chalkboard paint is a great way to make a doodles-welcome vase. Bottoms up.

1 Soak empty **wine or soda bottles** in soapy water to remove their labels.

2 Let them dry and spray them with a **spray primer** like Kilz.

3 When the primer is dry, coat them with **chalkboard paint,** added in thin, even layers with a paintbrush or applied as a spray if you can track that down. (We found some chalkboard spray paint for seven bucks at Jo-Ann Fabric.)

4 Doodle away with some **white or colored chalk.** (Draw a fake wine label, your name, a note to a guest, your favorite number, your last initial, whatever.)

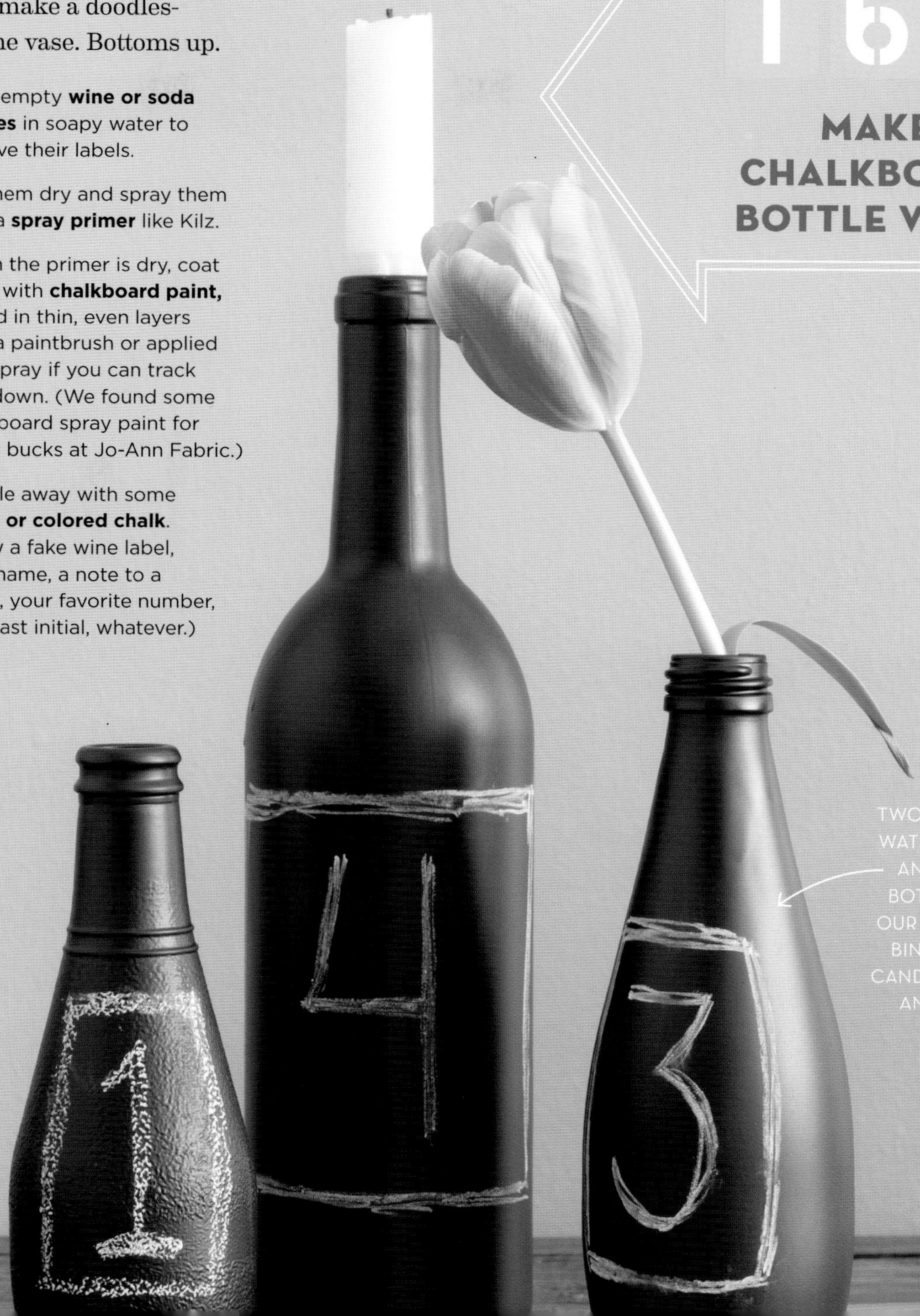

165

MAKE CHALKBOARD BOTTLE VASES

TWO SPARKLING WATER BOTTLES AND A WINE BOTTLE FROM OUR RECYCLING BIN ARE NOW CANDLEHOLDERS AND VASES.

166
ADOPT "SIGNATURE" ITEMS

Identify a few items that feel personal or meaningful—you know, stuff that can make your house feel like you. Taking a minute to think about what represents your relationship, your life, or your interests will make things nice and easy. That way when you see art or accessories in that vein, they'll pop out and call your name. Maybe you're drawn to icons or animals or letters or numbers. Here are a few of our favorites (and why).

1   The number 7 (We started dating on 7/7/05 and got married on 7/7/07.)

2   White ceramic animals, especially rhinos (Just because they make us smile.)

3   Photo-booth strips (We've probably posed for a hundred since we started dating.)

4   Keys (From old ones we've framed to oversized iron ones we've hung on the wall, for us they just have so much character and charm.)

5   Lemons and limes (They were the centerpieces at our summer wedding.)

6   Anything New York City–related (We met and fell in love there.)

7   Bees (They were on our wedding invitation, flying around a lemon tree.)

8   Maps (They're full of tiny details and texture, and they're especially meaningful when they feature places we've lived or visited.)

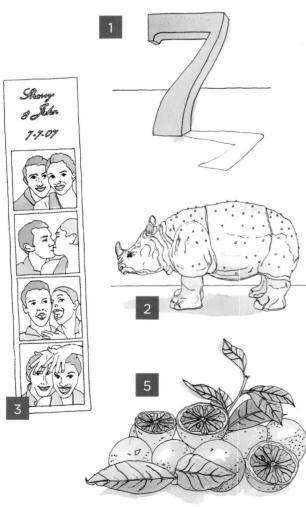

Refreshing a homely old wreath with glossy spray paint can add up to an almost ceramic look that's sleek and cheeky. Just find a wreath that's not made of real plants/leaves/flowers (go faux, baby) and that has an interesting shape. Apply as many thin and even coats of spray paint as you need to achieve full coverage. (Something with a built-in primer like Rust-Oleum Universal might be easiest.) When the wreath is dry, wrap some pretty ribbon in a loop around it and use that to hang it. This is great for dressing up a window or a mirror (just tape the ribbon behind the top edge of the mirror or add a small nail to the top of a window frame to hold it up).

167

MODERNIZE A WREATH

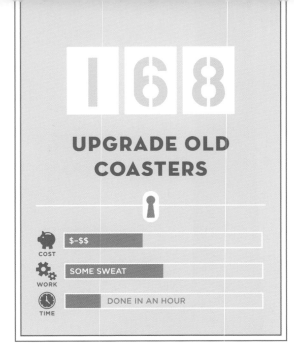

168

UPGRADE OLD COASTERS

🐷 **COST**	$-$$	
⚙️ **WORK**	SOME SWEAT	
🕐 **TIME**	DONE IN AN HOUR	

Scrapbook paper + glue = happy little coasters. For those who need a bit more detail, here you go.

1 Buy inexpensive **ceramic tiles** that are big enough to rest cups on from a home-improvement store, or grab **cheap coasters** from a thrift store (they're usually four for a dollar).

2 Pick up some **decorative paper** from the craft store for around fifty cents per sheet. (We like using four different patterns for a fun, eclectic look.)

3 Trace the shape of each tile (or thrift-store coaster) onto the back of your decorative paper with a pen or pencil and carefully cut it out.

4 Use **craft glue** to secure it in place atop the coaster or tile.

5 **Mod Podge** the top of the paper for extra durability once the glue has dried.

6 If you're working with tile, you might want to add small **felt pads** from a home-improvement store (the ones that go under chair legs to keep them from scratching the floor). Skip this step if you've found secondhand coasters that already have protective backing.

169

BRING THE OUTSIDE IN

Lots of outdoor stuff can work inside, like rocks, branches, moss, shells, sand, acorns, pinecones, leaves, and (duh) flowers. Even an old tree trunk remnant can be sealed to make a killer side table.

BONUS TIP
Say No to Bugs

Freezing things like acorns and pinecones before displaying them can ensure that there aren't any critters lurking inside. And leaving larger things in a holding area like a garage or a sealed sunroom before bringing them in enables you to check for bugs a day or two later.

1. Corral pencils and pens

2. Store ribbon or extra buttons and thread

3. Add some essential oils and wood skewers for an instant all-natural air freshener

170

USE CUPS FOR MORE THAN DRINKING

Here are five other ways to use a cup.

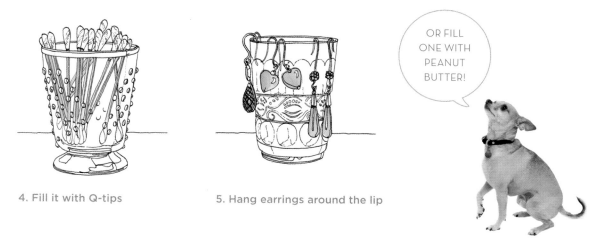

4. Fill it with Q-tips

5. Hang earrings around the lip

OR FILL ONE WITH PEANUT BUTTER!

171

TOP A TABLE WITH GREAT DECORATIVE FABRIC

COST	$-$$
WORK	SOME SWEAT
TIME	DONE IN AN AFTERNOON

If you have a table or desk that deserves a wake-the-heck-up memo, just grab a cool fabric remnant and a glass or Plexiglas top.

1   Measure the top of your table and purchase a **piece of glass** or **Plexiglas** cut to that size. Many home-improvement stores can do this on the spot with Plexiglas, or you can order a piece of glass from a local glass fabricator (just Google around for one in your area). We got our 20-by-30-inch piece of Plexiglas from Home Depot for twenty-six bucks.

2   Cut decorative **fabric** to fit the rectangular top of your table. (You can hem the edges for a polished look or leave them raw if you've chosen something rough, like burlap, or a fabric that doesn't fray.) **OPTIONAL:** lightly secure it in place with some **double-stick tape.**

3   Put your cut piece of glass or Plexiglas over the fabric to hold it in place. Done-zo.

Take a trip (for the day, the weekend, the whole week, whatever) and buy something meaningful somewhere else. Not a tacky souvenir, but a piece of art, a candle, a vase, or even a piece of furniture. It'll always have a fun little memory attached to it.

172

GET SOMETHING SPECIAL FOR YOUR HOUSE BY GETTING AWAY FROM IT

173

ADD BOLDNESS WITHOUT PAINTING THE WALLS

Can't paint your walls (due to fear of commitment or fear of your landlord)? Brightly toned pillows, art, rugs, and curtains can add just as much wow without breaking out the paintbrush. Lots of color-loving connoisseurs choose to have white walls to make their colorful accessories pop, so white walls don't have to be an obstacle when it comes to serious style. Even colorful smaller accessories like a stack of books or pretty bright bowls can add some great punch to a formerly flat-looking space.

174

PUT SOMETHING IN AN UNUSED FIREPLACE

There are lots of ways to dress up an old unused fireplace. Here are a few of our favorites.

• A mirror leaning in the back of the fire box with a tray of candles gleaming in front

• A big potted fern

• Stacks of hardcover books

• A large round woven basket

• Framed art (try three photos of varying heights layered in front of one another)

175

ADD A SLAP OF WHIMSY

At first we made the mistake of trying to keep things serious and "grown-up" in our first house, and surprise, surprise, it didn't feel like home at all. We thought beige walls, a matching furniture set, and "adult" accessories were the thing to do. But the second we went rogue and opted for things that we love (more color, fun accessories, and a nice serving of quirk) it felt a lot more like us. So if you feel like you live in a space that's a bit too safe or generic for your liking, add a few personal touches, be it a pair of turquoise pillows, a zebra-print ottoman, a large oyster shell–encrusted mirror, or anything else that takes the room from "it works" to "it's mine."

YAY, WHIMSY.

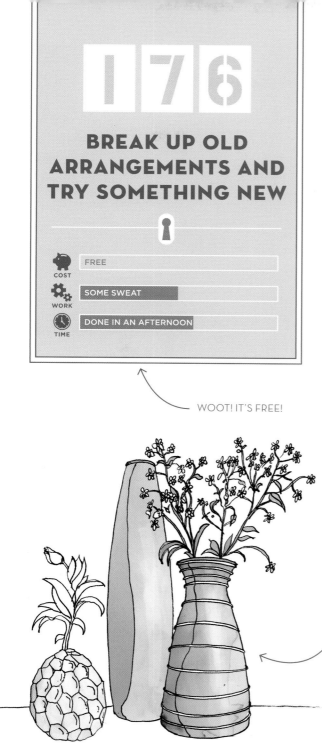

176

BREAK UP OLD ARRANGEMENTS AND TRY SOMETHING NEW

COST FREE

WORK SOME SWEAT

TIME DONE IN AN AFTERNOON

WOOT! IT'S FREE!

Gather every single decorative accessory that you own into one easy-to-survey spot (like a large dining room table or the kitchen floor). Seeing everything en masse will help you create new pairings (and break up those tired old ones) for a whole new look. Although you're using things you already have, they can look completely different if they're arranged with different items and in different color schemes. If you're having a hard time coming up with some fresh new arrangements, here are a few ideas.

- Dig up all your candlesticks (crystal, wood, glass, etc.) and group them on a mantel or a floating shelf.

- See if you have multiple items in the same general color (be it white, green, black, or hot pink) and work them all into a bookcase or china cabinet. Adding similarly toned decorative items to break up stacks of books or plates can look great.

- Grab a bunch of your brightest accessories from the pile and put them together on a console table or on a runner down the center of your dining table. Even though they're a variety of colors, sometimes bright just works with bright—even if it seems like it would compete.

- Play with textures and materials. Pick something that's smooth and shiny and pair it with something that's rough and rustic. Or place something patterned next to something clean and simple.

- Look for one item that's short, one item that's of medium height, and one item that's tall. Groupings of three and items of varied heights often look good together, even if those three things don't always seem like they'd go.

- Grab everything that's made of the same material (glass or wood or metal) and display it together for a nice cohesive tone-on-tone look.

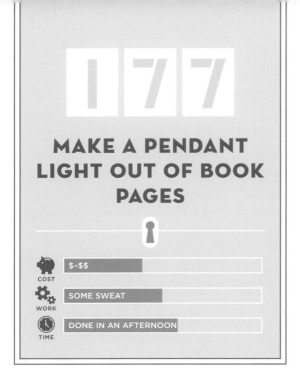

177

MAKE A PENDANT LIGHT OUT OF BOOK PAGES

COST $-$$

WORK SOME SWEAT

TIME DONE IN AN AFTERNOON

Try using pages from a children's book, a thrift-store novel, an old encyclopedia, or a book of botanicals.

1 Find an old **drum shade** at a thrift store or buy one from a decor store. Make sure it has a metal ring on top of the shade so it can be hung from above or attached to a light kit. (Some lampshades have metal arms with a ring at the top and others attach from the bottom.)

2 Find a **vintage book** and cut out the pages that you want to use by carefully running an **X-Acto knife** along the spine. (You can color copy the pages if you can't bear to rip a book apart.)

3 Cut the pages into 2-inch or 3-inch sections.

4 Tape four strips together in a staggered pattern like you see in the photo above (flip them over to hide the tape). Then fold the top of your staggered strip over the shade and tape it in place.

5 Continue folding and taping pages until the entire shade is covered by book page flaps that hang down to create a fringe-y effect.

6 Add a light kit (Ikea sells them for around five dollars) or just hang your new pendant on its own (without any wiring necessary) to add interest over a table in the corner.

CAPTAIN CAREFUL ALERT: Paper lampshades and lanterns are commonly used, so there's no fire hazard as long as heat can escape out the top and bottom of the shade, and the bulb has ample clearance (i.e., it isn't super close to or pressed up against the paper, tape, or shade). Using a CFL or an LED bulb is always a good idea too, since they put out significantly less heat than incandescent bulbs.

WE FOUND AN OLD EMILY POST BOOK AT A THRIFT STORE TO USE (FOR TEN CENTS!).

178

DYE PILLOW COVERS FOR A DREAMY, BLURRED EFFECT

COST | $
WORK | SOME SWEAT
TIME | DONE IN AN AFTERNOON

Who says the only way to make your own pillows is to sew them? You can definitely make premade pillow covers your own with dye!

1 First gather your supplies. You'll need a plain white **100-percent cotton pillow cover** and some **fabric dye**. (Check the instructions for additional supplies you may need for dyeing, like salt.) Ikea sells great inexpensive pillow covers like the one we used here.

2 Mix up a dye bath in your sink, tub, or spare bucket according to the dye instructions. We used Dylon dye in Jeans Blue for our pillow.

3 Fold the pillow cover in half and then in half again. Then submerge it about halfway in the dye bath. Hold it there as long as the dye instructions dictate.

4 Rinse and wash/dry the pillow cover according to the dye instructions, taking care to ensure that the color doesn't run onto the undyed parts of the pillow cover while you rinse it (wait for the water to run clear before washing or drying it to avoid any running).

5 Repeat to make as many pillow covers as you'd like.

WE USED AN OLD BUCKET FROM THE BASEMENT, BUT A SINK OR TUB CAN WORK TOO!

179

MAKE RECYCLED GLASS BOOKENDS

Dig glass jars out of your recycling bin (ours used to house pasta sauce) and remove the labels. Fill them with rocks, water, or sand—anything heavy enough to hold up some books. Then spray paint the heck out of them with their lids on, applying thin and even coats of whatever color you'd like. They'll be just as pretty as a glass vase or ceramic planter that might live on a bookcase and a whole lot cheaper to create. Ours were four dollars total!

180

UNDRESS YOUR HARDCOVER BOOKS

Slipping the jackets off of hardcover books may reveal gorgeous, less-busy fabric covers underneath. The stripped-down spines make for an easy way to posh up your bookshelf or coffee table.

181

UPGRADE A MIRROR WITH WASHERS

We bought thirty large metal washers for nine dollars at a home-improvement store and attached them to the frame of a four-dollar thrift-store mirror with Liquid Nails. After the glue dried, we taped off the mirror part and spray painted the frame with glossy white paint (Rust-Oleum's Universal, which has a built-in primer). Some other color options to try are oil-rubbed bronze, black, high-gloss red, soft coral, celery, or any other color that catches your eye.

RE-COVER A LAMPSHADE

COST	$-$$
WORK	SOME SWEAT
TIME	DONE IN AN HOUR

Look around for a fabric-covered drum lampshade. With less than a yard of fabric and a glue gun, you can completely reinvent it. The same-width-all-the-way-around shape of a drum pendant makes this type of shade the easiest to work with, and you can create a seam in the back that no one will ever see (like all lampshades have).

1 First choose a **fabric** you love. Anything from a rich neutral to a bold pattern can work, just try to stay away from heavy fabrics that will end up blocking lots of light (sheer and silky fabrics may also be harder to work with than something classic like lightweight cotton).

2 Measure the height and circumference of your **drum shade.** Add 2 inches to each measurement and cut your fabric to that size. If your fabric has a pattern, be sure to keep it straight as you cut it. You'll be left with a rectangle of fabric slightly larger than the shade.

3 Using a **hot glue gun,** secure one of the two short sides of your fabric rectangle vertically down the back seam of your lampshade (one long line of glue should hold that end in place).

4 It helps to have two people on hand for this step. Pull the fabric tightly around the shade and fold the end over about a half of an inch to create a nice finished edge. Meanwhile, have your helper place a line of glue over the original edge of the fabric that you already glued down.

5 Press the folded edge of fabric into the line of glue so it's held firmly around the shade. Your pattern may not match up perfectly, but that's okay since this seam will be in the back.

6 Fold over the excess fabric at the top and bottom edge of your shade and glue it along the inside lip. Again, it may be helpful to have someone man the glue gun while you press the fabric into the line of glue that's being applied and make your way around the shade. You may need to make small cuts to fold the fabric around the metal arms of the shade.

CAPTAIN CAREFUL ALERT: Most fabric lampshades are held together with glue, so there shouldn't be a danger of anything melting or dripping once the glue has set. (Shades are typically located a fair distance away from the bulbs, so the heat won't affect the glue.)

NOTE: For more photos and tips, visit younghouselove.com/book.

TURN THE PAGE TO SEE THE FINISHED PROJECT!

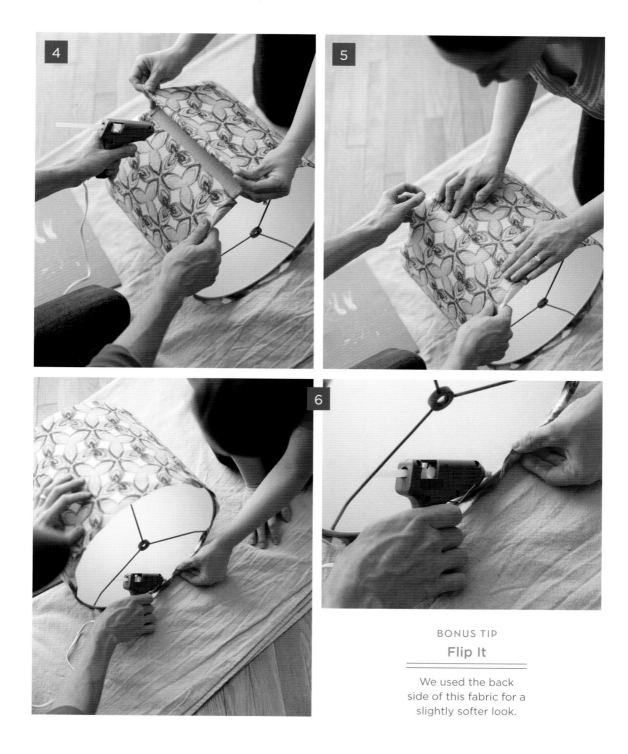

BONUS TIP

Flip It

We used the back
side of this fabric for a
slightly softer look.

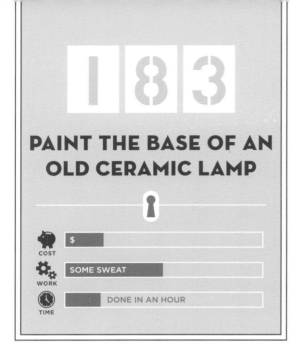

PAINT THE BASE OF AN OLD CERAMIC LAMP

COST $

WORK SOME SWEAT

TIME DONE IN AN HOUR

PAINT A LAMPSHADE

COST $-$$

WORK SOME SWEAT

TIME DONE IN AN HOUR

Sometimes adding one more pop of color can be that "something's missing" solution that cheers up a room. So grab a lamp you already have (or an oldie from the thrift store) and happy up your space.

1 Remove the shade and any shade hardware. Tape off the bulb socket and the cord with **painter's tape** to keep them from getting painted.

2 Apply a few thin coats of a **spray primer** to the lamp base, followed by three or four coats of **spray paint** in the color of your choice. See page 87 for some general spray-painting tips. You could also prime and paint the lamp base with a brush and latex paint if you prefer (we used Hibiscus by Benjamin Moore)—just always keep your coats thin and even.

3 Allow ample drying time before putting the shade back on and basking in the afterglow of a job well done.

Some unexpected interest on a lampshade can shake things up. Just use a cheap two-dollar tube of acrylic paint from the craft store for a whole new look. Try one of these designs or go rogue and dream up your own.

• High-contrast zebra stripes (Find an example online and lightly sketch your pattern on the shade with pencil before filling it in with paint.)

• Classic horizontal stripes (Use painter's tape as your guide.)

• A painted border or band at the top and bottom of the shade for drama (like the ones we added with the help of painter's tape)

• A monogram (Find a stencil at a craft store and gently stipple the paint on using a flat stencil brush and a dab-dab-dab motion.)

• Some mod or retro shapes like teardrops, repeating circles, hexagons, etc.

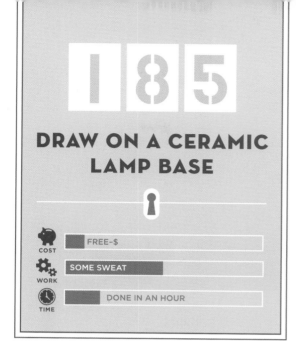

185

DRAW ON A CERAMIC LAMP BASE

🐷 **COST** — FREE–$

⚙️ **WORK** — SOME SWEAT

🕐 **TIME** — DONE IN AN HOUR

186

TRIM A LAMPSHADE WITH RIBBON

🐷 **COST** — FREE–$

⚙️ **WORK** — SOME SWEAT

🕐 **TIME** — DONE IN AN HOUR

Break out that paint pen (in silver, black, white, anything!) and draw on the base of a plain lamp to add some detailed texture and interest. Anything goes, from rough vertical stripes to irregular waves or even a ton of interlocking shapes. We used a Sharpie paint pen in white and drew some free-form leafy branches in about eight minutes.

TIP: Try practicing a few potential patterns on paper before going to town on your lamp base, just to master the technique before the pressure's on.

All you need for this project is a lamp, enough ribbon to wrap around the top and bottom of the shade, and a glue gun.

1 Hunt down the **ribbon** that you'd like to use. (Already have some laying around? Even better!) We love to use crisp accent colors like black, white, navy, lime, or chocolate against a neutral **lampshade.**

2 Wrap the ribbon around the top edge of your shade, leaving an extra inch or two to be safe, and cut it. Repeat around the bottom edge.

3 Using a **glue gun,** attach the ribbon around both edges, ensuring that the pieces meet on the same side of the shade (so that you can turn it to face the wall). Fold the end of the ribbon where it meets/overlaps before gluing it down for a cleaner edge.

187

GILD A GLASS LAMP BASE

🐷 **COST**	$-$$	
⚙️ **WORK**	SOME SWEAT	
🕐 **TIME**		DONE IN AN HOUR OR TWO

Glass + gold = awesome. And since you probably don't have gold bars sitting around waiting to be melted down, this might be the next best thing.

1 Use **gold craft paint** and a **small paintbrush** to dab a pretty decent amount of paint around the base of the lamp up to whatever horizontal line you'd like to establish (we used Deco Art Dazzling Metallics paint in Glorious Gold).

2 After one pretty thick coat (this might be the only time we encourage thick paint application), let it all dry. It'll probably look really bad at this point and you'll have zero faith that the project will work. We remember it well. But press on, my friend.

3 Once your first horrible-looking coat dries, apply your second coat, again being generous (apply it nice and thick—of course not gloppy and drippy, but we wouldn't describe it as thin either).

4 Allow for more drying time and then apply a third coat. (It took us three thick coats with ample drying time to get to a gleaming finished result—but when we got there we loved it so much that we wondered why we ever worried.)

5 Bask in the glory of a three-dollar craft-paint upgrade that looks like a million bucks.

Replacing old knobs for fresh shiny ones can make your house feel decades newer. And going to specialty stores like Anthropologie or even a salvage yard or thrift store for something with character and charm to update an old eighties brass knob can definitely wake up more than just your door—it can add polish to the entire room. We once toured a house with ebony wood floors and large white ceramic knobs on every door. The mixture of the dark floors and the glossy white knobs was amazing. Who knew knobs could make such a difference? They were like elegant little exclamation points all over the house.

188

SWAP OUT A DOORKNOB OR TWO

1 8 9

HOST A PILLOW SWAP

COST	FREE
WORK	NO SWEAT
TIME	DONE IN AN AFTERNOON

Ask five of your closest friends to bring over one or two accent pillows that they no longer love and pass them around until everyone ends up with something new. It sounds really weird, but we've done it, and it's fun. It's also free, so it's worth a shot, right? This works with lamps, vases, art, and bigger things like rugs and duvets as well. So you can host an anything-home-related swapfest if you'd like.

There are tons of ways to incorporate your relationship into your decor other than displaying wedding pics. For example, you can frame a napkin from your wedding's cocktail hour, a map of the place you honeymooned, or the menu from the restaurant where you went on your first date. You can also hang the numbers that represent your anniversary (or another special occasion) on a frame wall or use them as paperweights on your desk. Sometimes being mushy is A-OK.

1 9 0

THINK BEYOND WEDDING PHOTOS

191
TRY COLORED CHALKBOARD PAINT

You can now buy chalkboard paint in a ton of tones at craft stores, hardware stores, and even online, so purchasing your color of choice is pretty straightforward. And you can use it anywhere, like . . .

- On a mirror frame or picture frame
- On a serving tray
- On a storage box
- On a planter
- On a paneled door
- Over an existing chalkboard that you want to make over
- Pretty much anywhere else you'd like!

192
WHIP UP A BATCH YOURSELF

Here's a way to make small samples of chalkboard paint (you'll want to make and use it pretty quickly or it'll begin to harden). Combine 1 paint test pot in any color (we used 14 Carrots by Benjamin Moore) with 1 tablespoon of unsanded tile grout mix from a hardware store and stir it up to get rid of lumps. Use a small foam craft brush to apply your mixture in thin and even applications. Many thin coats might be necessary (you can prime the item beforehand for added durability). If it dries gritty, use 200-grit sandpaper to smooth things out. Then rub the side of a piece of chalk over the entire surface to condition it and wipe everything down with a moist rag.

193

SKETCH ON A PILLOW

COST	FREE–$	
WORK	NO SWEAT	
TIME	DONE IN AN HOUR	

Drawing on a pillow can definitely sound a little . . . questionable. But it can actually look really high-end if you choose a pattern and color scheme that elevate a boring old pillow cover. We went with gold and white for our colors, and just sketched variously sized rectangles to create a geometric pattern that we really like. And yes, we'll admit that it was scary at first. But scary/thrilling, not scary/nauseating.

1   Find any plain white or solid-colored **pillow** or **pillow cover** (we got this one for seven dollars at Ikea).

2   Use a **fine-tipped fabric marker** in any color to draw your design. (You can also use a Sharpie poster paint pen, but it may not be machine washable, so spot cleaning is recommended.)

3   To ensure that it won't bleed, test your marker in an inconspicuous spot on your pillow before going all out.

4   Anything from branchy or leafy designs to geometric shapes or even organic swirls can work. You might want to practice your pattern on scrap paper until you love it enough to move on to the pillow.

MY LINES WEREN'T PERFECT, BUT THAT'S PART OF THE CHARM.

194

EMBRACE WHAT MAKES YOU HAPPY

Things that you love can add so much flavor to your home. For example, if you love horses, don't stop at photos, try a 3-D object like a horse shoe or a horse-head bookend. If you're into a sports team, find a vintage print or item of memorabilia and display it. If you're obsessed with a certain band, find a cool show poster or T-shirt to cut into a square and frame. Or bring an old Polaroid camera (or a smartphone with a stylized picture app) to a concert and shoot a bunch of pictures to pin up in a grid on the wall. If you're into old cars, find vintage postcards of them—or even a cool car part, like an old steering wheel, which you can mount on the wall as a place to hang a coat or a dog leash.

Test tubes

Canning jars

Glass soda bottles (Izze ones are always charming)

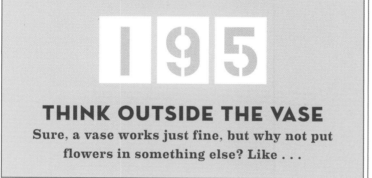

1 9 5

THINK OUTSIDE THE VASE

Sure, a vase works just fine, but why not put flowers in something else? Like . . .

An old ceramic cowboy boot (we see them at thrift stores)

An old soup can (an ode to Warhol)

Wine bottles (which can be wrapped with burlap, ribbon, or fabric)

196

MAKE SIMPLE SEASONAL CHANGES

Swapping a colorful linen or cotton throw for a large faux-fur blanket on the sofa can totally warm up or cool down your house to set the tone. Here are a few other things that you can switch up for some seasonal flavor.

- **ART AND THE MATS BEHIND IT.** Big, handsome red mats could be festive for the holidays if they're usually white during spring, summer, and fall.

- **CANDLES.** Certain scents are just so seasonal, like linen or daffodil in the spring, pineapple or watermelon in the summer, pumpkin or cranberry in the fall, and spruce or gingerbread in the winter.

- **TABLE RUNNERS OR CLOTH NAPKINS.** Think light linen in the spring; sunny yellow or big graphic blooms for the summer; jute or goldenrod in the fall; and white, ruby red, or lime green for winter.

- **PILLOWS.** Anything bright and punchy says spring and summer, while amber, gold, and chocolate might feel fallish, and fluffy mohair and velvet ones scream winter.

We got each of these random items for a dollar (at a thrift store and in the dollar bin at Target) and gave them a few thin coats of glossy white spray paint with a built-in primer (we used Rust-Oleum Universal) for a fresh ceramic look.

SEE THE FINISHED PRODUCTS ON THE BOOKCASE ON PAGE 155!

197

CERAMICIZE SOMETHING

Simple things like rotating the personal pictures in your frames can get you in the mood of that season. Beach photos are great to display over the summer, while skiing and Christmas pics from years past work in the winter. For easy storage, just keep one photo from each season in the frame (behind the main one on display). That way you can easily switch them up without having to hunt around.

198
SEASONALLY SWITCH
OUT FAMILY PHOTOS

NICOLE'S EASY VASE UPGRADE

GUEST BLOGGER IDEA

BLOGGER:
NICOLE BALCH

BLOG:
MAKING IT LOVELY
(WWW.MAKINGITLOVELY.COM)

LOCATION:
OAK PARK, ILLINOIS

FAVORITE COLOR COMBO:
PINK + GOLD

FAVORITE PATTERN:
CRAZY FLORALS

FAVORITE GO-TO TOOL:
A FIVE-IN-ONE PAINTER'S TOOL

I needed a plain white vase for a friend, so I came up with the idea to line a glass vase with paper. Then I decided it would be a whole lot more fun to switch out the white paper for different colors and patterns, so I got to work figuring out how to do it.

SUPPLIES

- Simple, straight-sided clear glass vase
- Large sheet of decorative paper
- Pencil
- Scissors
- Tape
- Smaller vase, container, or glass to fit inside *(to hold water if you plan to use it for fresh flowers)*

1 **TRACE THE VASE.** I set the vase on its side on top of the paper and traced along the top as I rolled the vase. Then I did it again along the bottom as I rolled it back.

2 **CUT THE PAPER.** Following the lines that I drew, I cut my paper template out and placed it inside my vase to check the fit.

3 **TRIM.** Mine was a bit too tall, so I just traced along the top rim of the vase (onto the paper) and used that mark to cut off the excess.

4 **TAPE IN PLACE.** Once I had the size right, I put the paper back in the vase and taped along the inside seam to hold the shape.

5 **FILL WITH SOMETHING PRETTY.** Finally, I was ready to place my smaller vase inside—to hold water along with some fresh flowers!

I love how quick and easy this little project is to do, and how inexpensive it is too. It's nice to have a container as pretty as the stems that go inside, and to know you made it yourself!

08

CHEERS

ENTERTAINING IDEAS

SHERRY SAYS

In what can only be called our most ambitious entertaining mission of all time, we actually hosted our own wedding in our backyard and decided to do nearly everything ourselves (yup, even the food— we made stuff in bulk beforehand and recruited family members to help man the grill to make gourmet blue-cheese sliders and chicken-apple sausage). We even convinced John's cousin and close friend to officiate at our ceremony.

To this day we have no idea what possessed us to take that on since up to that point the largest crowd we had "entertained" was five (and we usually ended up ordering pizza or making a big bowl of spaghetti).

But something got into us and we got crazy-excited to turn our big day in our backyard into something personal, memorable, special, and sweet. It all could have been intensely intimidating, but we tried to take things one project and one day at a time (a skill that would later prove to be invaluable when we began our home-improvement-slash-blogging journey). So first we just focused on finding color-scheme inspiration, which oddly came from a paper napkin covered in lemons and limes that we saw at Target.

That whole "napkin starting point" led to the idea of filling cylindrical glass vases with fresh lemons and limes and adding simple votive candles down the length of the table for flower-free ambiance. We also designed our own invitations with little lemon topiaries on either side of the card with small yellow bees flying around them. The fresh summer feeling even carried over in the strings of bulb lights that we hung above all the tables and the soft yellow woven runners that I made with discount fabric.

That day taught us that even people with zero experience can throw one heck of a party, just by finding a spark—some fun inspiration that leads to other ideas and sort of snowballs from there. So just remember to break big tasks down into bite-sized pieces to keep things from getting too overwhelming. If two novices like us can host a shindig for seventy-five people in our backyard, anyone can throw a little par-tay at their place without getting all clammy and breaking out in hives.

I bought this dress just two days earlier!

Ah, weddings, where no one faults you for putting your face on everything.

1. Sand and a pillar candle

2. Pistachios

3. Fortune cookies

200

SIX QUICK CENTERPIECE IDEAS

Modern cylindrical or square vases are super versatile when it comes to creating a variety of unfussy and non-face-blocking centerpieces. They can be filled with so many things in under two minutes and are simple and chic when running down the center of a rectangular table (or grouped in the middle of a round one).

4. Breadsticks or other longish treats like rock candy

5. Balls of twine or spools of thread

6. Fresh fruit (like green apples, lemons and limes, or oranges)

201

MAKE PERSONALIZED PLACE "CARDS"

Collect some smooth round rocks from outside or grab a bag of river rocks from a decor store and create monogrammed seating "cards" by adding stickers with each attendee's first initial. Or if you're hosting a baby shower, each rock could sport a sticker with the word *joy* or *sweet*, while a holiday party might call for a snowflake. They double as great take-home favors, and letters are just the beginning.

BONUS TIP
Bring It Down a Notch

You can also do this on a grain of rice to really impress your friends. (Just kidding—that would be really hard.)

202

BRING BALLOONS INDOORS

Nothing shouts festive like a ton of helium balloons just floating in a room. Pick a playful rainbow of colors for a child's birthday party and go with something sophisticated like gold or white for an adult New Year's celebration. Some soft and ethereal colors can even be used as a backdrop for a wedding or a shower. And a ton of black balloons might be fun for Halloween or even an over-the-hill party.

Banners and party garlands come in all shapes and sizes and can add a lot of ambiance, excitement, and cheerful color to your gatherings. You can make them from anything—like paper, fabric, or balloons swagged on ribbon or twine. Even tissue-paper pom-poms or hearts, circles, or stars punched from decorative paper can look great strung up around the house. Draping them over curtain rods, mantels, windowsills, and doorways is a quick way to slap your space with an extra dose of fun. We used alphabet stickers, decorative paper, ribbon, and string to make the three party animals above.

203

MAKE FESTIVE LET'S-PARTY GARLANDS

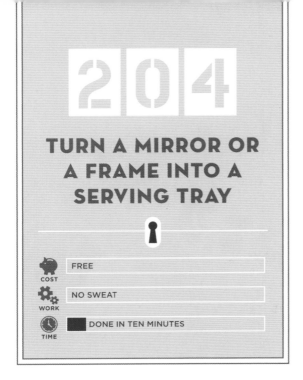

204

TURN A MIRROR OR A FRAME INTO A SERVING TRAY

COST	FREE
WORK	NO SWEAT
TIME	DONE IN TEN MINUTES

If you find yourself in desperate need of a serving tray with no time to run out and buy one, you can always use a wall mirror or a large frame. Many posh resorts serve things on mirrors and framed glass trays, so there's no shame in working with what you have!

1   Snag a mirror or frame from a room that your guests won't be entering, like a bedroom.

2   After giving the glass or mirror pane a quick wipe-down, set it out on the coffee table with little bowls or plates of hors d'oeuvres on top.

3   Marvel at the magic of dodging a party foul.

BONUS TIP
Stow the Bath Mat

Having a group of people over for a little gathering? Stash your bath mat in the hamper to instantly make the room feel cleaner and bigger, and to keep everyone from stomping all over it (which leaves it dirty and gross—and doesn't do your bathroom any favors).

They're certainly not expected at every house party you throw, but you might want to look around for inexpensive little things to leave on your guests' plates as a charming take-home favor. They don't have to be expensive—try a small ornament, a tiny bud vase with a single flower or sprig from the yard in it, or an individually wrapped candy. You can even get a bit cheeky (like some Smarties on everyone's plate or napkin for a graduation party). The extra thoughtfulness doesn't have to cost an arm and a leg, and it may just earn you "varsity hostess" status.

205

ADD EXTRA-CREDIT FAVORS

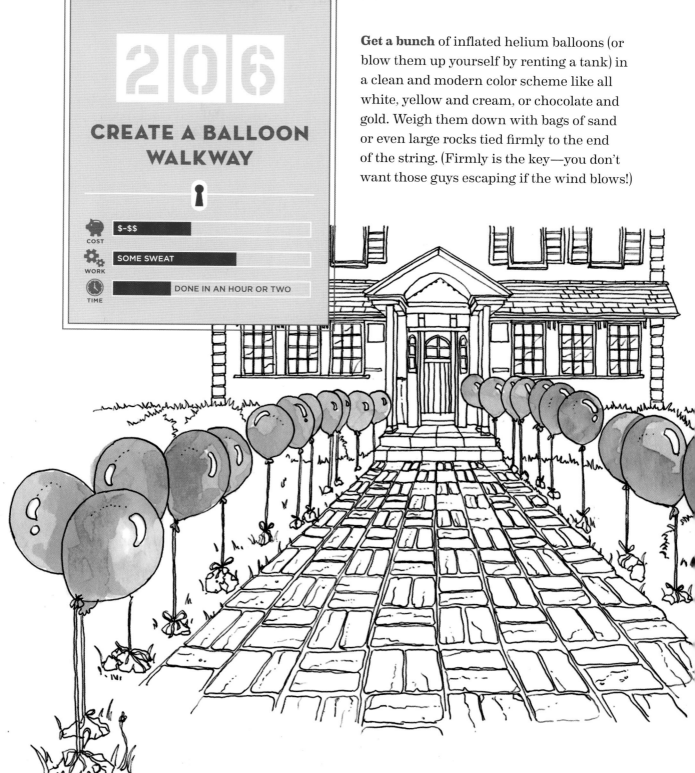

206

CREATE A BALLOON WALKWAY

COST	$-$$
WORK	SOME SWEAT
TIME	DONE IN AN HOUR OR TWO

Get a bunch of inflated helium balloons (or blow them up yourself by renting a tank) in a clean and modern color scheme like all white, yellow and cream, or chocolate and gold. Weigh them down with bags of sand or even large rocks tied firmly to the end of the string. (Firmly is the key—you don't want those guys escaping if the wind blows!)

207

ABBY'S SWEET CENTERPIECE

GUEST BLOGGER IDEA

BLOGGER:

ABBY LARSON

BLOG:

STYLE ME PRETTY

(WWW.STYLEMEPRETTY.COM)

LOCATION:

BOSTON, MASSACHUSETTS

FAVORITE DIY SIDEKICK:

ERIN OF *ERIN EVER AFTER*

FAVORITE ROOM IN MY HOUSE:

MY DAUGHTER'S BEDROOM

FAVORITE WAY TO FINISH A ROOM:

PINK FLOWERS

I'm always looking for beautiful ways to bring a sense of cohesion and style to wedding-day decor without breaking the budget. And when an idea can also work for a party you're throwing at home (or on your everyday table), well, that's even better.

SUPPLIES

- Collected vases, vessels, and glassware *(I used spare juice glasses and vases that had been delivered by florists over the years.)*
- Spray primer
- White gloss spray paint
- Liquid Leaf paint in Classic Gold
- Tupperware or bowl
- Paintbrush

1 **SPRAY ON PRIMER.** First, lightly coat the vases with primer. I used two coats, sprayed about 12 inches from the vessels, allowing about twenty minutes between coats.

2 **SPRAY THE VASES WHITE.** I used three very light coats, applied about 12 inches from each vessel, allowing thirty minutes between coats. It's much better to spray lightly than to overcoat and see drip lines. For opaque glasses, you might need an additional coat.

3 **GO GOLD.** Pour the gold Liquid Leaf paint into a Tupperware container large enough so the mouth of your vases can easily fit inside. Using a medium-sized paintbrush, paint the interior of your vases. I started with the bottom then worked my way up the side with the paint. The paint is rather forgiving if you use it liberally, and a few streak marks and drips only add to the handmade charm.

4 **DIP.** Slightly submerge the mouth of each vase into your pool of gold Liquid Leaf paint in the Tupperware container, twisting the vase around to create an easy, uneven effect over the top. This definitely doesn't have to look perfect—you're going for handmade charm and a sweet, casual look.

5 **LET DRY.** Hold the vase upside down for one to two minutes depending on the size of the

vase and the amount of gold paint that you used. This will help prevent drips from slipping down the sides of the vase when you set it upright. Allow everything to dry completely before using it. (The vases should dry to the touch in an hour, though I let them sit overnight before adding water and flowers.) If you worry about water touching your interior paint job, using smaller vases nested inside can keep it dry.

And there you have it! A collection of mismatched, found vases that have a new sense of handcrafted charm as pretty as any pricey vase you'd see in a store. Fill these beauties with some sweet stems and place them at the center of your table before a dinner party. You can even use this method on a series of nesting bowls to house your jewelry!

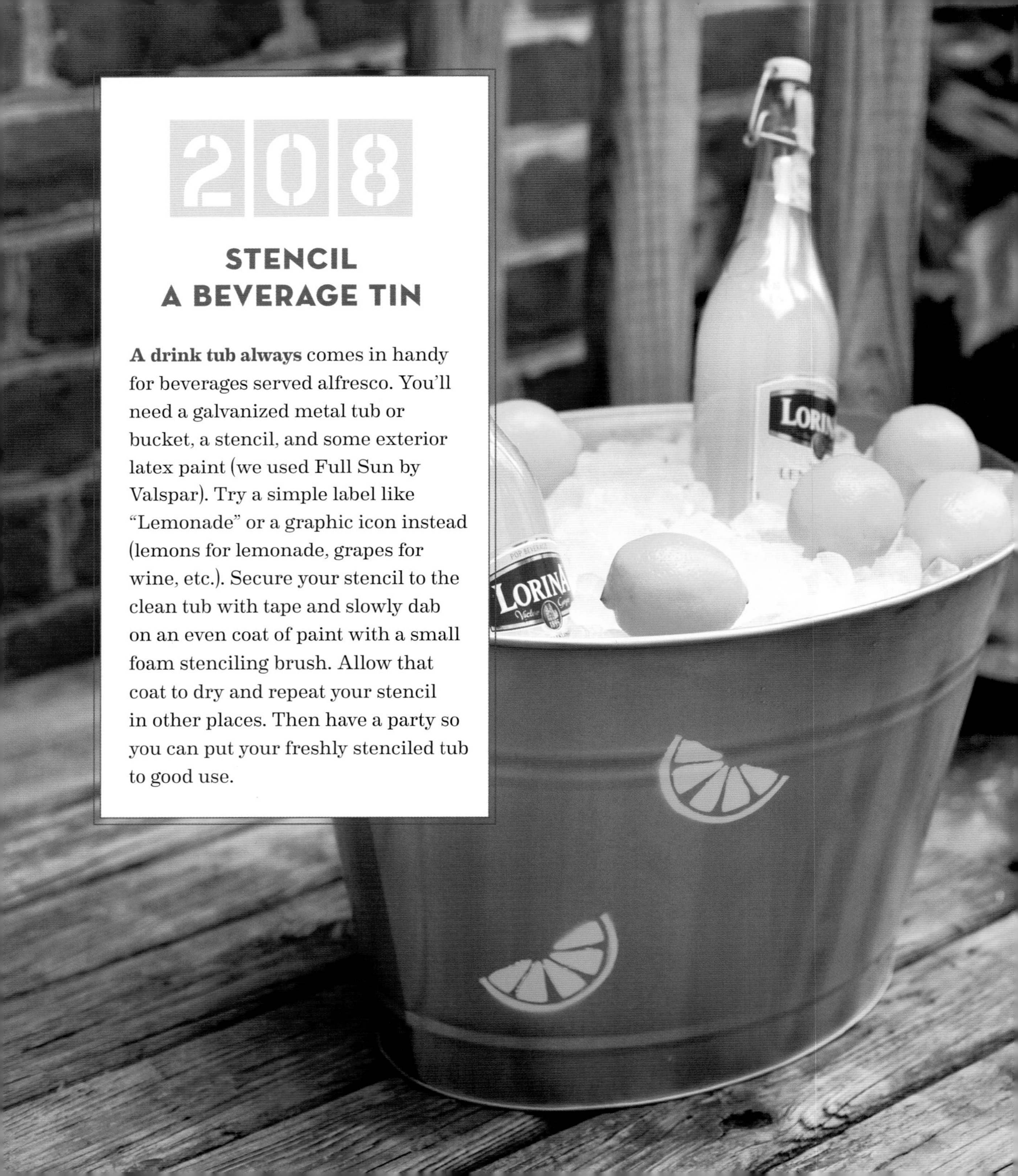

208

STENCIL A BEVERAGE TIN

A drink tub always comes in handy for beverages served alfresco. You'll need a galvanized metal tub or bucket, a stencil, and some exterior latex paint (we used Full Sun by Valspar). Try a simple label like "Lemonade" or a graphic icon instead (lemons for lemonade, grapes for wine, etc.). Secure your stencil to the clean tub with tape and slowly dab on an even coat of paint with a small foam stenciling brush. Allow that coat to dry and repeat your stencil in other places. Then have a party so you can put your freshly stenciled tub to good use.

209

PREP A SPARE BEDROOM FOR GUESTS

We know all about how intimidating it can be to host someone for a few days. One way to be sure that your guest room is comfortable and visitor-friendly is to spend the night in there yourself, just to see what's missing. You might find that there's nowhere to rest a glass of water or charge your cell phone, for example. Here are some other things to look for.

❏ Is there a spot for your guest to put their suitcase/bags?

❏ Is there a window shade, blind, or curtain to block light from streaming in the next morning?

❏ Is there a place to hang something up (even just a hook on the back of the door for a towel or a dress on a hanger)?

❏ Is there a mirror somewhere to check for crazy hair before emerging in the morning (a wall-mounted one or even a smaller tabletop option)?

❏ Is there something moderately entertaining to read (like a quirky book on dreams or horoscopes, a current magazine about something your guest enjoys, or a photo album with pics of them and other mutual friends)?

Just add small mint leaves or raspberries to the water in your ice cube tray before freezing it. You can even find cool square ice-cube trays (or other modern shapes, like long cylinders) instead of using standard ones.

210

MAKE INTERESTING DRINK OR COCKTAIL ICE CUBES

211

MAKE A FREE-FORM TABLE RUNNER

COST	FREE–$
WORK	SOME SWEAT
TIME	DONE IN AN HOUR

A table runner doesn't have to be one solid piece of fabric. Make a fun and festive one with colorful tissue paper cut into diamonds or long rectangular strips. Sprinkle it confetti-style down the middle of a table or even pile it into glass hurricanes clustered as a cheerful centerpiece.

BONUS TIP
Play Around

A few other free-form runner ideas might be candy corn, ribbons, peppermint candies, or leftover paint swatches.

212

FIND A STARTING POINT

Are you hosting a seasonal party and looking to gussy up your dining table or buffet? Sometimes finding a starting point is all it takes to get those decorating juices flowing. The idea of placing a quirky ceramic animal menagerie down the middle of the table for an Easter gathering might pop into your head (which could lead you to find small bird, bunny, deer, and other animal figurines at Goodwill and spray paint them in Easter colors like celery green and soft pink). Another decor starting point could simply be a pretty seasonal table runner that you already own or a specific dish that you want to serve. (Pomegranate punch can spark an all-red theme for food, drinks, and even decor.) Pinning down an inspiring image or item can be all you need to get the ol' ball rolling.

I'M AVAILABLE FOR ALL PARTIES WHERE FOOD IS SERVED.

09

SPLAT

PAINTING IDEAS

JOHN SAYS

I'm sure we're not the only ones who have

experienced this phenomenon: You spend a few years in white-walled dorms, followed by white-walled rental apartments, and over time this itch, this need, this urge to just paint a friggin' wall builds up until you feel like you could burst. Well, it happened to us. The pent-up paintless frustration—and the bursting part. And boy, did we burst a whole rainbow of color over our first house.

The excitement of finally owning a home and having the freedom to paint any wall any color got the best of us. We literally had conversations like this:

SHERRY: "Should the dining room be blue? Let's do turquoise!"

ME: "Yeah, and maybe the den is the bright yellow room?"

SHERRY: "Sure! Ooh, and the living room can be green! Yes, mint green!"

It was as if we were trying to meet some color quota by covering the entire spectrum. So the bedroom went blue. The living room went mint. The den went sunshine yellow. The dining room went turquoise, along with the bathrooms. And so on and so forth. And we were thrilled.

Then we started noticing that some other houses weren't painted in kaleidoscope colors. In fact, we visited friends who had painted every single room the same color. Our first reaction was "What restraint! Doesn't that get boring?!"

It wasn't until we toured a bunch of awesome local model homes looking for decorating ideas that something started to click. Their walls weren't the same color throughout, but they were painted in a tighter palette, which made the homes feel more cohesive and, to our surprise, a lot bigger too.

We had thought the key to making a small house look big was to show off how many rooms you had. ("Look, I have a room for every section of the color wheel!") But we learned that a house feels bigger when you remove the choppiness and unite the rooms through color. And it doesn't have to be boring.

So within a year of moving in, we found ourselves repainting nearly every single room in a cohesive palette of subtly shifting blues, creams, tans, greens, and even a bit of chocolate. Sort of like sea glass + sand + ocean + a big, plush chocolate beach towel. We even worked in a sky-blue ceiling, a geometric-stenciled sunroom floor, subtle horizontal stripes in the bathroom, and lots of other interest-adding paint-related touches. Our 1,300 square feet immediately felt bigger. And we, having gotten our Crayola-box selections out of our system, finally felt at home.

We dove right into bolder colors when we moved into our current house (deep teal! happy yellow-green! slate blue! lime!), but this time we knew the key was quality over quantity (i.e., not ten warring brights, each assigned to its own room) and that tempering our palette with classics like light gray, white, and charcoal would make all the difference. And oh, happy day, it does.

Look at that face. So giddy to paint anything and everything.

There's so much wrong with this picture.

Okay, I'll admit I still kinda like this color.

BRUSH VS. ROLLER

Wondering whether to use a paintbrush or a roller? There are lots of thoughts on this subject, so here's our take: We prefer using traditional 8-inch rollers to paint large expanses like walls and ceilings, and smaller foam rollers to paint things like cabinets, most pieces of furniture, and interior or exterior doors. (They tend to deposit less paint and are easier to control than larger rollers that you'd use on the wall.) We also rely on high-quality 2-inch angled paintbrushes to get into those hard-to-reach cracks and corners (from cutting in to painting trim).

Of course, you can't forget about spray primer and spray paint for smaller items like lamp bases, stools, or picture frames. We don't recommend spray painting larger items like tables or nightstands since most novices usually get less drippy and longer-lasting results with primer and paint applied thinly and evenly with a foam roller or a brush. (The pros use sprayers for large pieces all the time, but beginners can end up with a forever-tacky mess.) In fact, we've gotten such great results from our tried-and-true roller and brush formula that it's still our preferred method over a sprayer whenever we redo furniture.

213

CONQUER PAINT PARALYSIS

Are you frozen with fear when it comes to painting your walls? That's okay. It's totally normal and 100 percent curable. Just pick a color and give it a try. Really, it's that simple. If you hate it, you can always repaint. Whereas if you never try anything, you're a lot further from finding that perfect hue than you would be if you'd quit hemming and hawing and just picked up a paintbrush, goshdarnit. Here's the drill.

1   Decide to get off the couch and do it. Even if you're nervous, at least you're doing something instead of being frozen with indecision.

2   Bring home a slew of paint swatches and tape them up on the wall in the room that you'll be painting. Evaluating them in that space will combat the what-you-see-isn't-what-you-get phenomenon that occurs when people pick their favorite colors at the store instead of in their house (where the lighting is dramatically different).

3   After taping all the swatches up on the wall, take a step back to see what you think. Sometimes the swatch that you like most changes when it's hung on a vertical plane instead of being placed on a tabletop or held in your hand. And since you'll be painting the walls, looking at how the color reads on that surface is always helpful.

4   Try to really compare the swatches to each other. This will help you eliminate some that are "too pink" or "too dark" or "too pastel" instead of looking at each one in a vacuum.

5   Be sure to check out your swatches at all times of the day to confirm that your favorite daytime color doesn't get all weird and ugly at night (which actually happens quite often).

6   Many paint companies offer bigger swatches for a small fee, which can give you a poster-sized idea of what that color will look like on the wall. You can also buy a small pot of sample paint and apply a large square on the wall (use two thin and even coats) to be sure it's a color that you love before taking the plunge.

7   Paint already! You've considered a ton of colors, tested your favorites, and picked the best one among the group. March your confident paint-picking butt down to the store, get that big ol' gallon of paint, and get 'er done. The best thing about paint is that it's not permanent. It's actually one of the most inexpensive "mistakes" you can make, since it will cost only twenty-five to fifty dollars for another gallon to repaint if you hate the outcome. And more often than not, after completing the above steps, you won't.

PAINT CAN'T POSSIBLY BE SCARIER THAN CATS.

214

PAINT ALMOST ANY PIECE OF FURNITURE

🐷 **COST** $-$$

⚙️ **WORK** SOME SWEAT

🕐 **TIME** DONE IN A WEEKEND

Once you have this skill down, there's no stopping you when it comes to furniture transformations. We could wax poetic about how much of a difference paint can make, but you totally get that by now, right? So give yourself a few evenings or a weekend to have at it. Paint in your hair is so hot right now anyway.

1   Move your piece of furniture to any covered area where you can get a bit messy, like a garage, basement, or cleared-out corner of a room. Wipe the piece down with a damp rag to get rid of any dust or grime.

2   If your piece has an existing finish (i.e., feels a bit slick to the touch), you'll want to rough things up for the greatest durability. Break out some **low-grit sandpaper** and go over all surfaces (try a palm sander for large areas). Unlike when you're staining something, you don't need to remove as much of the previous coating, but you want to rough it up so primer and paint can take hold.

START HERE

3   Using a **small paintbrush** for nooks and crannies and a **foam roller** for larger surfaces (and to go over any brushed areas for a smooth result), apply one thin coat of **stain-blocking primer**. Don't fret if the coverage looks spotty during this step; primer always looks uneven. Just ensure that there aren't any drips and keep things thin and uniform.

4   Once the primer is dry (check the can for the proper waiting time), use the same application method to apply two or three coats of **latex paint** in a satin or semigloss finish. Be sure they're (you guessed it) thin and even. And allow each one to dry completely before moving on to the next one. Check the paint can for how much time you should allow between coats. We used Wasabi by Benjamin Moore.

5   If your piece will get lots of use and/or may encounter moisture (like in a dining room or kitchen), applying two thin coats of a clear **water-based sealant** can translate to tons of added durability. (Certain formulas can yellow, so we like water-based Minwax Polycrylic Protective Finish in clear gloss, found at any home-improvement store, or Safecoat Acrylacq, which is a low-VOC, nontoxic, and super-green alternative sold at eco boutiques or online.)

6   We know you're chomping at the bit to enjoy your new piece of furniture, but be sure to wait at least seventy-two hours before using it or putting anything on it. You don't want things to stick and leave marks after all your hard work! If your piece is tacky days after you're done, try leaving it out in the sun (that can speed up curing time) or even sprinkling some baby powder on it to absorb any stickiness. (It's best to wait at least a week to be sure it doesn't get stuck in the paint or poly.)

NOTE: Visit younghouselove.com/book for more tips.

2

4

EIGHT BUCKS
SCORED US
THIS THRIFT-
STORE FIND.

BONUS TIP
Check the Surface

This process works best on wood or
veneer furniture (laminate stuff might not
grab paint as well for the long haul).

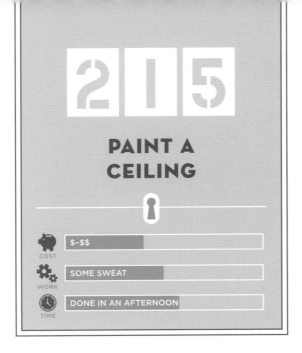

215

PAINT A CEILING

COST **$-$$**

WORK **SOME SWEAT**

TIME **DONE IN AN AFTERNOON**

A SOFT YELLOW-GREEN CEILING CAN WARM UP COOL BLUE-GRAY WALLS.

Put down this book and go find a white ceiling in a room that could stand to be a little more special. Then pick a soft color that makes you happy (a hint of pink? light blue? a paler version of the color that's already on the wall?). And don't worry about a painted ceiling making the room feel squat, dark, or claustrophobic. As long as it's light in tone it'll add interest without too much weight. (We recommend sticking to the lightest swatch on a paint chip and taping it up on the ceiling to see how it reads up there first.) Some experts even argue that a softly toned ceiling actually makes rooms feel taller since it's less jarring and in-your-face than a stark white ceiling (which can seem closer to the ground since it's harsher and more high-contrast). And achieving a loftier look isn't bad for under fifty bucks and a few hours of work.

1 Tape off the top of your walls or crown molding with **painter's tape.**

2 Move any furniture around the perimeter of the room and cover it and the floor with **drop cloths.**

3 Paint the ceiling with a **roller** (a rod extender can make it easier) and use a **2-inch angled brush** to get into the corners that a roller can't reach. **Flat latex paint** typically works best for ceilings (it hides imperfections).

216

STENCIL YOUR WALLS

COST	$-$$
WORK	LOTS OF SWEAT
TIME	DONE IN A DAY OR A WEEKEND

You might want to stencil an accent wall or a small nook, or go bold and stencil the whole room. If you want something subtle to add texture, low-contrast color is the way to go. (Think white on cream, tan on mocha, gray on lighter gray, slate on navy, etc.) We used Ashen Tan over Decorators White, both by Benjamin Moore. Meanwhile, a more high-contrast color pairing can make for a dramatic statement (like cream on chocolate or pale aqua on navy). Here are a few stenciling tips that we've learned along the way.

- Prep a room or wall for stenciling by clearing the area of rugs, window treatments, art, and any furniture that could accidentally get dripped on.

- We've had luck using Martha Stewart Crafts Stencil **Adhesive Spray** from Michaels, which you apply to the back of the stencil before taping it up on the wall. This helps the middle parts of the stencil stick to the wall for a nice crisp line. You should be able to reposition the stencil two or three times before needing to respray it with the adhesive.

- You'll want to use a large piece of cardboard or a **drop cloth** to lay your stencil on while you spray the back of it (so you don't get sticky stuff all over the floor) or spray it outside.

- Starting in the middle of the wall at the top and working out from there in all directions can help keep the pattern centered.

- We use **painter's tape** to attach the **stencil** to the wall at the top, bottom, and sides. It shouldn't pull off paint as you go (even though it seems like it could).

- A **small foam roller** meant for smooth surfaces without too much paint on it helps achieve a crisp appllication.

- If you fear that a bit of paint somehow got behind the stencil, before repositioning it on the wall for the next application, just wipe the back with a dry rag or paper towel to remove any stray paint.

NOTE: Visit younghouselove.com/book for more tips and a bonus behind-the-scenes stenciling video.

FIND COLOR INSPIRATION ALL AROUND YOU

You can pull a whole room's color scheme from a favorite outfit, book cover, coveted work of art, pretty candle's packaging, or anything else that grabs your attention. It's a great error-proof way to identify a color combo that you already know you love, and you can use that object (or collection of items) as a cheat sheet for selecting paint swatches.

THIS SCARF COULD INSPIRE BLUE WALLS WITH ORANGE BEDDING AND PINK BEDSIDE LAMPS.

Juicy Passionfruit

Dragon Fruit

Aqua Breeze

(ALL COLORS BY BEHR)

THESE CANDLES COULD LEAD TO GRAY WALLS WITH A NAVY SOFA AND A BOLD GREEN ARMOIRE. →

(ALL COLORS BY BENJAMIN MOORE)

Savannah Green

Edgecomb Gray

Twilight Blue

THESE DISHES COULD SPARK HAPPY YELLOW WALLS WITH A CHOCOLATE DINING TABLE AND A LARGE BLUE PAINTING. ↓

Jackson Glen

Java

Lemon

(ALL COLORS BY VALSPAR)

PAINT A GRAPHIC PATTERN ON A DESK OR DRESSER

COST	$-$$
WORK	LOTS OF SWEAT
TIME	DONE IN A WEEKEND

START HERE

THIS MID-CENTURY DESK WAS A WHOPPING TEN BEANS AT A THRIFT STORE.

Rich wood furniture is gorgeous, and we have it all over our house. But there's no denying that a few painted pieces layered into the mix can really take things from all-the-same-tone to interesting and intricate—especially if there's a cool pattern or detail going on to amp things up.

1 Follow steps 1–3 of the furniture-painting tutorial on page 278.

2 Once your piece is primed, apply two thin, even coats of **satin or semigloss latex paint** with a **small foam roller** on the area where you'll be adding your pattern. For this piece, we painted the entire front of each drawer with Martini Olive by Benjamin Moore and let it thoroughly dry before proceeding.

3 Use **painter's tape** to map out your pattern. (We used FrogTape to prevent bleeding.)

Vertical or horizontal stripes are always fun and easy, but we cut 3½-inch pieces of tape to create a basket-weave pattern. You can forgo the tape and draw something more organic (like waves or a leafy motif) by lightly sketching its outline with a pencil.

4 For those taping: Once your tape pattern is applied and firmly pressed down, apply two thin and even coats of **satin or semigloss paint** in your contrasting color over the entire area using a **small foam roller** (we used Hale Navy by Benjamin Moore over the taped-off drawer fronts and the rest of the desk). We recommend peeling the tape off while the second coat is still wet for the cleanest lines (if that's too scary you can always touch things up later after peeling off the tape).

5 If you didn't apply tape and opted to sketch something free-form, carefully paint your design with a **small paintbrush,** staying within the pencil lines that you drew.

6 Optional: You can seal your design with **polyurethane** for extra protection. We prefer to use a low-VOC version from Safecoat called Acrylacq or water-based Minwax Polycrylic Protective Finish in clear gloss since those two don't tend to yellow as much.

NOTE: Visit younghouselove.com/book for more tips and bonus behind-the-scenes pics of this project.

219

STEAL ONE OF OUR FOUR FAVORITE WHOLE-HOUSE PALETTES

There are infinite oh-my-gosh-I-love-it color combos to choose from, but here are a few of our favorite palettes to use throughout a home to add just enough interest without making things feel choppy and disjointed. (It's a delicate line to walk, and it's different for everyone.) Consider using some of these tones on the wall and others on items like accent pillows, curtains, and even painted pieces of furniture so there's a nice varied-yet-subtly-related feeling from room to room. The goal is for the whole house to go together without the rooms feeling too matchy, so keeping a few favorite tones in the mix while adding in different colors, textures, and materials from room to room can really spice things up and give each space its own flavor.

Bay Leaf, Persimmon Red, Crevecoeur, Heath by Martha Stewart				
Citron, Hibiscus, Baby Fern, Dragonfly by Benjamin Moore				
Hale Navy, Ashen Tan, Quiet Moments, Milano Red by Benjamin Moore				
Gobi Desert, Hazelnut Cream, Celery Ice, Lime Light by Behr				

Lay a collection of leaves on a plain burlap or cotton pillow cover and apply a few thin, thin, thin coats of fabric spray paint to create a cool organic shape when you lift the leaves off. We used Simply Spray in Brite Yellow from Jo-Ann Fabric for five bucks and a seven-dollar pillow cover from Ikea (the spray dried just as soft as the pillow cover felt originally). You could also use leaves to stencil a piece of fabric that you can frame, or even a roman shade. There are so many ways to go, and you can't beat using free greenery.

220

MAKE A STENCIL WITH SOMETHING NATURAL

TOTAL PROJECT COST: TWELVE DOLLARS!

221

SPICE UP WHITE ROLLER SHADES WITH GRAPHIC STRIPES

COST $

WORK SOME SWEAT

TIME DONE IN AN HOUR

This project can be especially inexpensive if you already have basic pull-down roller shades to begin with. (If not, grab them at your local home-improvement center, where they can be cut to size for you for free.)

1 Roll the **shade** out on a flat surface. Pull and secure it in its most unfurled position.

2 Use a **ruler** and **painter's tape** to measure and tape off whatever pattern you'd like (our stripes are 2½ inches wide and 1½ inches from the shade's edge).

3 Apply two or three thin, thin, thin (can you tell this is key?) coats of **semigloss latex paint** (we used Citron by Benjamin Moore) with a **small foam roller** to avoid cracking and peeling. Allow each coat to dry before applying the next one.

4 Wait at least forty-eight to seventy-two hours and then hang it up.

One semi-risky move like this can really add interest to a space. Think of your window, door, and baseboard trim as a bunch of giant picture frames of sorts. We all know that sometimes it's the frames that make the art. So try painting all the molding a not-white color that complements your walls. For example, a white room with gray molding (like the one on the right, where we painted the trim Gray Horse by Benjamin Moore) or a navy room with light celery trim could feel really fresh. You can also choose to paint your trim the exact same color as the walls, but in a high-gloss finish (for example, a blue-gray room with glossy blue-gray trim). Delish.

222

DO SOMETHING UNEXPECTED TO YOUR MOLDING

WE FRESHENED
THIS OLD SHADE
WITH
A THREE-DOLLAR
TEST POT OF
PAINT!

TEN BUCKS
CAN GET
YOU THREE
TEST POTS
OF PAINT TO
COMPLETE
THIS PROECT.

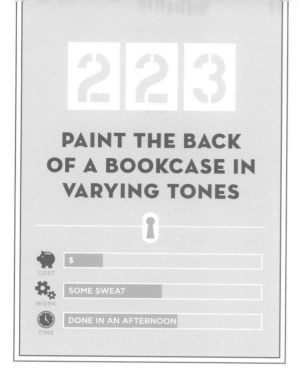

223

PAINT THE BACK OF A BOOKCASE IN VARYING TONES

COST $

WORK SOME SWEAT

TIME DONE IN AN AFTERNOON

Using different shades of the same tone or even painting a playful rainbow effect on the back wall of a bookcase can really perk up an entire room. You can even use test pots of paint to score different hues for just three to four dollars a pop.

1 With a pencil, mark the top and bottom of each shelf along the back of your bookcase. Remove the shelves if possible.

2 Apply one thin and even coat of a **stain-blocking primer** to the back wall of your bookcase with a **small foam roller** and a **2-inch angled brush** (to get into the corners). Try not to prime over your pencil lines if you need them as a guide. You may want to tape off the sides (and shelves if they don't come out) so you only get primer and paint along the back plane of the bookcase.

3 After the primer dries, follow it with two thin coats of a **satin or semigloss paint** in each of the colors that you've selected for each section of the bookcase (we used Wasabi, Exhale, and Silhouette by Benjamin Moore). Apply it with a brush and a small foam roller like the primer.

4 Let everything dry, and put the shelves back if you removed them. Yippie. Done-zo.

PICKING THE RIGHT PAINT FINISH

There are some general paint-finish recommendations, like using flat paint for ceilings (to hide imperfections) and semigloss paint for trim (it's easy to wipe down). But in most cases, your finish is a personal preference. So go with your gut, or ask the pros at the paint counter if you're still unsure.

■ **Flat.** This is the best at hiding imperfections, but it shows more wear than its glossier counterparts. It's the easiest finish to touch up without telltale outlines.

■ **Eggshell.** This is the first step up on the sheen scale, so it gives you a bit more wipeable protection but still looks matte on the walls.

■ **Satin.** You've get a noticeable sheen, but you haven't hit a real "gloss" quite yet. Many shine-averse people go with satin for bathrooms and kitchens (which is usually the lowest sheen that works well for those rooms).

■ **Semigloss.** This is a great choice for bathrooms, kitchens, and trim because it's easy to wipe down. It's harder to touch up than the flatter stuff, but the durability is nice.

■ **Gloss or High-gloss.** This finish provides the shiniest lacquerlike effect. It's super wipeable and durable, but can make imperfections really obvious and is the hardest to touch up.

2|2|4

PAINT A BRICK FIREPLACE

COST	$-$$
WORK	LOTS OF SWEAT
TIME	DONE IN A WEEKEND

If there's an old brick fireplace sucking the life (and light!) out of a room, we're huge fans of painting it. This is definitely one of those personal-preference things, though, so if you love your brick, don't you dare pick up that paintbrush.

1 Give the brick a good wipe-down with a damp rag to remove any dust, cobwebs, or soot.

2 Apply a coat of **stain-blocking primer.** If your brick isn't too rough, you may be able to get good coverage with a **high-nap roller,** but expect to use a **brush** to get into all of the crevices.

3 Once the primer is dry, use the same method to apply two coats of **latex paint** in the finish of your choice (we like wipeable semigloss). Brick likes to suck up paint, so you may need a third coat to ensure full coverage.

4 If it's a nonworking fireplace, painting the firebox charcoal is a great way to clean it up.

We've been lucky (unlucky?) enough to have wood paneling in our first home and in our current one. Good thing it takes just a few coats of paint to update things.

1 Clean your paneling with a damp rag to rid it of any dust, dirt, or grease that might be lurking, then wipe the paneling down with a rag moistened with **liquid deglosser** (we like Crown's NEXT, which is low in VOCs and biodegradable) to further remove any grime.

2 Use a **roller** to apply a thin and even coat of **stain-blocking primer.** Use a **short, angled brush** to get into any seams or edges that you can't reach with a **roller.** Don't worry if coverage isn't perfectly even; primer looks blotchy, but as long as you've made thin and even coats, you're good. Let everything dry completely.

3 Use the same method to apply two thin and even coats of **latex paint.** (We like an eggshell finish.)

2|2|5

PAINT WOOD PANELING

226

KATIE'S COFFEE TABLE TWIST

BLOGGER:
KATIE BOWER

BLOG:
BOWER POWER
(WWW.BOWERPOWERBLOG.COM)

LOCATION:
LOGANVILLE, GEORGIA

FAVORITE COLOR COMBO:
NAVY + WHITE + A GRASSY
GREEN = THE PREPPY TRIFECTA!

FAVORITE PATTERN:
TICKING STRIPES OR POLKA DOTS

FAVORITE ACCESSORY:
A BOLD THROW PILLOW

Our living room was sporting the nautical look, so I really wanted a coffee table that would fit in without being too precious for my very aggressive toddler. When I saw an old square table at Goodwill, I knew that it would be the right scale and shape for the room, but the wood finish was way off. I decided that a quick and easy paint makeover might be just the ticket to infuse a little more pattern and provide a place to kick up our feet—all while reminding us of our littlest family member.

SUPPLIES

- Primer
- Paintbrush
- White semigloss paint
- Gray semigloss paint
- Small foam craft brush
- O craft stamp
- 150-grit sandpaper
- Water-based polyurethane *(optional)*

1 **PRIME AND PAINT.** To start, I primed the entire coffee table. After the primer was dry, I painted the legs white (Bright White base by Valspar) and the top gray (Pewter Gray by Krylon). Two coats gives you bonus points . . . and in my case, extra coverage for my toddler!

2 **STAMP AWAY.** Using the foam brush, I painted my O craft stamp with the white paint I used on the legs. (It helped to keep the stamps very thin.) I blotted it with a paper towel when necessary and stamped directly onto the coffee-table top, creating an 8 shape. I continued until the entire coffee-table top was covered with even rows of 8s. (My son, Will, was born on April 8, so the 8s are for him!)

3 **WEATHER IT.** After the paint dried, I took my sandpaper and lightly sanded by hand in one direction. I was trying to achieve a more weathered look, not remove the paint entirely.

4 **SEAL IT.** This is optional, but for extra durability, I sealed my table with a few thin coats of water-based polyurethane.

I love this coffee table. Not only does it complement the room but it also adds a little interest. The pattern reminds me of a string of pearls. That's nautical, right? And not only do the 8s represent my son, the table works for our family. Having to worry about a toddler marking up a more pristine piece of furniture would be such a pain. I don't even have to worry about using coasters on this table—condensation rings blend right in!

1

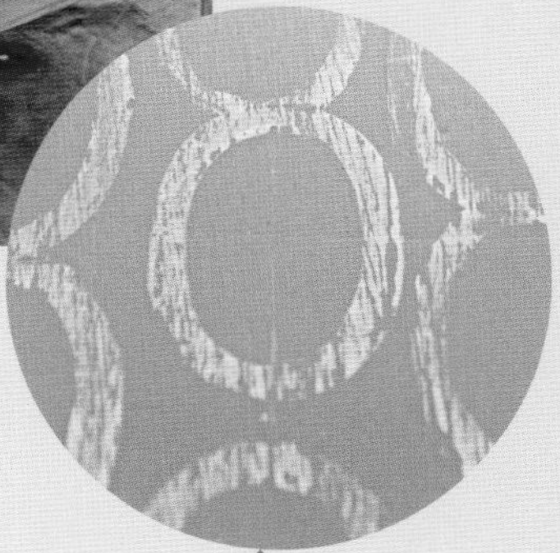

227

PAINT YOUR CURTAINS (YUP, PAINT THEM!)

COST: **$**

WORK: **SOME SWEAT**

TIME: **DONE IN AN AFTERNOON**

It might sound weird, but regular old latex paint on curtains can add up to lots o' drama (the good kind).

1 Wash and hem your **curtain panel** to fit your window (we used inexpensive Ritva curtains from Ikea for twelve dollars a pop).

2 Lay your curtain flat on a **drop cloth** and apply horizontal stripes of **painter's tape** across the entire curtain at equal increments (we did six stripes that were about 12 inches thick).

3 Thin your paint with **textile medium.** We used **latex paint** thinned out with Folk Art Textile Medium from the craft store. (Just follow the directions on the bottle.)

4 Using a **small foam roller,** apply two thin coats of paint for each of your stripes. We alternated between Benjamin Moore's Caliente and Berry Fizz to make our bold red and magenta stripes.

5 Carefully remove the tape as soon as you're done with your last coat of paint to get the cleanest lines and repeat the process on as many curtain panels as you'd like. When everything's dry, hang those babies up.

WE'LL ADMIT IT, PAINTING CURTAINS FELT WEIRD. EVEN FOR PAINT FREAKS LIKE US.

228

INVIGORATE A ROOM WITH BOLD COLOR

COST	$-$$
WORK	SOME SWEAT
TIME	DONE IN A DAY

Just give it a try. Be brave. It's only paint! Bold color on the walls doesn't have to feel crazy or overwhelming, especially if you balance it out with subdued wood or neutral-toned furnishings to keep things from competing. Bold color (we used Moroccan Spice by Benjamin Moore) can actually create a very cozy and enveloping space.

SEE HOW DIFFERENT THESE ITEMS LOOK WITH A COLORFUL WALL BEHIND THEM?

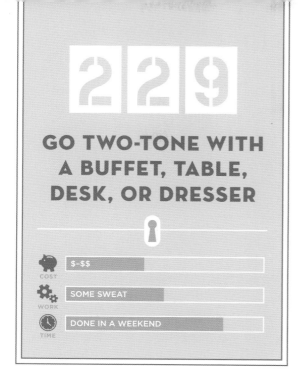

229

GO TWO-TONE WITH A BUFFET, TABLE, DESK, OR DRESSER

COST $-$$

WORK SOME SWEAT

TIME DONE IN A WEEKEND

There's something so polished about an item of furniture with two contrasting colors. So whether you have a dark wood buffet and opt to paint the top a glossy white or even decide to paint a dresser all white with sleek indigo drawers, the two-tone look is an easy one to master.

1 Remove any hardware that will get in the way of your paint job and wipe everything down with a **damp rag** to remove dust and grease.

2 Using a **palm sander** and **low-grit sandpaper,** give all areas you'll be painting a light sanding—enough to rough up a glossy finish. Use your rag to clean off any dust created by sanding.

NOTE: Before sanding an old painted piece, use a lead test stick from a home-improvement store to be sure you're in the clear.

3 Prime your piece using a **stain-blocking primer** and a **small foam roller** (use a brush to get into nooks and crannies). Removing drawers and painting them separately makes for the cleanest result. Allow the primer to dry completely.

4 Apply two thin and even coats of the **satin or semigloss paint** in your selected colors to the desired areas. We painted the drawers of this fifteen-dollar desk with Gray Horse and the frame of the desk with Decorators White, both by Benjamin Moore. Leaving something wood toned and painting only the top or the drawer fronts is another great way to score a sleek two-toned look. Just use **painter's tape** to keep paint from bleeding onto unwanted areas.

5 Optional: Apply two thin and even coats of **water-based polyurethane** for added durability (some formulas can yellow, so we like water-based Minwax Polycrylic Protective Finish in clear gloss or Safecoat Acrylacq).

6 Once it's fully dry (we like to wait at least seventy-two hours), reattach all the hardware and enjoy. We painted our hardware with a fresh coat of **oil-rubbed bronze spray paint** to further freshen things up before popping it back on.

NOTE: Visit younghouselove.com/book for more tips and another two-toned piece we tackled.

START HERE

THIS DESK WAS A FIFTEEN-DOLLAR CRAIGSLIST FIND!

230

PAINT A GRADIENT

COST	$
WORK	SOME SWEAT
TIME	DONE IN A WEEKEND

BONUS TIP

Go Short

On the subject of painting, to say that we're fans of a high-quality, short-handled 2-inch angled brush for cutting in or painting molding and trim is the understatement of the century. The control that it can give you is unbelievable, and it can literally cut your trim-painting time in half.

START HERE →

Nothing says I-am-dresser-hear-me-roar like awesome painted drawers that gradually shift tones from top to bottom. Using any item of furniture with lots of drawers can work. (We found this guy for cheap at a local thrift store!) Then all you need are some test pots of paint for a few bucks each. For color inspiration, it can be as easy as grabbing a paint swatch with at least as many colors on it as your number of drawers. Whether you go bright and playful or moody and muted, it's definitely one of those everybody-gravitates-toward-it projects (we used White Wisp, Gray Owl, Sea Haze, Desert Twilight, Durango, and Char Brown by Benjamin Moore). And you don't even have to tape things off while painting. Just remove each drawer, take off the hardware, stand it on a drop cloth so the drawer front faces up, and apply a thin coat of stain-blocking primer, followed by two thin and even coats of paint, with a small foam roller. Check out more furniture-painting tips on page 278.

SIX TEST POTS
OF PAINT +
ONE THRIFT-
STORE PIECE =
LOVE

OUT

EXTERIOR IDEAS

JOHN SAYS

Exterior spaces can be scary. In fact, one of the main reasons that I second-guessed our decision to buy our first house was because of the yard. There. Was. So. Much. Yard.

Okay, maybe not that much yard (it was nearly an acre, not the size of a national forest), but it seemed like a small farm compared to what we were used to while living in Manhattan. Sherry (who is the dreamer and schemer in our relationship) saw loads of potential in the expanse of land surrounding our home to be. I, on the other hand, fulfilled my role as the nervous naysayer by raising concerns about "all that mowing" and the likelihood that we'd kill lots of plants along the way.

Obviously, we bought the house, and I was forced to face my fears about the little section of Earth we now owned. Even better? Facing my fears had a deadline: our wedding. That gave us about fourteen months to transform the dirt-floored forest that obscured our house from the street, where mulch, leaves, and pine needles had once been (yes, we inherited an overgrown wooded plot as a front yard), into a wide-open and welcoming landscape with greenery and grass. No pressure, right?

So we hired a professional tree service to remove a bunch of poorly placed/dead trees that threatened our house's safety. Sure, it did wonders when it came to letting natural light flood our once-dark house and solving the neighborhood mystery of "Is there really a house back there?" . . . but it also left us with a big expanse of ugly brown nothing.

This is where we learned that yard work can be backbreaking. I have distinct ~~flashbacks~~ memories of spending an otherwise lovely Saturday toiling away with Sherry as we raked, shoveled, and hauled wheelbarrow after wheelbarrow full of mulch and pine needles into the woods behind our house. By dark we had finally uncovered raw dirt. Beautiful, grass-seed-ready dirt. Spreading and watering the grass seed was a walk in the park by comparison, and when that green carpet finally started to fill in, we were left with a house that we were proud to use as our "wedding venue."

Of course that wasn't the last of our trials and triumphs with exterior spaces. But it proved to us that with some patience and a bit of sweat (okay, a lot of sweat), exterior spaces don't have to be so scary after all. Now picture me holding out my arms as various birds and woodland creatures perch on my fingers.

Paul Bunyan, eat your heart out.

Proof that we actually bought a house (and not just a forest).

231

PAINT YOUR FRONT DOOR

COST	$-$$
WORK	SOME SWEAT
TIME	DONE IN A DAY

Putting a fresh color on the front door can wake up your whole house and add curb appeal for under fifty dollars. We love a bright red door (like Fabulous Red by Valspar). It's unexpectedly versatile—it even works with a rusty redbrick facade. A happy daffodil-yellow door (like Full Sun by Valspar) can also charm things up in a snap. Or try a deep eggplant, a soft celery or sage tone, or even just something sophisticated like slate blue, smoky gray, or glossy black.

1   Tape paint swatches up on the door (you want to see them on the actual plane that will be painted) and step back and evaluate them in the morning, at midday, and in the evening after the sun has set with the porch light on. That way you'll pick something that looks good at all times of the day and complements the rest of your house.

2   If you're a pro painter, you might not need to cover your hinges with **painter's tape** to protect them, but it's definitely a great step for any beginner. We have never removed an exterior door to paint it, and have always been happy with our results, so we're members of the keep-it-hanging camp. (Others may prefer to take their doors down and paint them that way.)

3   The next step is optional, because you can tape these things off as well, but we prefer to remove any hardware that isn't necessary to keep the door hanging (i.e., hinges stay, but knobs come off).

4   It never hurts to rough things up with some **sandpaper** before priming and painting to ensure that you'll get strong adhesion and a nice smooth end result. Then wipe things down with a **liquid deglosser.**

5   A **stain-blocking oil-based primer** can combat bleeding and cut down what might require five or six coats to two or three. It also helps with adhesion and will keep paint from cracking or peeling if your door was previously painted with oil-based paint. Totally worth the trouble, right?

6   Once your primer has dried, apply your **semigloss exterior latex paint** with a **small foam roller** in extremely thin and even coats. (You can also use a **2-inch angled brush** to get into any recessed panels or crevices; just follow that with a foam roller to eliminate brush strokes as you go.) Thin and even is the key to avoiding any smears or drips, so take your time and enjoy that pop of hello every time you drive up.

NOTE: Visit younghouselove.com/book for more door painting tips and pics.

BONUS TIP
Be an Early Bird

Start this project early in the morning so you can close the door and lock up by evening. Giving the paint five to seven hours of drying time with the door cracked before closing it is ideal.

232

HANG NEW HOUSE NUMBERS

Upgrading your house number is such an easy and affordable way to add curb appeal.

Some charming placement ideas for house numbers include:

- Your front door
- The riser of your front porch steps
- Next to your door on the house's facade
- A glass transom above your door
- A large stone or plaque in the corner of your yard

233

ADD SOMETHING CHARMING UNDERFOOT

🔑

🐷 **$** | COST

⚙️ **SOME SWEAT** | WORK

🕐 **DONE IN AN AFTERNOON** | TIME

Basic doormats can be personalized with spray paint and some painter's tape for a whole new look. We got ours for under five bucks at Ikea and used leftover oil-rubbed bronze spray paint to have some fun with it. Just tape off your design and use any exterior-grade spray paint to evenly coat your mat a few times. Peel off the tape, and voilà. When it comes to the design, you can create stripes, grids, zigzags, or asterisks, or stencil on your house number. We've even made antlers for a cheeky holiday effect.

234

PAINT A CONCRETE BIRDBATH A BOLD, HAPPY COLOR

Yellow, lime, red, or even plum or turquoise works on a birdbath, so the choice is yours! (We used Full Sun by Valspar.) Two to three coats of regular old latex exterior paint applied with a brush should do the trick—just don't paint the inside, so the birds' drinking water isn't affected. It's a great way to draw attention to any garden or cheer up an otherwise bland backyard.

235
PLANT SOMETHING EDIBLE

COST	$-$$	
WORK	SOME SWEAT	
TIME	DONE IN A DAY	

If you have an empty area in your yard, consider planting herbs or vegetables instead of ornamental bushes or grasses. Nothing beats growing your own fresh food, and it might help you enjoy your yard more (since you'll be trekking out there for basil and tomatoes all the time).

A good friend of ours likes to say that rain barrels remind her of kegs. This is true, but they also provide free water for car washing and flower watering and can be hidden so their keglike appearance is less apparent. Try adding one to a downspout near a garden and then attaching a soaker hose. Just opening the spout for fifteen minutes a day will water your garden on autopilot (and cost you nada). You can screen your keg—er, barrel—with lattice, a small wood fence, shrubbery or vines, or other green stuff. And you can even apply a few coats of exterior spray paint meant for plastic (like Rust-Oleum's Universal) so it blends in with the color of your house or the greenery that surrounds it.

236
GET A RAIN BARREL

A craftsman-ish lantern in oil-rubbed bronze is always a classic choice.

This polished chrome fixture adds industrial interest with a cool cage around the bulb.

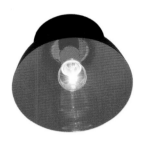

This is actually an interior sconce, but it shows how you can wake up an outdoor one with some bold spray paint.

237

UPGRADE EXTERIOR LIGHTS

Swapping out a drab old outdoor light fixture can add a ton of personality. Here are a few options.

I CAN'T DO MY BUSINESS IN THE DARK.

This frosted shade with a modern shape adds clean lines and simple style.

This cylindrical option shines light out the top and bottom for a cool modern effect.

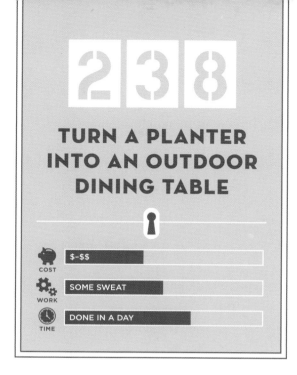

238

TURN A PLANTER INTO AN OUTDOOR DINING TABLE

COST $-$$

WORK SOME SWEAT

TIME DONE IN A DAY

Top an oversized planter (ideally around 28 inches tall) with a large round of wood (found at a local lumber yard, home improvement center, or thrift store) and use it as an outdoor dining table. Just be sure the planter is wide enough to support the wooden top without feeling unsteady and use heavy-duty construction adhesive to attach it once it's stained and sealed for outdoor use. Then just pull up a few chairs and get comfortable.

BONUS TIP
Score Some Free Help

Speaking of easy transformations, you can turn a negative into a positive when it comes to yard work. If you ever have a tree, shrub, or patch of ground cover that you'd like gone, try posting a "You Dig It and It's Yours" ad on Craigslist. Someone else is usually happy to take something off your hands for free, and they'll provide all the labor in exchange for the greenery.

239

HANG BIG-BULB STRING LIGHTS

COST	$-$$
WORK	SOME SWEAT
TIME	DONE IN AN AFTERNOON

Places like Pier 1, Target, and World Market sell cheap string lights, and hanging them up around a fence, an arbor, or a pergola, or just in a few trees, can really set the mood for a nice alfresco dinner. You can even leave them up permanently (or seasonally). Who says you have to throw a party to bask in the glow of some party lights?

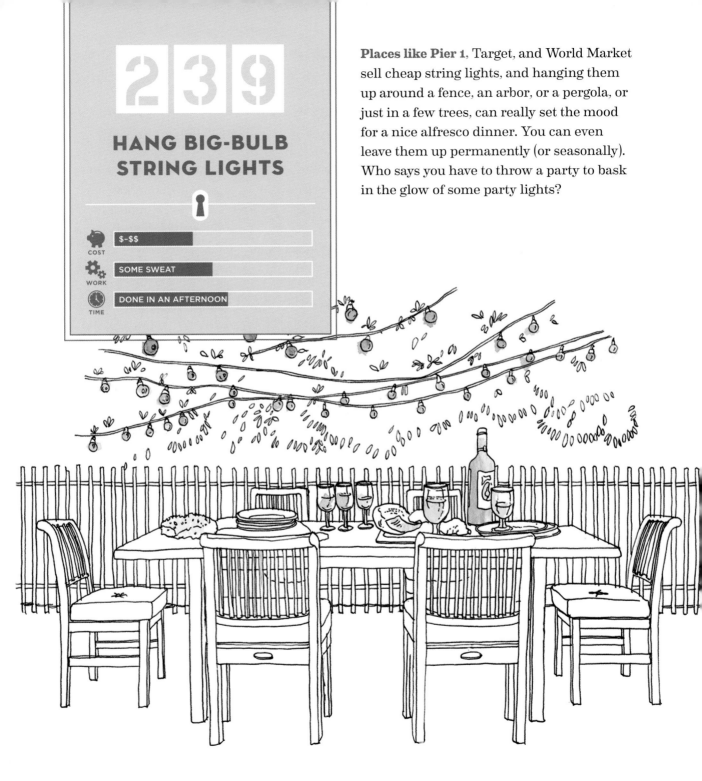

2|4|0

GIVE WOODEN PLANTERS SOME POP WITH PAINT

COST $-$$

WORK SOME SWEAT

TIME DONE IN AN AFTERNOON

Painting wood planters can take them up a few notches in an afternoon. And it's as easy as it sounds. Choose an exterior paint in a semigloss finish (we used Chamomile by Benjamin Moore) and apply it with a brush or a small foam roller in a few thin and even coats (priming first wouldn't hurt, but we've gone without and had nice results). When the paint is dry, pop any plants that you'd like inside and marvel at the cheerful loveliness.

A basic wood planter is handsome on its own.

But if your yard could use some color, bold paint cheers things right up.

241

BENITA'S OUTDOOR UPGRADE

BLOGGER:
BENITA LARSSON

BLOG:
CHEZ LARSSON
(WWW.CHEZLARSSON.COM)

LOCATION:
STOCKHOLM, SWEDEN

FAVORITE PATTERN:
DOTS

FAVORITE GO-TO TOOL:
I LOVE MY MOUSE SANDER!

FAVORITE DIY SIDEKICK:
MINI, ONE OF MY KITTIES, WHO'S ALWAYS THERE TO GIVE ME A PAW.

When I moved into my new old house with Wille, my teenage son, and my two cats, Mini and Bonus, it had been in the same family since it was built in 1954. While there are still some lovely original features inside, the area next to my front door didn't look its best. I'm afraid the weedy look wasn't doing anything for me.

SUPPLIES

- Rake and shovel
- Weed-blocking membrane
- Gravel or other paver base
- Latex paint (for door)
- Watering hose
- Concrete blocks
- Polymeric sand
- Pea gravel or other landscaping stones

1 **CLEAR YOUR SPACE.** I started the whole project by removing the grass (what little there was of it) and weeds (plenty of those) and then laid down a special membrane that keeps weeds from reappearing while still allowing water to drain through. I used the same method at my old house and it works really well. A few little weeds may still appear after a few years, but they come from above, which makes them easy to pull out.

2 **LAY YOUR BASE.** On top of the membrane, I shoveled a 4-inch sand/rock mixture as a paver base, which not only keeps the membrane down but also evens out the surface. If this were a driveway it would have been essential to compress the sand/rock mixture with a heavy-duty tamping machine, but we only walk and park bikes on our path, so I flattened it all down by watering it and then dancing around on it, pounding it down with a flat rake as I went. I bet this was quite a sight for my new neighbors.

3 **CREATE A STOOP.** After the sand/rock foundation had been pounded down, I laid three rows of concrete blocks that run along the length of the addition. (There had been just one pallet-sized thing in front of the door before.) The blocks are simply placed next to each other,

and weed-resistant polymeric sand was brushed into the crevices between them and watered down.

4 SPREAD THE STONE. To cover the path and the area next to the concrete blocks, I used a 1¼-inch layer of gray sea-pebble gravel. I just love the contrast of the round, soft pebbles next to the rough, square concrete stoop.

5 ADD SOME COLOR. The final flourish to the project was simply painting the door my favorite shade of green (try Seaweed by Benjamin Moore for a similar look) and adding a doormat.

It has all come together the way I hoped; it's clean, simple, and welcoming. I love it.

242

ADD A DOOR DECAL

COST	$
WORK	NO SWEAT
TIME	DONE IN AN HOUR

Decals aren't just for your interior walls; they're a sweet way to quaint up the curb appeal and score at least a few compliments from the neighbors.

1 Hunt down a **vinyl decal** that you like online. (We found ours on Etsy for six dollars by searching "address decal.")

2 Find the center of the door and carefully tape up the decal so that it's centered and level. (Using a **level** and a **yardstick** or **ruler** to check this can save you tons of frustration.)

3 Apply the decal according to the instructions provided. Ours just required us to rub it onto the door and peel back the paper.

4 Accept praise graciously from various neighbors.

243

ADD WINDOW BOXES

Window boxes can bring some awesome charm and dimension to a bland facade (on the windows and even a porch railing), and filling them with colorful blossoms will upgrade your entire exterior. To hang the window boxes just follow the directions that come with them (since they vary by type). You can find them at many big-box stores, as well as at specialty garden centers, online, or even at salvage yards.

A FEW PARTING WORDS

So here it is—the end of the book. Picture us standing on the dock waving and crying as your ship sails off into the sunset and you embark on your own home-sprucing journey. Even though it's the end of this book, it's only the beginning of your adventures on the home front. The greatest thing about house makeovering is that it's an ongoing project—and you can keep reimagining and reinventing things to suit your ever-changing tastes and needs. Just remember that home decorating is not a sprint. So quit rushing and try to relax and enjoy the ride. Our mantra is usually "one project at a time" (alternate mantra: "whoa, Nellie"), so we remember to take things slowly and not get too overwhelmed along the way.

Promise us that you'll never settle for something that you don't absolutely love. Especially when you can pick up a paintbrush or a hammer and make it even more customized, functional, or just plain beautiful. And in return we'll promise you that there's an amazing amount of pride and satisfaction when you change something for the better— even if all you're making are super-cheap and easy tweaks. So all the sanding and priming and painting and hanging and hammering and rearranging and drilling and hemming (and hawing) and worrying and laughing and crying and daydreaming will be worth it in the end. And best of all, your house will feel like home. Like you. Just have fun and never stop thinking "What if . . ."

Happy house loving to one and all!

PSST . . .

Visit younghouselove.com/book to see lots of behind-the-scenes videos, photos, and extra project details!

Wanna know where something's from? We've compiled this source section for virtually all of our photos in this book. It's arranged by tip number, and if you can't find info on a specific item, please check page 336 (and visit younghouselove.com/book for updates).

Preface

DEN AFTER

Curtains, armchair, frame over fireplace, faux sheepskin rug on sofa, cork planter: Ikea (ikea.com); art: homemade; desk: West Elm (westelm.com); lampshade on fan, frames in grid, ottomans, slipper chair, side table, media console, TV, white horse head, green tray: Target (target.com); mirror, green and yellow bowls, capiz storage box: HomeGoods (homegoods.com); sofa, area rug, decorative horns: Pottery Barn (potterybarn.com); green pillows: Marshalls (marshallsonline.com); floor lamp: Lowe's (lowes.com); iron bull head: flea market; glass hurricane lantern: Linens N Things (lnt.com); fireplace screen: yard sale; faux flower: eBay (ebay.com); faux topiary: Crate & Barrel (crateandbarrel.com); floor: Lumber Liquidators (lumberliquidators.com); side walls color (Wishes) and fireplace wall color (Water Chestnut) by Glidden (glidden.com)

KITCHEN AFTER

KraftMaid cabinets, Stonemark Granite counters, Arietta range hood: Home Depot (homedepot.com); Frigidaire appliances: Lowe's (lowes.com); rug: The Company Store (thecompanystore.com); Price Pfister faucet: eBay (ebay.com); pendant: West Elm (westelm.com); cutting board: Marshalls (marshallsonline.com); clamshell fruit bowl: Z Gallerie (zgallerie.com); floor: Lumber Liquidators (lumberliquidators.com); wall color: Gentle Tide by Glidden (glidden.com)

LIVING ROOM AFTER

Sofa, sofa pillows: Rowe (rowefurniture.com); table lamps: Linens N Things (lnt.com); wood blinds: Walmart (walmart.com); curtains, frames, dandelion art: Ikea (ikea.com); other art: homemade; slipper chair: Target (target.com); pillow on slipper chair: Crate & Barrel (crateandbarrel.com); area rug: Pottery Barn (potterybarn.com); coffee table: thrift store; shell ball: Kohl's (kohls.com); oversized glass vases: Z Gallerie (zgallerie.com); antler candlestick: West Elm (westelm.com); concrete greyhound: Great Big Greenhouse (greatbiggreenhouse.com); wall color: Sand White by Glidden (glidden.com)

Introduction

LIVING ROOM NOW

Sofa, frames, curtains: Ikea (ikea.com); mirror, ottoman, Safavieh rug, desk chair: Joss & Main (jossandmain.com); art: Sherri Conley (etsy.com/shop/SherriConley); pillows: Target (target.com), Ikea (ikea.com), Etsy (etsy.com), Bed Bath & Beyond (bedbathandbeyond.com), and homemade; console table: homemade; lamps behind sofa: Marshalls (marshallsonline.com); garden stool, blue and green lanterns on desk: HomeGoods (homegoods.com); desk: West Elm (westelm.com); lamp on desk, ottoman under desk, media console, TV: Target (target.com); wall color (Moonshine) and beam color (Shaker Gray) by Benjamin Moore (benjaminmoore.com)

OFFICE NOW

Chandelier: unknown (came with house); chandelier paint (Indigo by Valspar): Lowe's (lowes.com); shade for chandelier: The Decorating Outlet (shadesoflight.com/SOL_Retail.php?SOL_Store=OUT); frames: Ikea (ikea.com) and Target (target.com); octopus art: A Vintage Poster (avintageposter.com); map art: Studio Savvy (studiosavvydesign.com); chairs: thrift store with Ivy Leaf spray paint by Krylon (krylon.com) and Robert Allen Khanjali Peacock fabric from U-Fab (ufabstore.com); desk cabinets: thrift store; desk top: homemade with wood from Home Depot (homedepot.com); desk lamps, green artichoke vase: HomeGoods (homegoods.com); basket, armchair, round ottoman: Target (target.com); rug: Joss & Main (jossandmain.com); wall color (Moonshine with half-tint paint for stencil) and accent color (Sesame) by Benjamin Moore (benjaminmoore.com); stencil: Royal Design Studio (royaldesignstudio.com); crochet cacti: Lazymuse Productions (lazymuse.etsy.com)

KITCHEN NOW

Backsplash tile (Penny Round Moss): The Tile Shop (thetileshop.com); shelves: homemade with wood and brackets from Home Depot (homedepot.com); bowls, plates, and accessories: various sources; clamshell fruit bowl: Z Gallerie (zgallerie.com); teakettle: KitchenAid (kitchenaid.com); Frigidaire appliances: Lowe's (lowes.com); cabinets: Quaker Maid (quakermaid.com); cabinet paint (Cloud Cover) and wall color (Sesame) by Benjamin Moore (benjaminmoore.com); counters: Glacier White by Corian (dupont.com); pendants: Shades of Light (shadesoflight.com); bar stools: School Outfitters (schooloutfitters.com); bar stool paint: Tropical Oasis by Valspar (valsparpaint.com); art print: Samantha French (samanthafrench.com); yellow vase, yellow bowls: HomeGoods (homegoods.com); rug: Urban Outfitters (urbanoutfitters.com); cork flooring: Lumber Liquidators (lumberliquidators.com)

LAUNDRY ROOM NOW
Clothespin pendant light, shelves: homemade; knobs on cabinet doors: Hobby Lobby (hobbylobby.com); washer and dryer: Whirlpool via Lowe's (lowes.com); planter and shoe cabinets: Ikea (ikea.com); pink vase: Target (target.com); bee hook: thrift store; picture frame: Pottery Barn (potterybarn.com); baskets: Michaels (michaels.com); cork flooring: Lumber Liquidators (lumberliquidators.com); wall color: Sesame by Benjamin Moore (benjaminmoore.com)

01 Chill

001 FAUX WALLPAPER THE BACK OF YOUR BOOKCASE
Wrapping paper: The Gift Wrap Company (giftwrapcompany.com) via Mongrel (mongrelonline.com); silver plate: Crate & Barrel (crateandbarrel.com); coral: eBay (ebay.com); blue fish: Target (target.com); frame: Ikea (ikea.com); butterfly art, fabric box: homemade using Mingei fabric by Premier Prints (premierprintsfabric.com); ceramic octopus: Plasticland (shopplasticland.com); vase: Target (target.com); hurricane lantern: HomeGoods (homegoods.com); ceramic rhino: Z Gallerie (zgallerie.com); shell ball: Kohl's (kohls.com); gold box: West Elm (westelm.com); bookcase shelves color: Dove White by Benjamin Moore (benjaminmoore.com)

002 STENCIL A SISAL OR JUTE RUG
Runner: Ikea (ikea.com); stencil: Royal Design Studio (royaldesignstudio.com); Jessica Simpson red shoes: Dillard's (dillards.com); paint for stencil: Vintage Vogue by Benjamin Moore (benjaminmoore.com)

003 INVENTORY ALL THE TEXTURES IN YOUR ROOM
Curtains: Ikea (ikea.com); art: homemade; chair, floor lamp, pouf: Joss & Main (jossandmain.com); throw pillow, woven basket: Target (target.com); throw: HomeGoods (homegoods.com); drinking glass: World Market (worldmarket.com); coaster: Anthropologie (anthropologie.com); rug: Pottery Barn (potterybarn.com); wall color (Carolina Inn Club Aqua by Valspar): Lowe's (lowes.com)

005 MAKE OVER A BAR CART WITH CHALKBOARD PAINT
Bar cart: thrift store; chalk paint: Chalkboard by Krylon (krylon.com); green bowl: HomeGoods (homegoods.com); Core Bamboo blue bowl, green tray: Joss & Main (jossandmain.com); wineglasses, napkin: Crate & Barrel (crateandbarrel.com); wine opener: Bed Bath & Beyond (bedbathandbeyond.com); curtains: homemade with Robert Allen Khanjali Peacock fabric from U-Fab (ufabstore.com); wall color (Moonshine) and paint for bar cart (Dragonfly) by Benjamin Moore (benjaminmoore.com)

006 BRING HIGH CEILINGS DOWN SO THEY'RE COZY (AND EASIER TO PAINT)
Frames: Target (target.com) and Ikea (ikea.com); U.S. map: eBay (ebay.com); table lamp, green bowl, solid-colored pillows: HomeGoods (homegoods.com); duvet cover used as tablecloth: Designers Guild (designersguild.com); drinking glass: World Market (worldmarket.com); daybed, green zebra pillow: West Elm (westelm.com); blue and white pillow: Surya (surya.com); bedsheet: Target (target.com); wall color: Quiet Moments by Benjamin Moore (benjaminmoore.com)

009 MAKE SIMPLE NO-SEW CURTAINS
Curtain fabric (Gazebo Cloud by Braemore): U-Fab (ufabstore.com); HeatnBond no-sew hem tape: Michaels (michaels.com); frames: Ikea (ikea.com); Richmond city map: eBay (ebay.com); monogram art: homemade; faux topiary: Crate & Barrel (crateandbarrel.com); side table, Jill Rosenwald decorative tray, Safavieh rug: Joss & Main (jossandmain.com); wall colors: Moonshine and Shaker Gray by Benjamin Moore (benjaminmoore.com)

010 ONE IKEA LACK TABLE THREE WAYS
One Table as a Shelf: Shelf, vases, file cabinet: Ikea (ikea.com); ceramic bird: yard sale; woven ball: Target (target.com); postcards, wood printing blocks, globe: thrift store; numbered ceramic balls: Pier 1 Imports (pier1.com); bowls, ceramic pears: HomeGoods (homegoods.com); wall color above chair rail (Moonshine, with half-tint paint for stencil), and accent color (Sesame) by Benjamin Moore (benjaminmoore.com); stencil: Royal Design Studio (royaldesignstudio.com)

Two Tables as a Headboard: Headboard, curtains, bedding: Ikea (ikea.com); throw pillow, wall mirror, red box: Target (target.com); table lamp: HomeGoods (homegoods.com); side table: yard sale; wall color (Plumage by Martha Stewart): Home Depot (homedepot.com)

Three Tables as a Cube Bookcase: Bookcase, curtains: Ikea (ikea.com); rhino trophy, rhino figure: Cardboard Safari (cardboardsafari.com); wooden cactus: Plan Toys (plantoys.com); radio: Tivoli Audio (tivoliaudio.com); black lacquered box, yellow artichoke vase: HomeGoods (homegoods.com); metal file box: thrift store; wall color: Moonshine by Benjamin Moore (benjaminmoore.com)

015 ONE SOFA THREE WAYS
Sofa: Crate & Barrel (crateandbarrel.com); frames: Ikea (ikea.com); art: Sherri Conley (etsy.com/shop/SherriConley); rug: World Market (worldmarket.com)

Blue version: Solid blue pillow, floral pillow, striped pillow, throw: Pier 1 Imports (pier1.com)

Red version: Pillows (second from left, far right): Dermond Peterson (dermondpeterson.com); all other pillows: Target (target.com); red throw: The Company Store (thecompanystore.com)

Yellow version: Yellow pillows: Target (target.com); long patterned pillow: HomeGoods (homegoods.com)

020 GUSSY UP A THRIFT-STORE MIRROR
Spray paint: Aubergine by Rust-Oleum Painter's Touch (rustoleum.com); gray vase, scallop bowl: Target (target.com); wall color: Moonshine by Benjamin Moore (benjaminmoore.com)

021 REFINISH WOOD FURNITURE
Table: thrift store; stain: Dark Walnut by Minwax (minwax.com); glass cloche: yard sale; faux potted plant: Ikea (ikea.com); bowls: Linens N Things (lnt.com); wall color: Dove White by Benjamin Moore (benjaminmoore.com)

023 PAINT A CHEAPO PAPER LANTERN
Paper lantern: World Market (worldmarket.com); paint (Viridian Hue by Reeves): Main Art Supply (mainartsupply.com); shelves: homemade; wall color: Proposal by Benjamin Moore (benjaminmoore.com)

024 TRY WALLPAPER
Wallpaper: Darcy by Graham & Brown (grahambrown.com); dog bookends: Z Gallerie (zgallerie.com); small plate: West Elm (westelm.com); console table, storage box, faux succulents: Target (target.com); console knobs: Anthropologie (anthropologie.com)

025 MIX HARDWARE FINISHES
Wall mirror: Hobby Lobby (hobbylobby.com); desk lamp: Marshalls (marshallsonline.com); desk: West Elm (westelm.com); Safavieh chair: Joss & Main (jossandmain.com); green vase: Crate & Barrel (crateandbarrel.com); bronze pig, bronze urchin: HomeGoods (homegoods.com); silver tray: thrift store; wall color: Moonshine by Benjamin Moore (benjaminmoore.com)

028 COLLAGE YOUR WALL
Vintage postcards: eBay (ebay.com); blue vases: Z Gallerie (zgallerie.com); plates: thrift store; ceramic octopus: Plasticland (shopplasticland.com); side table: Joss & Main (jossandmain.com); wall color: Moonshine by Benjamin Moore (benjaminmoore.com)

029 ADD A PAINTED DETAIL TO YOUR PANELED DOORS
Dark accent paint (Silhouette) and light accent paint (Moonshine) by Benjamin Moore (benjaminmoore.com); bedding, faux sheepskin rug: Ikea (ikea.com); throw pillow: Target (target.com); wall color (Carolina Inn Club Aqua by Valspar): Lowe's (lowes.com)

030 MAKE THE SHELF THE STAR
Shelf, silver vase: Target (target.com); painter's tape to make stripes: FrogTape (frogtape.com); faux flower: eBay (ebay.com); bird photo clip: HomeGoods (homegoods.com); wall color (Sunburst) and paint for stripes (Silhouette) by Benjamin Moore (benjaminmoore.com)

033 MAKE A DRIFTWOOD-ESQUE TWIG MIRROR
Mirror: thrift store; twigs: found outside; adhesive: Home Depot (homedepot.com); spray paint for mirror: Fossil by Rust-Oleum Painter's Touch (rustoleum.com); faux topiary: Crate & Barrel (crateandbarrel.com); blue vase: Pier 1 Imports (pier1.com); faux starfish: Kohl's (kohls.com); black lacquered box: HomeGoods (homegoods.com); bar cart: see page 324, Make Over a Bar Cart with Chalkboard Paint; wall color: Moonshine by Benjamin Moore (benjaminmoore.com)

034 HANG TEXTURED WALLPAPER FOR A TIN-CEILING EFFECT
Wallpaper: Small Squares Paintable Wallpaper by Graham & Brown (grahambrown.com); shell ball: Kohl's (kohls.com); glass vase: Michaels (michaels.com); fabric container: homemade using Mingei fabric by Premier Prints (premierprintsfabric.com); ceramic horse: Target (target.com); wallpaper paint color (Quiet Moments), wall color (Moonshine), and bookcase colors (Dove White on shelves and Dragonfly on back) by Benjamin Moore (benjaminmoore.com)

035 SHOP AT GARDEN CENTERS
Planter: HomeGoods (homegoods.com); wrapping paper: Target (target.com) and Mongrel (mongrelonline.com)

02 NOSH

038 THREE EASY DIY BACKSPLASH IDEAS
Counter: Glacier White by Corian (dupont.com);
cabinet paint: Cloud Cover by Benjamin Moore
(benjaminmoore.com)

Tin: Tin panels: Home Depot (homedepot.com);
orange container: Pier 1 Imports (pier1.com);
glass canister: West Elm (westelm.com); white
bowl: Bed Bath & Beyond (bedbathandbeyond
.com)

Beadboard: Beadboard panels: Home Depot
(homedepot.com); yellow canister: Pier 1 Imports
(pier1.com); vase, cutting board: HomeGoods
(homegoods.com)

Frames: Fabric (Iman Zahra Leaf Luna): U-Fab
(ufabstore.com); frames: Ikea (ikea.com); Core
Bamboo bowls: Joss & Main (jossandmain.com);
plates: Linens N Things (lnt.com); flatware: Crate &
Barrel (crateandbarrel.com)

**039 MAKE HAPPY HERB POTS
FOR YOUR KITCHEN**
Decorative tape, terra-cotta pots: Michaels
(michaels.com); counters: Glacier White by Corian
(dupont.com); wall color: Sesame by Benjamin
Moore (benjaminmoore.com)

040 A FRUIT BOWL FIVE WAYS
Wire basket and cake stand: thrift store; wood
bowl, metal hex basket: Target (target.com); faux
clamshell: Z Gallerie (zgallerie.com)

041 THREE WAYS TO SET THE TABLE
Colorful: Tall drinking glass: Ikea (ikea.com);
wineglass: Joss & Main (jossandmain.com); plate,
napkin: Target (target.com); bowl: HomeGoods
(homegoods.com)

Modern: Blue drinking glass: Joss & Main
(jossandmain.com); bowl, plate: Linens N Things
(lnt.com); napkin: Target (target.com)

Natural: Woven drinking glass: Sur La Table
(surlatable.com); plate: Linens N Things (lnt.com);
napkin, bowl: Target (target.com); bee candy
container, flatware: thrift store

048 SPIFF UP AN OLD BRASS CHANDELIER
Chandelier: thrift store; spray paint: Gloss Purple by
Rust-Oleum Painter's Touch (rustoleum.com)

049 STASH YOUR KNIVES
Glass container: Ikea (ikea.com); knives: Bed Bath &
Beyond (bedbathandbeyond.com); backsplash tile
(Penny Round Moss): The Tile Shop (thetileshop
.com); shelves: homemade with wood and brackets
from Home Depot (homedepot.com); counters:
Glacier White by Corian (dupont.com)

050 REMOVE SOME UPPER CABINETS
Art by Emerald Grippa: Quirk Gallery (quirkgallery
.com); bowl: Target (target.com); ceramic apple:
thrift store; radio: Tivoli Audio (tivoliaudio.com);
drinking glass: Ikea (ikea.com); counter: Glacier
White by Corian (dupont.com); cabinet hardware:
Amerock (amerock.com); cabinet paint (Cloud
Cover) and wall color (Sesame) by Benjamin Moore
(benjaminmoore.com)

**051 MAKE ETCHED-GLASS CONTAINERS FOR
YOUR COUNTER**
Glass containers: Target (target.com); etching
cream: Michaels (michaels.com); Avery white sticker
paper: Office Depot (officedepot.com); wall color:
Moonshine by Benjamin Moore (benjaminmoore.com)

054 REUPHOLSTER A DINING CHAIR
Chair: thrift store; fabric (West Elm Ikat Ogee):
U-Fab (ufabstore.com); red lantern: Ikea (ikea.com);
candle: Target (target.com); rug: The Company Store
(thecompanystore.com); wall color: Moonshine by
Benjamin Moore (benjaminmoore.com)

**055 MAKE QUIRKY SHADOW-BOX ART
FOR THE KITCHEN**
Frame: Ikea (ikea.com); white and yellow cups: thrift
store; ceramic pear: HomeGoods (homegoods.com);
bowls: Target (target.com); backsplash tile (Penny
Round Moss): The Tile Shop (thetileshop.com);
shelves: homemade with wood and brackets from
Home Depot (homedepot.com)

**057 THINK BEYOND POTPOURRI FOR VASE
FILLERS**
Glass hurricane lantern: HomeGoods (homegoods
.com); pillar candle: Target (target.com)

058 STENCIL A TABLE RUNNER
White runner: Pottery Barn (potterybarn
.com); lace for stencil, vase, napkins, flatware: thrift
store; fabric spray paint (Copper by Stencil Spray):
Jo-Ann Fabric and Craft Stores (joann.com); woven
drinking glasses: HomeGoods (homegoods.com);
plates: Linens N Things (lnt.com); table, chairs: Pier
1 Imports (pier1.com); wall color: Moonshine by
Benjamin Moore (benjaminmoore.com)

060 MAKE A BRANCH CANDLEHOLDER
Branch: found outside; glass votive holders,
runner: Target (target.com); votive candles, plates,
wineglasses, table, chair: Pier 1 Imports (pier1.com);
flatware: thrift store

 **DOZE**

061 MAKE AN UPHOLSTERED HEADBOARD
Fabric (Modernista Citrine): U-Fab (ufabstore.com);
batting, frame: Michaels (michaels.com); bedding:
Ikea (ikea.com); throw pillow: Target (target.com);
table lamp: HomeGoods (homegoods.com); side
table: homemade; wall color: White Dove by
Benjamin Moore (benjaminmoore.com)

062 ONE BED THREE WAYS
Headboard, bed skirt: Target (target.com)

Luxe Brown bedding: Target (target.com); white
bedding: Ikea (ikea.com); lumbar pillow, yellow
throw blanket, ceramic garden stool: HomeGoods
(homegoods.com)

Lively: Pillow shams: Pottery Barn (potterybarn.com);
lumbar pillow, yellow artichoke vase: HomeGoods
(homegoods.com); white bedding: Ikea (ikea.com);
yellow sheets: Garnet Hill (garnethill.com); side table:
Target (target.com)

Moody: Throw pillows: Joss & Main (jossandmain
.com); blanket, white bedding: Ikea (ikea.com);
concrete whippet statue: Great Big Greenhouse
(greatbiggreenhouse.com); faux antlers by The
New Woodsman: Quirk Gallery (quirkgallery
.com); wall colors Moonshine by Benjamin Moore
(benjaminmoore.com)

**065 HAND-STAMP A DUVET / 068 PAINT A
HEADBOARD ON THE WALL**
Paint for headboard (Hale Navy) and wall color
(Dove White) by Benjamin Moore (benjaminmoore
.com); green pillows: HomeGoods (homegoods
.com); white duvet cover: Garnet Hill (garnethill
.com); stencil, fabric paint for duvet (Met Olive Green
from Lumiere by Jacquard): Jo-Ann Fabric and Craft
Stores (joann.com); foam brush: Michaels (michaels
.com); floor lamp: Joss & Main (jossandmain.com)

**070 LINE YOUR DRAWERS WITH PATTERNED
PAPER**
Dresser: thrift store; gift wrap: The Gents and
Fox paper, both by Nineteen Seventy Three
(nineteenseventythree.com) via Mongrel

(mongrelonline.com); egg crate: Crate and Barrel
(crateandbarrel.com).

072 ONE NIGHTSTAND THREE WAYS
Nightstand: Target (target.com)

Wood nightstand: Metal pull: Liberty Hardware
(libertyhardware.com); roll of cork: Jo-Ann Fabric
and Craft Stores (joann.com); casters: Home Depot
(homedepot.com); cork planter: Ikea (ikea.com);
metal coin bank: West Elm (westelm.com)

White nightstand: Spray paint: White by Rust-Oleum
Universal (rustoleum.com); antler candleholder:
West Elm (westelm.com); glass cloche: yard sale;
faux potted plant: Ikea (ikea.com); wood tray:
Core Bamboo (corebamboo.com) via Joss &
Main (jossandmain.com); green bowl, capiz box:
HomeGoods (homegoods.com)

Blue nightstand: Spray paint: Lagoon by Rust-Oleum
Painter's Touch (rustoleum.com); decorative knob,
bowl: Anthropologie (anthropologie.com); ceramic
pig speaker: West Elm (westelm.com); drinking glass:
World Market (worldmarket.com); coaster: Jonathan
Adler (jonathanadler.com); red throw: HomeGoods
(homegoods.com)

073 MAKE A WEATHERED-WOOD HEADBOARD
Wood: Home Depot (homedepot.com); stain: Dark
Walnut by Minwax (minwax.com); yellow pillow
shams, white duvet: Garnet Hill (garnethill.com);
stuffed giraffe: Jellycat (jellycat.com); wall color
(Moonshine) and beam color (Shaker Gray) by
Benjamin Moore (benjaminmoore.com); for mirror,
see below, Make a Spiky Branch Mirror

074 MAKE A SPIKY BRANCH MIRROR
Branch wreath: Michaels (michaels.com); round
mirror: Jo-Ann Fabric and Craft Stores (joann
.com); yellow spray paint: Sun Yellow by Rust-Oleum
Painter's Touch (rustoleum.com)

075 MAKE WHIMSICAL CLOUD SHELVES
Shelves, crayon holder, faux succulent: Target
(target.com); sock monkey: Pier 1 Imports (pier1.com);
toy animals: Hobby Lobby (hobbylobby.com); faux
butterfly art: flea market; fabric letter: Beyond the
Seam on Etsy (etsy.com/shop/BeyondTheSeam);
wooden blocks: homemade gift; wall color
(Moroccan Spice) and paint for clouds (Decorators
White) by Benjamin Moore (benjaminmoore.com)

076 USE WALLPAPER TO AMP UP A DRESSER
Dresser: Ikea (ikea.com); wallpaper: Vivid Wallpaper

by Graham & Brown (grahambrown.com); faux succulent: Target (target.com)

04 RINSE

05 STOW

06 HANG

Home Depot (homedepot.com); wall color: Sesame by Benjamin Moore (benjaminmoore.com)

155 MAKE SIMPLE SILHOUETTES
Frames: Ikea (ikea.com); America Retold ceramic pig hook: Mongrel (mongrelonline.com); Richmond city map: eBay (ebay.com); wall color: Moonshine by Benjamin Moore (benjaminmoore.com)

156 MAKE FINGERPRINT ART / 157 MAKE FAMILY BOTANICALS / 158 MAKE A STAMP FAMILY TREE / 159 PAINT YOUR MAT
Frames (on top and bottom left): Target (target.com); frames (on top and bottom right): Ikea (ikea.com); stamps: Packard's Rock Shop (804-794-5538); alphabet stamps for labeling botanicals, ink pad for fingerprints: Michaels (michaels.com); wall color (Plumage by Martha Stewart): Home Depot (homedepot.com)

 TWEAK

P.217 Bookcase Ceramic horse: Target (target.com); fabric container: homemade using Mingei fabric by Premier Prints (premierprintsfabric.com); faux butterfly art: homemade in Ikea frame (ikea.com); white shell, ceramic bird: thrift store; silver wrapped box: homemade; glass hurricane vase: HomeGoods (homegoods.com), ceramic rhino: Z Gallerie (zgallerie.com); bookcase colors (Dove White on shelves and Dragonfly on back) by Benjamin Moore (benjaminmoore.com)

160 ADD SOMETHING RED
Pillow cover: Ikea (ikea.com); fabric spray paint: Brite Yellow by Simply Spray via Jo-Ann Fabric and Craft Stores (joann.com); stencil: leaves from yard; chair: Target (target.com); wall color: Moonshine by Benjamin Moore (benjaminmoore.com)

162 PLAY MUSICAL CHAIRS WITH YOUR ACCENT PILLOWS
Pillows (from top to bottom): West Elm (westelm.com), Surya (surya.com), HomeGoods (homegoods.com), West Elm (westelm.com); chair: thrift store; wall color: Moroccan Spice by Benjamin Moore (benjaminmoore.com)

165 MAKE CHALKBOARD BOTTLE VASES
Bottles: recycled wine and sparkling water bottles; chalk paint: Chalkboard by Krylon (krylon.com); wall color: Moonshine by Benjamin Moore (benjaminmoore.com)

167 MODERNIZE A WREATH
Wreath: thrift store; spray paint: White by Rust-Oleum Universal (rustoleum.com); ribbon: Michaels (michaels.com); curtains: homemade with Robert Allen Khanjali Peacock fabric from U-Fab (ufabstore.com)

168 UPGRADE OLD COASTERS
Decorative paper: Michaels (michaels.com); coasters: thrift store; drinking glass: World Market (worldmarket.com)

169 BRING THE OUTSIDE IN
Oversized glass vase: Z Gallerie (zgallerie.com)

171 TOP A TABLE WITH GREAT DECORATIVE FABRIC
Desk: West Elm (westelm.com); fabric: Undulating Bud by Robert Allen via U-Fab (ufabstore.com); mirror: Joss & Main (jossandmain.com); table lamp, hurricane lantern, pillar candle: Target (target.com); jar candle: Pure Light Candles (804-934-9171); bronze pineapple vase: thrift store; chair: eBay (ebay.com); wall color: Moonshine by Benjamin Moore (benjaminmoore.com)

173 ADD BOLDNESS WITHOUT PAINTING THE WALLS
Painting: Lindsay Cowles (lindsaycowlesart.blogspot.com); chair: Target (target.com); pillow: Dermond Peterson (dermondpeterson.com); table lamp: Linens N Things (lnt.com); side table: thrift store; cork planter: Ikea (ikea.com); bowls: HomeGoods (homegoods.com); rug: Pottery Barn (potterybarn.com), drinking glass: World Market (worldmarket.com); wall color: White Dove by Benjamin Moore (benjaminmoore.com)

174 PUT SOMETHING IN AN UNUSED FIREPLACE
See page 332, Paint a Brick Fireplace

175 ADD A SLAP OF WHIMSY
Wood bird: Anthropologie (anthropologie.com); bowl: Target (target.com)

177 MAKE A PENDANT LIGHT OUT OF BOOK PAGES
Lampshade, book for pages, fabric in frame: thrift store; frame: Ikea (ikea.com); coaster: Jonathan Adler (jonathanadler.com); wall color: Taupe Fedora by Benjamin Moore (benjaminmoore.com)

178 DYE PILLOW COVERS FOR A DREAMY, BLURRED EFFECT
Pillow cover, couch: Ikea (ikea.com); dye (Jeans Blue by Dylon): Jo-Ann Fabric and Craft Stores

(joann.com); desk (in background): West Elm (westelm.com); solid blue pillow, decorative lanterns: HomeGoods (homegoods.com); wall color: Moonshine by Benjamin Moore (benjaminmoore.com)

179 MAKE RECYCLED GLASS BOOKENDS / 180 UNDRESS YOUR HARDCOVER BOOKS
Jars: recycled pasta sauce containers; spray paint: Brass by Krylon Metallic (krylon.com); bookcase: Target (target.com); wall color (Moonshine) by Benjamin Moore (benjaminmoore.com)

181 UPGRADE A MIRROR WITH WASHERS
Mirror: thrift store; washers, construction adhesive: Home Depot (homedepot.com); spray paint for mirror: White by Rust-Oleum Universal (rustoleum.com); wall color (Carolina Inn Club Aqua by Valspar): Lowe's (lowes.com)

182 RE-COVER A LAMPSHADE / 183 PAINT THE BASE OF AN OLD CERAMIC LAMP / 184 PAINT A LAMPSHADE / 185 DRAW ON A CERAMIC LAMP BASE / 186 TRIM A LAMPSHADE WITH RIBBON
Lamps from left to right:

Fabric for lampshade: Jo-Ann Fabric and Craft Stores (joann.com); lamp base: Linens N Things (lnt.com)

Lamp: Target (target.com); paint for base: Hibiscus by Benjamin Moore (benjaminmoore.com)

Lamp: HomeGoods (homegoods.com); paint for shade: Taupe Fedora (bottom) and Decorators White (top) by Benjamin Moore (benjaminmoore.com)

Lamp: Target (target.com); paint marker: Sharpie (sharpie.com)

Lamp: HomeGoods (homegoods.com)

Wall color: Moonshine by Benjamin Moore (benjaminmoore.com)

187 GILD A GLASS LAMP BASE
Lamp: HomeGoods (homegoods.com); dresser: see page 333, Paint a Gradient.

188 SWAP OUT A DOORKNOB OR TWO
Doorknob: Anthropologie (anthropologie.com); frames: Ikea (ikea.com); Safavieh chair: Joss & Main (jossandmain.com); pillow: Marshalls (marshallsonline.com); faux topiary: Crate & Barrel (crateandbarrel.com); side table: Target (target.com);

wall color: Moonshine by Benjamin Moore (benjaminmoore.com)

191 TRY COLORED CHALKBOARD PAINT
Planter: Ikea (ikea.com); paint used for DIY chalkboard paint recipe: 14 Carrots by Benjamin Moore (benjaminmoore.com); colored pencils: Target (target.com)

193 SKETCH ON A PILLOW
Pillow cover: Ikea (ikea.com); chair: Target (target.com); bronze fruit: Pier 1 Imports (pier1.com); ceramic garden stool: HomeGoods (homegoods.com); paint (Plumage by Martha Stewart): Home Depot (homedepot.com)

194 EMBRACE WHAT MAKES YOU HAPPY
Canvas: Michaels (michaels.com); horseshoe: thrift store; horse bookend: thrift store; paint for bookend: Sun Yellow by Rust-Oleum Painter's Touch (rustoleum.com); chevron box: Target (target.com)

197 CERAMICIZE SOMETHING
Slinky, elephant toy: Target (target.com); pineapple: thrift store

198 SEASONALLY SWITCH OUT FAMILY PHOTOS
Frame: Pottery Barn (potterybarn.com); wall color: Moonshine by Benjamin Moore (benjaminmoore.com)

 CHEERS

201 MAKE PERSONALIZED PLACE "CARDS"
Stone: found outside; alphabet sticker: Michaels (michaels.com); napkin: Crate & Barrel (crateandbarrel.com); plate: Linens N Things (lnt.com); table: Pier 1 Imports (pier1.com)

203 MAKE FESTIVE LET'S-PARTY GARLANDS
Top garland: Colorful craft paper, alphabet stickers, embroidery thread: Michaels (michaels.com)

Middle garland: Ribbon, embroidery thread: Michaels (michaels.com)

Bottom garland: Colorful craft paper, embroidery thread: Michaels (michaels.com)

208 STENCIL A BEVERAGE TIN
Beverage tin: Target (target.com); lemon stencil: eBay (ebay.com); paint: Full Sun by Valspar

(valspar.com); Lorina lemonade: Trader Joe's (traderjoes.com)

210 MAKE INTERESTING DRINK OR COCKTAIL ICE CUBES
Drinking glasses: Ikea (ikea.com)

211 MAKE A FREE-FORM TABLE RUNNER
Tissue paper: Michaels (michaels.com); cake stand: Marshalls (marshallsonline.com); cupcakes: Martin's Food Market (martinsfoods.com); woven drinking glasses, table, chairs: Pier 1 Imports (pier1.com); Core Bamboo bowls: Joss & Main (jossandmain.com); plates: Linens N Things (lnt.com); flatware: Crate & Barrel (crateandbarrel.com)

09 SPLAT

213 CONQUER PAINT PARALYSIS
Paint can (Sunburst) and paint fan deck (Color Stories paints) by Benjamin Moore (benjaminmoore.com); stir stick, paint can opener, drop cloth: Home Depot (homedepot.com)

214 PAINT ALMOST ANY PIECE OF FURNITURE
Chair: thrift store; primer (Zinsser Smart Prime): Virginia Paint Company (virginiapaintcompany.com); curtains: Ikea (ikea.com); shoes: DSW (dsw.com); wall color (Moonshine) and chair paint (Wasabi) by Benjamin Moore (benjaminmoore.com)

215 PAINT A CEILING
Ceiling color (Hibiscus) and paint for mirror (Decorators White) by Benjamin Moore (benjaminmoore.com); wall color (Carolina Inn Club Aqua by Valspar) and mirror: Lowe's (lowes.com); painter's tape: FrogTape (frogtape .com); ceiling fixture: unknown (came with house); white vase, light fixture (in mirror): Ikea (ikea.com); ram trophy (in mirror): T.J. Maxx (tjmaxx.com); oversized glass vase: Z Gallerie (zgallerie.com); round frame: Anthropologie (anthropologie.com); capiz box: HomeGoods (homegoods.com); soap pump: Target (target.com)

216 STENCIL YOUR WALLS
Stencil: Royal Design Studio (royaldesignstudio.com); wall color (Decorators White) and stencil color (Ashen Tan) by Benjamin Moore (benjaminmoore.com); dresser: hand-me-down; round frame: Anthropologie (anthropologie.com); rectangular frame, white storage box: Target (target.com); bee candy containers, flower pot: thrift store; tray: Marshalls (marshallsonline.com)

217 FIND COLOR INSPIRATION ALL AROUND YOU
Scarf: Pier 1 Imports (pier1.com)
Candles: Market Street Candles: Joss & Main (jossandmain.com)

Table setting: Plate: Linens N Things (lnt.com); bowl: Target (target.com); cup, saucer, spoon: thrift store

218 PAINT A GRAPHIC PATTERN ON A DESK OR DRESSER
Desk: thrift store; painter's tape to make pattern: FrogTape (frogtape.com); desk lamp: Linens N Things (lnt.com); gray foo dog, faux succulent: Target (target.com); laptop: Apple (apple.com); chair: eBay (ebay.com); wall color (Moonshine), blue paint for desk (Hale Navy), and green accent paint for desk (Martini Olive) by Benjamin Moore (benjaminmoore.com)

220 MAKE A STENCIL WITH SOMETHING NATURAL
See page 330, Add Something Red.

221 SPICE UP WHITE ROLLER SHADES WITH GRAPHIC STRIPES/ 222 DO SOMETHING UNEXPECTED TO YOUR MOLDING
Roller shade: Home Depot (homedepot.com); green chair: thrift store with Ivy Leaf spray paint by Krylon (krylon.com) and Robert Allen Khanjali Peacock fabric from U-Fab (ufabstore.com); side table: yard sale; table lamp: HomeGoods (homegoods.com); yellow bowl: Anthropologie (anthropologie.com); wall color (Dove White), window trim color (Gray Horse), and paint for stripes (Citron) by Benjamin Moore (benjaminmoore.com); painter's tape to make pattern: FrogTape (frogtape.com)

223 PAINT THE BACK OF A BOOKCASE IN VARYING TONES
Bookcase, picture frame, gray vases, white basket, white box: Target (target.com); yellow bowl, floral bowl: Anthropologie (anthropologie.com); ceramic frog: thrift store; ceramic flower: Marshalls (marshallsonline.com); wall color (Moonshine) and bookcase colors (top to bottom: Wasabi, Exhale, and Silhouette) by Benjamin Moore (benjaminmoore.com)

224 PAINT A BRICK FIREPLACE / 225 PAINT WOOD PANELING
Frame: Ikea (ikea.com); faux antlers: Hobby Lobby (hobbylobby.com); paint for antlers: White by Rust-Oleum Universal (rustoleum.com); yellow planter: Target (target.com); gray ottoman: Joss & Main (jossandmain.com); wall color (Gray Horse) and fireplace box color (Temptation) by Benjamin Moore

(benjaminmoore.com); fireplace color (Olympic Premium base white): Lowe's (lowes.com)

227 **PAINT YOUR CURTAINS (YUP, PAINT THEM!)**
Curtain, frame, faux sheepskin rug: Ikea (ikea.com); wall color (Moonshine), beam color (Shaker Gray), and paint for red stripe (Caliente) and pink stripe (Berry Fizz) by Benjamin Moore (benjaminmoore .com); Folk Art textile medium for paint: Michaels (michaels.com); table lamp: see page 331, Re-cover a Lampshade; monogram art: homemade; desk: West Elm (westelm.com); ottoman: T.J. Maxx (tjmaxx.com); oversized glass vases: Z Gallerie (zgallerie.com)

228 **INVIGORATE A ROOM WITH BOLD COLOR**
Wall color before (White Dove) and after (Moroccan Spice) by Benjamin Moore (benjaminmoore.com); painting: Lindsay Cowles (lindsaycowlesart.blogspot .com); chair, side table, faux succulent: Target (target.com); table lamp: HomeGoods (homegoods .com); throw pillow: Surya (surya.com); area rug: Pottery Barn (potterybarn.com)

229 **GO TWO-TONE WITH A BUFFET, TABLE, DESK, OR DRESSER**
Desk: thrift store; paint on desk: Decorators White and Gray Horse by Benjamin Moore (benjaminmoore .com); spray paint for metal details on desk: Oil Rubbed Bronze by Rust-Oleum Universal (rustoleum .com); purse: T.J. Maxx (tjmaxx.com); pencil holder: Target (target.com); lamp: see page 331, Paint the Base of an Old Ceramic Lamp; chair: eBay (ebay.com); scarf: Old Navy (oldnavy.com)

230 **PAINT A GRADIENT**
Dresser: thrift store; paint for dresser drawers (top to bottom: White Wisp, Gray Owl, Sea Haze, Desert Twilight, Durango, and Char Brown) and frame (Char Brown) by Benjamin Moore (benjaminmoore.com); glass cloche: yard sale; faux potted plant: Ikea (ikea.com); fan: Bed Bath & Beyond (bedbathandbeyond.com); planter (in background): HomeGoods (homegoods.com); wall color (Carolina Inn Club Aqua by Valspar): Lowe's (lowes.com)

P.304 **BONUS TIP: GO SHORT**
Paint: Moroccan Spice and Chamomile by Benjamin Moore (benjaminmoore.com); paintbrush: Wooster Brush Company (woosterbrush.com)

10 OUT

233 **ADD SOMETHING CHARMING UNDERFOOT**
Doormat: Ikea (ikea.com); spray paint: Oil Rubbed Bronze by Rust-Oleum Universal (rustoleum.com); painter's tape to make pattern: FrogTape (frogtape .com); yellow door paint (Full Sun by Valspar's Eddie Bauer Home line): Lowe's (lowes.com); wood planters: Home Depot (homedepot.com), paint for planters: Greenwich by Ralph Lauren Home (ralphlaurenhome.com)

234 **PAINT A CONCRETE BIRDBATH A BOLD, HAPPY COLOR**
Birdbath: unknown (came with house); exterior paint: Dazzling Daffodil by Glidden (glidden.com)

240 **GIVE WOODEN PLANTERS SOME POP WITH PAINT**
Planter: Central Garden & Pet (central.com); paint color: Chamomile by Benjamin Moore (benjaminmoore.com)

242 **ADD A DOOR DECAL**
Custom decal: Single Story on Etsy (etsy.com/ shop/singlestory); yellow door paint (Full Sun by Valspar's Eddie Bauer Home line): Lowe's (lowes .com); wood planters: Home Depot (homedepot .com); paint for planters: Greenwich by Ralph Lauren Home (ralphlaurenhome.com); doormat: see Add Something Charming Underfoot, above; door hardware, porch light: unknown (came with house)

A Few Go-To Sources

Since we often get asked where to look for specific furnishings and accessories, we've compiled a giant list for you on our website at younghouselove .com/book. But since we can't resist sharing some love with a few local favorites in Richmond (many of whom we visited more times than we can count while making this book), here they are: U-Fab, Mongrel, Quirk Gallery, William's & Sherrill, Caravati's, Clover, Pleasant's Hardware, Love of Jesus Thrift, Diversity Thrift, the Habitat for Humanity ReStore, Consignment Connection, Class and Trash, Virginia Paint, Ruth & Ollie, The Decorating Outlet, Shades of Light, Main Art Supply, and La Difference.

STUFF WE LOVE

Magazines We Love

- *Atomic Ranch*
- *Better Homes & Gardens*
- *Canadian House & Home*
- *Coastal Living*
- *Do It Yourself*
- *Domino*
- *Dwell*
- *Elle Decor*
- *Fresh Home*
- *HGTV Magazine*
- *House Beautiful*
- *Livingetc*
- *Martha Stewart Living*
- *The Nest*
- *Real Simple*
- *Southern Living*

eZines We Love

- centsationalgirl.com
- highglossmagazine.com
- houseoffifty.com
- lonnymag.com
- puregreenmag.com
- ruemag.com

Design Sites We Love

- BHG.com
- doityourself.com
- floorplanner.com and google.com/sketchup (for making floor plans)
- HGTV.com
- houseandhome.com
- housetohome.co.uk/livingetc
- houzz.com
- mydeco.com, olioboard.com, and polyvore.com (for making mood boards)
- myhomeideas.com
- pinterest.com (for organizing inspiration)
- stylelist.com/home

Home Blogs We Love

- abchao.com
- absolutelybeautifulthings.blogspot.com
- alifesdesign.blogspot.com
- allthingsgd.blogspot.com
- ana-white.com
- anh-minh.com
- aninchofgray.blogspot.com
- annesage.com/blog
- apartmenttherapy.com
- aphrochic.blogspot.com
- ashleyannphotography.com/blog
- beachbungalow8.blogspot.com
- bellemaison23.com
- blackwhiteyellow.blogspot.com
- blog.effortless-style.com
- blog.urbangrace.com
- bowerpowerblog.com
- bromeliadliving.blogspot.com
- brooklynlimestone.com
- brynalexandra.blogspot.com
- bspokeblog.com
- bungalow23.com
- casasugar.com
- centsationalgirl.com
- chezlarsson.com
- cococozy.com
- cocokelley.blogspot.com
- copycatchic.com
- cotedetexas.com
- decor8blog.com
- designformankind.com
- design-milk.com
- designmom.com
- designspongeonline.com
- desiretoinspire.net
- doorsixteen.com
- emilyaclark.com
- 4men1lady.com
- habituallychic.blogspot.com
- hollymaus.blogspot.com
- hookedonhouses.net
- houseofturquoise.com
- housetweaking.com
- howaboutorange.blogspot.com
- isabellaandmaxrooms.blogspot.com
- ishandchi.blogspot.com
- isuwannee.com
- jenloveskev.com
- jennskistudio.blogspot.com
- journeysofmangonett.blogspot.com
- karapaslaydesigns.blogspot.com
- katie-d-i-d.blogspot.com
- kfddesigns.blogspot.com
- layersofmeaning.com
- littlegreennotebook.blogspot.com
- lovelylittledetails.com
- madebygirl.blogspot.com
- makingitlovely.com
- makingthishome.com
- maxxsilly.com
- mikeandmcgee.blogspot.com
- mrsblandings.blogspot.com
- mrshowardpersonalshopper.com
- mustardseedinteriors.com
- mysweetsavannah.blogspot.com
- newlyweddiaries.blogspot.com
- ohdeedoh.com
- ohhellofriendblog.com
- ohjoy.blogs.com
- oneprettything.com
- oneprojectcloser.com
- orangebeautiful.com/blog
- ourhumbleabowed.wordpress.com
- paloma81.blogspot.com
- pancakesandfrenchfries.com
- paulagracedesigns.blogspot.com
- pbjstories.com
- poppytalk.blogspot.com
- prettylittlethingsforhome.blogspot.com
- prudentbaby.com
- purestylehome.blogspot.com
- ramblingrenovators.blogspot.com
- remodelista.com
- restyledhome.blogspot.com
- savethedate4cupcakes.com
- 7thhouseontheleft.com
- sfgirlbybay.com
- simplifiedbee.blogspot.com
- simplygrove.com
- 6thstreetdesignschool.blogspot.com
- southernhospitalityblog.com
- stylebyemilyhenderson.com
- stylecarrot.com
- stylecourt.blogspot.com
- stylemepretty.com
- tenjuneblog.com
- the-brick-house.com
- thediyshowoff.blogspot.com
- thehappyhomeblog.com
- thehouseofsmiths.com
- theinspiredroom.net
- thelettedcottage.net
- thenester.com
- thestylishnest.com/blog
- thishomesweethome.blogspot.com
- thriftydecorchick.blogspot.com
- urbannestblog.com
- vivalabuenavida.blogspot.com
- youstirme.com
- yvestown.com

> You can find more blogs to check out back at our place (younghouselove.com). And please please please forgive us if we somehow left you off the list—our brains were oatmeal by the time we got to the final read-through, and there are so many amazingly inspiring blogs that it's impossible to name them all!

THANK YOU

A MILLION AND ONE THANKS go out to Rachel Sussman, Judy Pray, Jen Renzi, Kip Dawkins, Marcie Blough, Susan Victoria, Emma Kelly, Susan Baldaserini, Ann Bramson, Trent Duffy, Molly Erman, Bridget Heiking, Sarah Hermalyn, Michelle Ishay, Sibylle Kazeroid, Allison McGeehon, Nancy Murray, Barbara Peragine, Lia Ronnen, and Kara Strubel, who helped us turn a pile of scrap paper and scribbles into a book. We still can't believe it. And of course we can't thank our friends and family enough—for keeping us sane, making us laugh, and telling us when we have paint in our hair (most of the time). We'd love to list them all by name, but let's face it—we have big families. We definitely couldn't have pulled this off without our amazing parents, who stepped in to wrangle Clara and remind us to eat when we couldn't remember our own names. Another huge thank-you goes out to Stefanie, Kate, Jessica, Layla, Kevin, Ana, Dana, Nicole, Abby, and Benita—we love you guys! Thanks so much for the inspiring guest projects! And to Katie B and Cat, who provided such great encouragement (and comic relief) along the way—smooches, for real. While we're at it, we might as well send a giant thanks to all the other bloggers, designers, and people in general who inspire the pants off us on a daily basis (figuratively speaking, of course). And let's get really sappy for a second. To our blog readers. Our dear, amazing, and wonderful readers. We are acutely aware that you guys make what we do possible, and we can't thank you enough for your love, support, kind words, and encouragement. We're so grateful for the opportunity to share our adventures with you. So thanks for reading. You make our day, every day.

PHOTOGRAPHY CREDITS

The credits below are arranged by tip number, and you can check out the Photo Frenzy section on page 14 for more info.

PREFACE
Family portrait courtesy of Katie Bower Photography

010 ONE IKEA LACK TABLE THREE WAYS
Image of table courtesy of Ikea

014 GET ONE (OR ALL SEVEN) OF THESE CLASSICS
Clockwise from top left: images courtesy of Joss & Main, Joss & Main, Ballard Designs, Joss & Main, Joss & Main, Joss & Main, Crate & Barrel

016 DON'T FORGET THE HALLWAY
Image courtesy of Katie Bower Photography

019 SPICE UP YOUR STAIRS
Image courtesy of *Lowe's Creative Ideas for Home and Garden*

036 REPLACE "BLAH" LIGHT FIXTURES
Clockwise from top left: images courtesy of Lamps Plus, Ikea, Lamps Plus, Lamps Plus, Shades of Light

042 REFRESH OLD KITCHEN CABINETS WITH NEW HARDWARE
Top row: images courtesy of Anthropologie; middle row (left to right): images courtesy of Anthropologie, Anthropolgie, MyKnobs.com, Anthropologie; bottom row (left to right): images courtesy of Liberty Hardware, Hobby Lobby, Anthropologie, Anthropologie

043 MIX AND MATCH YOUR TABLE AND CHAIRS
First and fourth rows: images courtesy of Z Gallerie; second and third rows: images courtesy of Ikea

044 PAINT YOUR KITCHEN CABINETS
Image courtesy of Benjamin Moore

046 PAINT YOUR ISLAND A DIFFERENT COLOR THAN YOUR CABINETS
Image courtesy of Kohler Co.

047 REMOVE YOUR CABINET DOORS FOR AN OPEN FEELING
Image courtesy of *The Lettered Cottage*

052 UPGRADE YOUR COUNTERS AFFORDABLY
Image courtesy of Ikea

056 DON'T BE SCARED OF FLOWERS
Clockwise from top left: images courtesy of Joss & Main, Z Gallerie, Joss & Main, Crate & Barrel, Z Gallerie, Z Gallerie

082 GET INSPIRED BY YOUR FAVORITE GEMSTONE
Top row (left to right): images courtesy of The Container Store, Ikea, Anthropologie; middle row (left to right): images courtesy of The Container Store, Ikea, Ikea; bottom row (left to right): images courtesy of The Container Store, Ikea, Joss & Main

085 ADD STYLISH BATHROOM STORAGE
Top row (left to right): images courtesy of Ikea, Ikea, The Container Store; bottom row: all images courtesy of Ikea

086 REPLACE YOUR BATHROOM FAUCET
Image courtesy of Moen

093 ADD FUNCTION AND STYLE WITH HOOKS
Top row (left to right): images courtesy of Joss & Main, Anthropologie, Anthropologie; bottom row (left to right): images courtesy of Anthropologie, Liberty Hardware, Anthropologie

095 BASKETS SOLVE (ALMOST) EVERYTHING
Top row (left to right): images courtesy of The Container Store, The Container Store, Crate & Barrel; bottom row (left to right): images courtesy of The Container Store, Crate & Barrel, Crate & Barrel

098 CONQUER SHOE PILES
Image courtesy of Ballard Designs

099 TAME YOUR MAIL
Images courtesy of The Container Store

101 PIMP YOUR CLOSET
Image courtesy of The Container Store

114 STORE STUFF STYLISHLY
Clockwise from top left: images courtesy of The Container Store, The Container Store, The Container Store, Z Gallerie, Crate & Barrel

125 FILL AN ENTIRE WALL WITH FRAMES, A GIANT CORKBOARD, OR A HUGE CHALKBOARD
Image courtesy of *Lowe's Creative Ideas for Home and Garden*

189 HOST A PILLOW SWAP
Images courtesy of Z Gallerie

231 PAINT YOUR FRONT DOOR
Image courtesy of Benjamin Moore

232 HANG NEW HOUSE NUMBERS
Image courtesy of Heath Ceramics; photography: Jeffery Cross

237 UPGRADE EXTERIOR LIGHTS
Clockwise from top left: images courtesy of Lamps Plus, Lamps Plus, Shades of Light, Lamps Plus, Lamps Plus